SUNDAY PUNCH

EDWIN NEWMAN

SUNDAY PUNCH

BOSTON

HOUGHTON MIFFLIN COMPANY

Copyright © 1979 by Edwin Newman

Library of Congress Cataloging in Publication Data
Newman, Edwin.   Sunday punch.   I. Title.
PZ4.N54945Su   [PS3564.E9156]   813'.5'4
ISBN 0-395-28050-8   79-1289

Printed in the United States of America

v 10 9 8 7 6 5 4 3 2

SUNDAY PUNCH

1

I HAVE A FRIEND named Sam Franklin. (I also have friends who are not named Sam Franklin, but this is a claim anyone can make and I do not intend to dwell on it.) Sam, who is more often called Fogbound — and not entirely unfairly, but also because sportswriters, like caricaturists, exaggerate a single characteristic to get an interesting effect — is a fight manager. More precisely, he is a manager of prize fighters, the prize being, for some of the fighters, fame and fortune, often accompanied by splattered noses, tin ears, and a ringing sensation in the head, and for the managers, less fame and usually less fortune, but with the nose, ears, and head more or less intact.

It is surprising, given the number of graduate students in the United States and the emergence of such academic disciplines as "Sports in American Society" and "Recreation," that nobody has written a doctoral thesis on how fight managers come to be, what leads them into the field, and what qualities are called for. Few other occupations escape. Journalism certainly doesn't. I am a mere editorial writer, not long since removed from the sports page, but I spend a fair amount of time giving gracious and evasive answers to students of journalism who write, at the behest of their professors, that they are examining communication processes in the context of prevailing social/political situations and want to know how to relate to editors and how to motivate sources.

One reason Fogbound and his fellow managers have not been examined is that they are not as important as they used to be. Many athletes have declared their independence and feel able to make incorrect decisions for themselves, or if unable to do so, with the help of financial counselors. Moreover, television networks may sign up young fighters if they so much as glare impressively. The networks then look for opponents whose ability has not taken them beyond such boxing centers as Opelousas, Louisiana, Snyder, Texas, and Wolf Point, Montana; these are dispatched while the network commentators become highly emotional; and soon the young men are performing in prime time.

This relieves the manager of a large part of the managerial function, if he is fortunate enough to have a fighter who promises to get what the television people call "big numbers" in the ratings. If he is not so fortunate, he may want to thank the government for the existence of the Comprehensive Training and Employment Act, and seek to acquire marketable skill in another line of work.

For a time, Fogbound had no such fighter. He had no fighter at all. The well had run dry. Too many of his recent battlers had been either too sensitive about being hit or unable to avoid it. An example of the former, Sugar Ray Titulescu, a lightweight, might otherwise have earned the loyalty of the nation's Rumanian-American community, which would have welcomed renown unrelated to its connection with Count Dracula. An example of the latter was Sailor Bill Bentley, so called thanks to a short spell in the Navy, during which he did $250,000 in damage to a diesel engine, whether because of an inability to read a maintenance manual or a distaste for sea duty was not determined. On being ushered out of the Navy, Sailor Bill had had a brief career as a lightheavyweight before Fogbound, who is not of the "They can't hurt us" school of managers, mercifully brought it to an end. So had it come about that Fogbound, who was prepared to manage, who wanted to manage, lacked a managee.

During the months that Fogbound sorrowed over this, he did not know that help was on the way, in a manner he could not have foreseen. He would not have put it in these terms if he had known, but the old world was coming to the aid of the new. His life was about to change. Months later, telling me the story, he still didn't quite believe it.

We ran into each other in Paddy Hanrahan's Bar on Third Avenue, where I had gone to re-create the careless rapture of my days as a sportswriter. Indeed, it was in those days that I had met Fogbound. He had pointed me in the direction of a couple of stories — he was a kindly man and, as a source, needed no special motivation — and we had remained friends. Giving a convincing imitation of his name, he was standing at the bar and staring through the cigar smoke at the bottles on the shelf behind it. This was not because Fogbound was obsessed by drink; on the contrary, he was relatively abstemious; it was rather that the decor of Hanrahan's invited the eye to fix on the bottles rather than any other vista. When I spoke to him, he turned, and his bumpy face relaxed into a smile. It was a process a little like boulders rearranging themselves.

"Did you know," I asked him, "that the highest tribute a

Tibetan man can pay his dead father is to fashion a trumpet out of his father's thighbone?"

Fogbound did not answer me. He gave no sign of having heard the question, but this was not an act of discourtesy. Journalists enjoy sharing the fruits of their superior access to newsworthy information with those not fortunate enough to be in the business. I left the headlines to others. I, as Fogbound knew, supplied the material that plugs small holes on inside pages, a habit I had picked up on my first newspaper job, when I graduated from copy boy to reporter and drew the assignment of compiling fillers. They still stick in my mind, and there isn't much else you can do with the knowledge that seals sleep only five or six minutes at a time, and that the German composer George Philipp Telemann wrote more than 1400 cantatas.

"This is a great pleasure," said Fogbound, who was not above stating the obvious. "What brings you here, Joe, so near the Sportitorium?" (This was a reference to an all-purpose athletic arena built in New York with Arab oil money. Control of it lay in Qatar, on the Persian Gulf. This had no discernible effect on Sportitorium policy, but it did lead to the occasional presence in its corridors of Qatari citizens, burnoosed and flowingly robed, who were there either as ornaments or to count the house.) "Old times' sake?"

I nodded, and here I had better explain that I am not without vanity, and that when I nod, it is not only to indicate agreement but also to show a becoming directness and lack of affectation.

"I'm surprised never to see you in a bar," Fogbound said. "Editorial writers don't drink?"

"They patronize a different sort of place, usually with English sporting prints or framed front pages on the wall."

"Have you found out why they made you an editorial writer?"

"They said they wanted new blood on the editorial page. Mine was slightly used but it had had only one owner."

"How do you like it?"

I said that it was harder than I had expected, though that was partly my doing. I had, because I had read other people's editorials, posted rules for myself:

1. Do not describe any development as a step in the right direction.
2. Do not say that the burden of proof is on those who advocate change.
3. Do not say that acting as though the end justifies the means makes us no different from our communist competitors.
4. Do not use the words *scenario* and *option*.

One result of these interdictions was that I was often still working when the other editorial writers had finished. Sometimes I thought I would have to give way, especially over rules one and four. Still, it seemed worth it.

Not that I gave Fogbound these details. He would not have been interested. Instead, I asked him about business. Was there any?

"I can't complain," he said, then stopped and thought for a moment. "I'm not so sure. I forgot about Aubrey."

"Who's Aubrey?"

"I know his face is not a household word," Fogbound said, "but you, a newspaperman, you never heard of Aubrey, my English tiger? You ever met a tiger interested in economics? That's Aubrey."

"I never heard of an English tiger. The only tigers they

have in England are in zoos. Even tigers born there are denied citizenship."

"Pardon me," Fogbound said elaborately. "I forgot. You're an editorial writer now, not a sportswriter. My English fighter."

"Your English fighter? Sam, English fighters cut in a high wind. Their jaws make a tinkling sound when struck, and the main function of their skin is to split and allow blood to escape, preferably running into the eye and blinding the bleeder. You believe that they should be allowed to fight only outside the three-mile limit. I've heard you say so. What's happened?"

"I changed policy," Fogbound said. "I'm adoptable."

"Tell me everything," I said, "beginning with the name. What kind of name for a fighter is Aubrey?"

"You should hear the rest of it. Philpott-Grimes. Aubrey Philpott-Grimes."

I stopped Fogbound at this point and invited him to join me in a meal. He declined but sat at one of Hanrahan's tables while I ordered a Mediterranean Salad, which was, in airliner-menu language, a healthy sampling of sunny tastes, made up of crisp cucumbers, sweet red onion rings, slivers of salami, and mild feta cheese, tossed with garden-fresh greens, garnished with sliced radishes, and served with a zesty Caesar dressing, followed by the tender eye of the rib from specially aged and selected beef, carefully roasted, carved to order, and served with creamy horseradish sauce. Rough approximations of these arrived while Fogbound was going through his story.

At about the time I became an editorial writer and had begun thinking large thoughts suitable to elaboration in 400 to 750 words, Fogbound's wife had decided that travel was broadening, and that broadening was what her husband needed. He did not quash the idea at once, for he thought that it would die of itself. He believed his wife incapable of remaining away from her kitchen long enough to make the trip. He remembered occasions on which she had tiptoed into the bedroom while he was taking a nap, gently nudged him awake, held a packet of meat before him, said proudly, "Look at these lamb chops," and tiptoed out, the while urging him to go back to sleep.

Even as her plans progressed, he was confident that she would eventually back out, especially on being told, as he arranged to have her told by a widely traveled friend, that the British did not use dollars and cents as money but pounds and pence, that they drove on the left side, and that their time was different from that in New York — all evidence, it seemed to Fogbound, of intolerable willfulness and out-and-out enmity to Americans. But his wife had accepted this information with equanimity. Relatives of hers had visited England and come through. And while she wasn't sure about the Queen, Prince Philip had a kind face. She was prepared to risk it.

Eventually, Fogbound ceased his resistance. He did so for tactical reasons. A specter was haunting Fogbound at this time, though I did not favor him with this literary allusion because, with his way of half-listening and half-understanding, he would have replied, "Abe Spector? That's what he's doing now?" Nonetheless, there the specter was, just alongside the usual cloud no bigger than a man's hand. It was the specter of early retirement. Fogbound's failure to come up with another fighter had turned his wife's thoughts in that direction; she was, she told him, "looking into it"; pamphlets flowed in from the Social Security Administration in answer to her queries, and from retirement communities in Florida.

"The phamphlets," Fogbound told me. "I don't like them. They remind me what's ahead — books and museums and sitting in the sun. Completely nothing. It gives me a headache."

The trip to England was intended by Mrs. Franklin to give her husband a taste of life without work, to serve as a brief orientation course. Fogbound played along. Staying in New York, without a fighter, would only have made his wife more determined.

"You should have seen me," Fogbound said. "I had a blue denim suit and a camera around my neck on a strap. A regular tourist."

Mrs. Franklin also held the theory that her husband worried too much and needed a change. She made him promise to forget boxing and everything connected with it. Given the Titulescu and Bentley chapters, he was not, at first, against the idea. After accompanying his wife through Windsor Castle and the Tower of London, however, as well as the food halls at Harrods and Petticoat Lane — "Like the East Side in the old days," said Fogbound. "What's the fuss?" — his good intentions waned. They disappeared after a visit to Westminster Abbey where, stumbling dutifully through the west cloister, he came upon the tombstone of Elizabeth Broughton in time to hear someone explain that she was the wife of John Broughton, an eighteenth-century heavyweight considered the father of English pugilism.

"Respect," Fogbound told his wife. "Even here."

The incident removed any lingering guilt Fogbound felt about seeking his usual relaxation. He took himself to the Royal Albert Hall.

"Such a place, I never saw," Fogbound said. "One night a concert, next a dance, next a political meeting, next a fight.

That's where I found Aubrey. His build, you wouldn't believe. Skinny, and pale like boiled halibut." He broke off his account. "The English eat boiled halibut. I saw. That's how I know Aubrey looks like that. But he has a good left hand and plenty of guts. The other guy hits him one in the stomach, I thought his hand would come out the other side. But no, Aubrey keeps the left going, he doesn't worry, and he wins.

"After the fight," Fogbound went on, "I went to the dressing room to see him, first explaining to the bobby who I am. Bobby, that's what they call their cops. Who can understand such people?" He shrugged, then resumed. "In the dressing room, he looks even skinnier. Muscles? Not even a pimple. You ever saw a stovepipe? He's it."

As Fogbound told it, the stovepipe had some difficulty in convincing himself that people like Fogbound existed. Once he accepted the idea, they became friendly. Fogbound asked him what he did when he wasn't fighting and Aubrey said, "I'm a clerk, sir. Jobbing."

Fogbound picked up only the first half of it and, not wanting to sound ignorant, said, "That's one of those big families?"

The stovepipe entered into what he thought was the spirit of the thing. "Very," he replied.

Then Fogbound asked him where he had learned to fight, and Aubrey said he'd had to learn to protect himself against bullies who picked on him because he was so thin. "Jolly good fun," he said. "I enjoyed having a go with the other chaps."

"Where was this?"

"In the brigade, sir."

It seemed to Fogbound that anybody seeing Aubrey in a

soldier suit would have concluded at once that his country relied for its defense on machines. "In the *army*?"

"The Boys Brigade."

"England has *boys* in the army?"

Aubrey laughed. "It's a boys' organization. That led into amateur boxing, and here I am."

Fogbound watched Aubrey in the ring once more and became convinced that he had possibilities.

"Even if you are a Clark, you may need the money, anyway," Fogbound told him. "If you do, you should turn pro. For an Englishman, you're pretty good."

"Thanks, Mr. Franklin," Aubrey said.

Meanwhile, Mrs. Franklin was complaining that they had come to England for a change of scenery, and all he was doing was going to fights.

"You've seen this Albert Hall?" Fogbound asked her.

"No," said Mrs. Franklin, "and don't ask me."

"Well," said Fogbound, "take my word. If that isn't a change of scenery, nothing is. That's a change from everything. Who Albert is, I don't know, but in his place, I'd take my name off it."

Mrs. Franklin had her way. Fogbound attended no more fights and after being unable to squirm out of going with her to Stratford-on-Avon where, as he explained, Shakespeare wrote "To Be or Not to Be," and where he dined on, among other things, water crest soup, they came home. All that remained of the trip were a few memories and some things Mrs. Franklin had bought in the silver vaults — "What's the matter, they don't have silver in New York?" Fogbound had asked — and he never expected to see Aubrey again.

Nonetheless, a few months later, an intruder among the retirement literature, a letter arrived, in which Aubrey explained that he had found only one Samuel Franklin listed in the New York telephone directories at the United States Embassy in Grosvenor Square and had taken the chance that he would be the American fight manager who had been so encouraging to him. Fogbound was less impressed by Aubrey's resourcefulness than by the fact that New York telephone directories were freely available at the Embassy in London. Would this also be the case in Moscow? If it was, could the Russians be trusted with them?

Fogbound had the letter with him. He was proud of having correspondence from overseas, and he read from it as he went along. Aubrey wanted to take his advice and turn pro, and ventured to ask for help because he wanted to do his fighting in the United States. Purses were higher there, and he could do more for his country. Fogbound took this last phrase to mean that Aubrey hoped to bring glory to England through his fighting and that the United States, as the international capital of boxing, was the place to do it.

He read on once more. Aubrey needed a sponsor. Were he an established fighter, Aubrey wrote, the need would not arise, for a promoter booking him on a card could bring him in. Were he a person of — and here Aubrey began using quotation marks to show that he was referring to the United States immigration regulations — "distinguished merit and ability coming temporarily to the United States to perform services of an exceptional nature requiring such merit and ability, except that a graduate of a medical school coming to perform services as a member of the medical profession may come solely to teach or conduct research at a public or nonprofit private educational or research institution, or agency," the need would not arise.

"You hear?" Fogbound said. "Official."

He continued. Were Aubrey coming temporarily as a trainee other than to receive graduate medical education or training, the need would not arise. The consul had thought about that last one, but in the end she concluded that Aubrey's circumstances most resembled those of an alien going to the United States to take a specified job and being imported by an employer. That employer was Fogbound.

Fogbound had seen Aubrey hit plumb in the stomach without folding, and he had seen him hit around the eye and cheekbone and, in a thoroughly un-English manner, keep his blood to himself. He thought he could pick up enough fights for Aubrey to break even, at least; he admired his courage and spirit of adventure; and he had, after all, suggested that he turn pro. He obtained the necessary forms, was disappointed when handed them casually, without being searched or questioned, and bit the bullet.

Fogbound, a patriot, did not take the obligation lightly. He noted that aliens who are not mentally sound and physically fit, and those over 16 years of age who cannot read and understand some language or dialect, may be denied admission; that drug addicts and chronic alcoholics may not enter, and that an alien's past crime may be enough to bar him. Also, that among other excludable aliens are those who are, or at any time have been, members of or affiliated with any organization that advocates or teaches the overthrow, by force or violence or other unconstitutional means, of the Government of the United States or of all forms of law, or who advocate the economic, international, and governmental doctrines of world communism or the establishment in the United States of a totalitarian dictatorship, or who are members of or affiliated with any organization that so advocates. Fogbound considered that a member of a family as distinguished as the Clarks would hardly have such flaws of character and that Aubrey was not likely to be denied admission.

The form, "Job Offer for Alien Employment," U.S. Department of Labor Manpower Administration MA7–50B, of which Fogbound proudly showed me a copy and which I noted had replaced Form ES–575B, was more troublesome. Question 15, "Would you hire a qualified U.S. worker if available?" called for a "Yes" or "No" answer. Reasoning that if he had had one or two good boys at the moment, he would not have gone to England, Fogbound marked the "Yes" box. Question 16 asked what efforts he had made to fill the job. Sparing the government the story of Sugar Ray Titulescu, Fogbound wrote that he needed a good fighter and he thought Aubrey might be it. Question 17 asked how he had learned that alien named above was available. "Alien named above told me," Fogbound replied.

Under the job description, Fogbound was asked to list equipment operated and working conditions. He mentioned the heavy bag and the light bag and the skipping rope and the medicine ball, and under working conditions, he wrote, "None."

"Type and degree of supervision alien will receive" stopped Fogbound only momentarily. "Mine," he wrote.

There remained the declaration: "Under penalties of perjury, I declare that I have examined this application, supplements thereto, and all accompanying documents, and to the best of my knowledge and belief the information presented thereon is true, correct, and complete." As Fogbound explained it to me, he sat up straight in his chair, squared his shoulders, then his jaw, and signed.

2

DURING THE NEXT FEW WEEKS, out of curiosity, I dropped in at the gym from time to time to watch Aubrey train. One afternoon, I came upon him and Fogbound standing together inside an otherwise empty ring, breathing deeply and in unison. I thought that they might be practicing a form of meditation, or that perhaps they had bravely volunteered to risk contracting a respiratory disease in a scientific experiment financed by a large foundation.

It was neither of these. Fogbound had discovered that the prevailing aroma of British boxing was different from that in the United States, and traceable, he believed, to the difference between British and American cigarettes. "Another climate altogether," he said. He had, therefore, instituted breathing exercises for Aubrey and, to help along, he breathed with him. They made an unusual sight. When Fogbound inhaled and exhaled, most of the action took place below his beltline. Aubrey made breathing sounds, but with no visible effect. His chest was evidently incapable of expanding, and his stomach was almost concave.

Whatever these methods may have contributed, Aubrey did well. Not only did he win, but his appearance was so unlikely that the sportswriters took to him, even though he was only fighting preliminaries. "Angular Aubrey," they called him, and "The toothpick that walks like a man," and "The lengthy Limey." I read these names with some nostalgia, especially the alliterations. One did not alliterate in editorials, which were a higher calling.

Fogbound, sensing that he might have something out of the ordinary, brought Aubrey along with special care. Every time his man was hit in the stomach, he watched for the vertebrae to bounce all over the ring. They never did. He also nursed the fear that Aubrey's Adam's apple, an abnormally large feature, would get in the way of a glove. That never happened, either. Aubrey rolled along, a good boxer, courageous, with a long reach that partly offset his lack of punch.

One day, not long after the deep-breathing incident, I ran into Fogbound on the street. He was on his way to his office, I to mine, and we stood outside a shop that sold souvenirs and a variety of small items and which was conducting its final close-out sale, at the time in its seventh year.

"How's Aubrey?"

Fogbound rolled his eyes upward.

"What's the trouble?"

"Economics. He's crazy over economics. He sits for hours embossed in a book, reading and figuring. He knows parts of the paper I never heard of before."

"There are worse things to be interested in."

"Not before a fight," Fogbound said emphatically. "He fights tonight, the semifinal, and right now I bet he's studying his economics and not sleeping like I told him."

"Who's he fighting?"

"McGrath."

"Tough?"

"Like a tank." Fogbound shook his head mournfully. "They're not very comparative statistically."

"Sam," I said. "I am not worried. I think you have a man of destiny. Which reminds me: When Alexander the Great founded the city of Bucephalia in 326 B.C., he named it after his favorite horse, Bucephalus. Traces of the city, in what is now Pakistan, still exist. Get me a ticket."

"I'll see you at the fight," Fogbound said.

With this meeting, I became part of the chain that linked Fogbound and Aubrey and, as time went by, a company that included a gangster, a gangster's moll, an aging actress — who was, however, aging at the same chronological rate as everyone else — and a member of Congress. Also an obsessive giver of parties. And a British diplomat in the rare condition known as secondment. At some of the events to be described, I was present. Some I was told about. Some I was told about only after asking — this is now called investigative journalism. The account is reliable.

That night the ring at the Sportitorium was filled with the usual toweled, sweatshirted, and robed figures as Fredda Plantagenet, the aging actress, arrived. Fredda was sometimes described as a star of stage, screen, and television — "Not inaccurate," I once heard her say with satisfaction — and was a staple item for the gossip columnists, and, because of her devotion to boxing, a friend of Fogbound's. She had been named the ninth most admired woman in the United States in a public opinion poll, and had won a "Compassion in Media" award because a dog had been cured of distemper as part of the action in one of her television dramas.

She nodded to me — we were acquainted through Fogbound — and introduced her escort, Makepeace Guggenheim, before they sat down in the row in front of mine. "Mercer, *Star-Telegram*," I mumbled, hoping to sound semiofficial, which calls for more artful inflection than the full status does. She wore a cape with a red lining, and under that a black dress given the task of maximizing the points that indicated that she was far from finished and minimizing those that indicated how close to being finished she was. Her hair was an artificial and unidentifiable shade of brown — at any rate, it was unidentifiable to me without one of those color charts you get at a paint store, though I knew that it was fashionable.

Guggenheim I also recognized. He was an actor much employed in television commercials, in one of which he caused happy astonishment in his wife by asking for a second cup of coffee, this after she had changed brands. In another, he foolishly pronounced a cereal delicious, not realizing that it was a high-fiber cereal, while his wife winked at the camera. In a third, he told an investigator who recorded it all on videotape that he was indeed interested in the relative softness of toilet paper and wished that his wife (who was watching, profoundly gratified) would get one more delicate in texture.

Now the ring announcer took over. He described the match about to take place as the semifinal and penultimate event of the evening. He pointed toward a corner with his left hand, to a short, heavily muscled, glaring man, hopping up and down, his robe tossed over his shoulders. The pertinent facts about him were that he was Jim McGrath, came from San Francisco, and weighed one hundred fifty-nine pounds. His introduction brought forth a moderate roar from the crowd, and he danced forward, waving his gloves about his head.

The announcer thrust out his right hand toward an extraordinarily elongated man, his thin, obedient blond hair slicked down on his head. He had a pink face and in addition to his targetlike Adam's apple, a nose longer than seemed advisable. His robe was in danger of slipping off because his shoulders were so narrow, but he clutched it to him with his left hand and raised his right glove above his head. As he did so, his robe opened enough for me to see "A P-G" monogrammed on the front lefthand corner of his trunks. The announcer intoned that this was Aubrey Philpott-Grimes, the new English favorite from Steeple Bumpstead, England, weighing one hundred fifty-seven and a half.

In the ring, there was a brief conference as the referee gave his instructions, and then the two men returned to their corners and took off their robes. There was a gasp and some laughter as Philpott-Grimes removed his. His skin was pure white, almost transparent, and no hint of muscle disturbed its symmetry. It seemed doubtful that he would have strength enough to get his hands into fighting position, let alone move them in the direction of his opponent.

"Oh, come on," said Fredda. "That's no fighter. He looks like a flagpole."

"I can't see how they let him in there," Makepeace Guggenheim said. "Where did they say he was from?"

"Somewhere in England," Fredda said. "I couldn't make it out. I wonder whether they expect him back."

The bell rang and a look of apprehension crossed Fredda's face as she waited for Philpott-Grimes to be hit and to collapse. She winced when McGrath made a threatening move, but after a minute, she grew accustomed to the sight of Philpott-Grimes, with his gaunt figure, engaging in a prize fight, behaving as though he had engaged in one before, and generally conducting himself as though he had legitimate business in the ring. For somehow he had his hands up where they belonged and every so often the left snaked out and popped against McGrath's head. It did no damage but it did keep McGrath at a safe distance.

"I like him. He's so brave. And calm, too," Fredda said, as the bell rang for the end of the first round. "He doesn't seem concerned at all."

"Wait till McGrath hits him. He won't be able to be."

"You're mean, Makie."

"I'm a realist."

The second round found Philpott-Grimes continuing his methodical popping of McGrath's head. Whenever McGrath got in close, Philpott-Grimes's long arms, looking like white string against Manila hemp, tied him up. Fredda listened for the sound of bones cracking in the clinches, but it did not come.

"As I see it," Fredda said during the interval before round three, "even though McGrath is not very smart, he's going to figure out some way to hit him in the stomach. And that will be the end."

McGrath opened the third round by belting Philpott-Grimes smartly in the stomach. The tall Englishman, without changing expression, continued to pump out his left. As the round wore on, he added an occasional right cross. These, too, had no effect on McGrath's skull.

By round four, Fredda was calling Philpott-Grimes "Aubrey," laughing when he hit McGrath, and groaning when McGrath hit him.

"Isn't he wonderful?" she squealed. "I think he's wonderful."

By round six, the pattern of the fight was established. Aubrey was outscoring McGrath two and three to one, and every time his left landed on McGrath's head, it looked as though somebody had built a rickety bridge between a lamp-post and a fire hydrant. I made a note of this impression in case I should ever go back to sportswriting, then spoke to myself in sportswriter's language. "McGrath's punches carry more power," I advised myself, "but they leave Phil-pott-Grimes apparently unruffled."

I then replied: "It must be said that many a fighter left apparently unruffled by his opponent's blows turns out later to have been severely ruffled and eventually caves in from a shot that appears to be no more ruffling than those that went before."

I waited for this to happen to Aubrey, but it didn't, though in round seven, the fight did come to a sudden and violent end. Soon afterward, I found out why. McGrath, weary of sorting out his limbs after each clinch, growled, "Quit wrestling, you skinny Limey." Aubrey replied, "You shouldn't have called me that. I consider that an insult. That rouses me to fever pitch."

Thus roused, Aubrey took the offensive. His left moved out faster than ever, and, as McGrath tried to protect himself, Aubrey swung a right as though he were tossing a lariat. It caught McGrath on the point of the chin, and he fell flat on his back and was counted out. During the count, Aubrey leaned against the ropes in a neutral corner, smiling in an embarrassed way. Fogbound's mouth was open in astonishment, but he came to and climbed into the ring to embrace him.

Fredda was beside herself. "Oh, you sweetheart," she shouted. "Oh, you doll. You're wonderful, Aubrey." She turned to her escort. "Isn't he wonderful? Isn't he?"

"It looks like a fix to me," Guggenheim said. "He can't hit that hard. I think McGrath took a dive."

"He looked out to me," Fredda said. "I think I know a tank job when I see one. I also know Sam Franklin. He wouldn't go for anything like that. And if McGrath was faking, he's a better actor than some I've been working with. Which I admit," she said, "isn't saying much."

I leaned into the conversation. "Mercer, *Star-Telegram*," I said. "You're right on both counts, Miss Plantagenet. Sam wouldn't be connected with a tank job, and McGrath is a better actor than some you've worked with. Even when he's unconscious."

Fredda nodded to me regally, and rose. "Shall we go?"

"That was only the semifinal," Guggenheim said. "The main bout's still to come."

"Too many plays continue when the curtain should be down. The curtain here is down now."

"I'd like to see the main event," Guggenheim said.

"You've seen it. It just wasn't called that. Now come along. I intend to exit, enjoying the stares of the curious."

Guggenheim stood up and took her arm, but Fredda turned to me. "Philpott-Grimes. May I take it that he does not have a cockney accent? He doesn't fight like a man with a cockney accent."

"Not a trace. Even that roundhouse right was delivered without one."

Fredda said, "Fortunate," nodded once more, and they left.

I had the feeling that she was right. The rest of the evening no longer mattered. Fate was loose among us.

$\mathfrak{3}$

FOGBOUND'S OFFICE was not a place in which most people would choose to while away time without an excellent reason. It was in a ramshackle building served by a rickety elevator with wrought-iron sides, and was possessed by dust and damp. The office itself, on the eighth and topmost floor, commanded a view of a side street in the West Fifties and, if one's neck were craned painfully, of Eighth Avenue. Nobody came for the view. In the office were a desk, a rack for hats and coats, a wooden swivel chair with a seat of imitation leather, a couch also in imitation leather, a straight-backed wooden chair, a calendar, and pictures of fights and fighters. It had once boasted a cuspidor, but this had gone in a metal drive during the Second World War.

Making for this retreat, Fredda might have been said to be overdressed, though this was caused less by her costume, a restrained suit available only to those with large fortunes intact, than by the griminess of the precincts. Her appearance drew a compliment from Fogbound, whose interest in such matters normally was less than acute. This, however, may have been mere playing for time, for as he continued to look at Fredda, whose perfume was struggling with the building's resident odors, a sudden and unwelcome realization swept over him and he closely resembled a man preparing for the worst. It came quickly. Fredda explained that she wanted to look her best for Aubrey. He was a stranger in the country and she wanted to make him welcome.

"He's English," Fogbound said, throwing up a quick defense.

"And what is the significance of that remark?"

"I thought you should know."

"I do know," Fredda said, "but I may be willing to overlook it." She gazed with interest at one of the dozens of photographs on the wall. "Who's this fellow?"

"One of my old boys. Tarzan Hepburn."

"Did I ever meet him?"

"Not that I know of, Fredda."

"Why not?"

"You didn't have time. There was then a Mr. Brinsmead who played jazz on the flute."

Fredda looked at the couch, looked at what she was wearing, hesitated, saw me half-rising in a limited exhibition of courtesy, said, "Ah, the sardonic newspaperman," hesitated again, then bravely sat down. "What time did you say Aubrey would be here?"

Fogbound hesitated.

"Come on, Sam."

Fogbound sighed. "Any minute now he'll be here. And it's a pleasure to hear myself called Sam. You and my wife and Joe here and Aubrey, you're the only ones who do it. He's a nice boy," Fogbound went on. "Very serious. All the time studying. Too much, if you ask me. In his free time, he should relax. And Greek sayings. He's always ready with Greek sayings."

"What does he study, boxing?"

"Economics." Fogbound delivered the word as though he expected it to topple Fredda off the couch. "All the time economics. Sterling's area, things like that. And he has a photogenic memory. In all my life, I never heard such talk from a fighter. Yesterday, he was telling me about mackerel economics. I like fish, but to be so interested in mackerel isn't normal."

Fredda let Fogbound's comments pass. She established later, in consultation with me, that Aubrey had been speaking of macroeconomics which, as any editorial writer knows, takes the economic system as a unit, thereby distinguishing it from microeconomics, which in its benighted way studies the economic system through its components. I had recently written a stirring editorial coming down on the macro side and thought it only a matter of time before microeconomics gave up the unequal struggle. "What's his background?" she asked.

Fogbound looked impressed. "He's from one of those big English families. Aristocrats. All in all, quite a fella."

Fogbound had not told me of Aubrey's aristocratic forebears, and I was about to question him when there was a knock on the door and Philpott-Grimes walked in. He wore a black jacket, with a black waistcoat and black trousers. The stiff detachable collar of his white shirt housed a tightly knotted gray tie. Black shoes, bowler, and rolled umbrella completed the costume. When he saw Fredda, he bowed. She nodded gravely.

"Aubrey," Fogbound said, looking fearfully at Fredda, "this is the famous actress, Fredda Plantagenet. She came here especially to meet you. A great fight fan."

Aubrey bowed again and declared himself honored. Fredda extended a gloved hand. Then she said that she had seen him fight on the preceding night and that he had been wonderful. This led to a discussion of Aubrey's right hand, during which she congratulated him on his Sunday punch, and Aubrey replied that he didn't have one but that McGrath's calling him a Limey — one thing he could not stand — had brought on anger that added power to the blow.

"I'm sure it won't happen again," he said. "Mind you, it's far easier than all that jabbing. It's rather like a bulk purchase compared to a succession of small transactions, with the terms negotiated each time."

"Economics," Fogbound advised Fredda. "You hear?"

Inevitably, Fredda called England a lovely place, noted that she had been there a number of times, and had played the Old Vic.

"Old Vic," Fogbound said to me later. "Another one."

She guessed that Aubrey missed England. Aubrey, who by now had hung his bowler and umbrella on the rack and was watching Fredda with keen interest, admitted that he did miss it a bit.

In pursuit of a subject with which to keep the conversation going for more than a few sentences, Fredda next announced that according to Fogbound, Aubrey came from an old English family. Fogbound confirmed this, adding that it would be excellent publicity material when he was ready to let it out.

Aubrey turned to Fogbound. "Where did you get that idea?"

Fogbound was startled. "I thought you told me you came

from one of those big English families where nobody has to work."

"I never said anything of the kind."

"You said you were a Clark."

"I was."

"Spell it," said Fredda.

Aubrey did.

"You're a clerk," Fogbound shouted, "a clerk. Over there, I can see they don't teach so good. Learn to say clerk. Speak right and you'll get ahead faster."

"If I were a C–l–a–r–k," Aubrey asked, "why would my name be Philpott-Grimes?"

"I wondered about that," Fogbound said, "but I don't like to ask personal questions."

Fredda tried again. "I gather you're a student of economics. Isn't that an unusual interest for a fighter?"

"I don't know." Aubrey grinned shyly. "Boxing is like a nation's balance of payments. One wants to export more than one imports."

Fredda smiled in a gingerly way, and I half expected her to look around at Tarzan Hepburn's photograph again.

"You ever heard such a thing?" Fogbound turned to Aubrey. "You'd be better off studying boxing. Economics can come later."

"I'm doing rather well."

"More you can always learn. What the real pros did. The smart men."

"Like one Benny Leonard?" Aubrey asked. "I've read about him."

"A wonder," Fogbound said. "The best."

"Benny Leonard," I said for Fredda's benefit. "Born Benjamin Leiner. Lightweight champion, 1917–1925, when retired.

Came back as welterweigh, 1931. Over the hill and out of shape, knocked out by Jimmy McLarnin in six. Retired second time."

"If newspaper morgues could broadcast, they'd sound like you," Fredda said.

Aubrey cleared his throat. "I have read about Leonard's fight with one Lew Tendler — "

"Later the proprietor of a well-known Philadelphia restaurant," I said, to show that my spirit was unbroken.

" — in 1926." He turned to Fredda. "An aprocryphal tale, more than likely. Still, the story goes that when Tendler caught him with a left hook, Leonard concealed how bady hurt he was by asking whether that was as hard as Tendler could hit. Let us say that the story is true. Do you know what I should have done — had I been Tendler, of course?"

"No," Fogbound said. "What should you have done?"

"I should have said, 'Yes, but I do hit jolly often. Like this.' And I should have crossed my right and thoroughly discouraged him."

"You should have discouraged one Benny Leonard?" Fogbound asked.

"I should indeed," said Aubrey.

"You should indeed be ashamed of yourself," Fogbound said, and trying to impress upon Aubrey the enormity of his crime, he added, "speaking that way about a former immortal."

"You two have argued long enough," Fredda said. "I think that Mr. Philpott-Grimes had better come with me."

Fogbound looked wretched. "He's so thin, Fredda."

Fredda regarded him balefully. "I don't intend him to miss any meals."

"Where are you taking him?"

"To see a television show. My television show." She seemed suddenly to remember Aubrey's physical presence. "That is, of course, if he wants to go and" — she looked at Fogbound — "if he feels it's safe."

"*Quocumque duces*," Aubrey said cheerfully.

"What?" asked Fogbound.

"Wherever you lead," Aubrey explained.

"Greek again. I thought I had an English fighter, at least he'd speak English," Fogbound said.

Fredda rose. "Sam, I thank you. We're leaving."

"You won't be too busy rehearsing?" Fogbound asked hopefully.

"Not too busy," Fredda said. "Besides, Mr. Philpott-Grimes may find the rehearsal interesting."

Aubrey announced that he was sure he would.

Fogbound fired a last, forlorn shot. "He goes to bed early, remember." As they left, he shook his head sadly. "And just when Aubrey was beginning to make himself imminent." He thought for a moment, then accepted the inevitable. "Between consulting adults, how can I object?"

"Mark this well," I said. "We have seen the beginning of a liaison of high significance. Someday, we may dandle our grandchildren on our knees and tell them about it."

"I have no children," said Fogbound. "Neither have you. You're not even married. How can we dangle our grandchildren?"

I retreated. "Are you worried, Sam?"

"With a fighter who thinks half the time in Greek, and ruins his eyes reading economics, and now there's Fredda? I'm worried."

4

WHEN TWO WORLDS MEET, there should, at the very least, be
a crash and some dislocation. The Plantagenet–Philpott-
Grimes meeting brought no such consequences. Both worlds
walked away from the collision measurably happier than before, Fredda regarding Aubrey as an exotic bloom and Aubrey
reflecting that his experience included no such woman as this.
The United States, he told himself, was a great country.

Fogbound remained nervous. Fredda was an old friend,
and he was fond of her, and ordinarily he would not have
been troubled by her taking an interest in one of his fighters,
at any rate when they were not in training, but these were
not ordinary circumstances. First Aubrey was an Englishman. An Englishman might, for all he knew, be upset by
Fredda's tendency to take over.

"Proud, the English," Fogbound told me. "Of what, I
don't know. I read it."

His Englishness apart, Aubrey was so far from the usual
type of fighter that Fogbound was puzzled by him and there-

fore feared complications. "I had a fighter maybe something like Aubrey once," he said. "A college man. He spoke like you. It was a strain being with him."

Before I could thank him for this compliment, Fogbound went on to his third cause for nervousness: Aubrey's improbable physique. He did not altogether expect his man to wither and blow away if he became friendly with Fredda, but he felt a growing concern.

"Samson and Delilah," Fogbound said. "You think she cut his hair?" With his right hand he made snipping motions near the halo of gray hair that rimmed his head. "In those days, they couldn't say things as plain as today. Aubrey's thin. He has to save his strength."

When Aubrey came in, the morning after meeting Fredda, Fogbound was half afraid to look. I wasn't quite sure what he thought he might see — a stooped posture perhaps, a dragging gait, cheeks more sunken than before. In any case, his reluctant gaze revealed nothing missing or damaged, and Fogbound did not ask Aubrey to strip so that he could check further.

"We don't have women like Fredda in England," Aubrey said.

I said that the species, though not endangered, was fairly rare generally. Aubrey, a dreamy look on his face, appeared not to hear me. Fogbound, feeling his way, said, "She took your mind off economics?"

"On the contrary," Aubrey replied. "She is deeply interested in economics. It is merely another facet of her remarkable personality."

Fogbound, happy to have Aubrey back at all, abandoned the inquiry.

As time went by, Aubrey and Fredda grew closer and more

deeply attached, with salutary results for both. Aubrey soon had an autographed picture of Fredda in the bedroom of his small apartment.

"I could fairly be described," he told me, "as a man of the world."

I said that I was familiar with the type, though as a newspaperman never rich enough to qualify myself, and that I readily recognized him as an exemplar. It was the first time I had used that word in conversation. It came out unbidden. Being an editorial writer had enlarged my working vocabulary. I was gratified and decided that I would soon say exemplar again.

As for Fredda, whose disposition was made uncertain and even rancid by lack of affiliation, she became kind, considerate, and tender. Aubrey congratulated her on her understanding.

"Intuition and experience," she replied. "I know all about boys. I played Peter Pan when I was younger."

"I wish I had seen her doing it," Aubrey told me. "I love Peter's audacity."

Fogbound still made occasional tentative and fruitless inquiries — "You and Fredda are still reading economics?" and "Fredda's not taking her show to the coast or anything like that?" — and once, he asked me how I thought Aubrey looked. I told him it was possible that Aubrey's cells were deteriorating, but there were no outward signs of physical decline.

By this time, I had become a regular caller, in part so that they would not fail to know that children born in Italy in 1348, the year of the Great Plague, grew no more than 24 teeth, instead of the normal 32, and partly to keep up with what was going on. I suggested that Aubrey wear a monocle as a publicity stunt, but Fogbound, after learning that this was an eyeglass, worn in one eye only, vetoed the idea. With the possible exception of Aubrey's connection with Fredda, he wanted to keep things just as they were. Success was not to be tampered with. "No molecules," he said.

One day in Fogbound's office, as I questioned Aubrey about the advantages of a wardrobe made up entirely of identical costumes, including four black umbrellas, he began bubbling — it was low key, but bubbling nonetheless — and said, "Joe, do you remember my telling you that Fredda was sweet and unaffected?"

I did.

"The more I know her," Aubrey said, "the more I realize how right I was."

"You don't have to tell me," I said. "I remember it from the first time you told me."

"I know you do," Aubrey said, "but I wanted to tell you I was right."

The conversation seemed to me one that could be entered or left at any point without loss, so I pronounced a blessing on Aubrey, and another on the two of them together, and pulled a pipe out of one pocket, a pouch of tobacco out of another, and matches from a third. "This is my day off," I said, "but it's just about four o'clock and that's when we have the daily editorial conference. All the others draw in smoke before exhaling thoughtfully and making sage remarks. You can't make a sage remark at an editorial conference without allowing smoke to escape first. I'm practicing. If I didn't do it, no one would listen to me."

I drew in the tobacco smoke, gagged, let it escape, and said, "Some days, I can hardly see across the room. My eyes smart. I may put in for workmen's compensation."

"Perhaps you should go back to sportswriting."

"I've thought about it. I've also thought about a television career." This was true. I had been on a few times, on shows with titles like "The Hidden Sources of Public Opinion," and it seemed to me that I might have a future in commercials, recommending books and wines and walking sticks and other things that a thoughtful man would know about. I might say, for example, that I had been sitting in a certain easy chair when I conceived the editorial calling for a renewal of limited United States cooperation with the International Labor Office. A producer I consulted had suggested that I ought to be more shaggy. "We can get your hair cut shaggy," he told me. "Like sculpted." This, however, was his only idea, and I had not pursued the matter.

For the moment, I knocked the pipe against the heel of my shoe, watched the tobacco fall into the wastebasket near Fogbound's unoccupied desk, and put the pipe in my pocket. "You still interested in economics?"

"More than ever."

"How do you find time for it?"

"If Fredda were less understanding and less adventurous intellectually, I couldn't. But we read together. We finished a biography of John Maynard Keynes last week. Quite lively, really."

"If I were a gossip columnist," I said, "an item like that could keep me going for years. You two planning to be married?"

Aubrey blushed. "I did tell her the other day that I'd like her to meet my parents."

"Another item. What did she say?"

Aubrey hesitated.

"You can trust me," I said. "I have no professional interest in these fugitive matters. I'm an editorial writer. You've seen my pipe. You even saw me smoke it."

Aubrey blushed again. "She said I was precious."

"A noncommittal reply. She has not dealt you a resolute rebuff of the kind so often administered to greedy imperialists by the united socialist peoples. Neither has she grasped your initiative in a way that foreshadows favorable consideration. She has reserved her position. When's your next fight?"

"Sam's working on it now. We may know today."

He picked up an analysis of the trigger price system as a means of deterring unwanted imports, and I was on my way out when Fogbound came up on the elevator. Because of its convulsive state, parts of him, pockets of flesh here and there, continued to shake even when he stood on the unmoving floor. He persuaded me to re-enter the office with him, for he often felt the need of an ally when dealing with Aubrey. He brightened when he noticed the book in Aubrey's hand.

"How's Fredda?" he asked.

"All right, I imagine," Aubrey said.

"You haven't seen her?"

"Not since last night."

Fogbound ploughed ahead. "That's what I like to see. More people should read economics. I wish I had the time."

Aubrey put aside his book. "You, Sam, what a nosy parker! Forever tiptoeing around the point. I thought that Americans were bluff and hearty."

"Who's not bluff and hearty?" Fogbound said indignantly.

"Sam, I don't intend to discuss my private affairs with you. I'll put it this way. I'll have all my strength for my next fight. And I might as well tell you that since meeting Fredda, I have known mental peace, and that's important for a fighter. Now then, did you sign?"

"I almost forgot." Fogbound was happy to change the subject. "I signed. Palmer. We fight him in five weeks."

"Good," Aubrey said. "I don't want to get rusty."

"How tough is he?" I asked.

"Mostly, he doesn't bother you." Fogbound stood up, took a fighting position, feinted with his hands, moved his shoulders, ducked his head and moved it from side to side, covered up, and skipped in and out. "Not many punches. But sometimes he makes the other guy look bad."

Aubrey said, "I like the footwork, Sam, but the lino slows you down. When do we go into training?"

"Tomorrow."

"Very well. I'll tell Fredda tonight. She'll be pleased."

Fogbound guarded his silence.

5

IN MOTION PICTURES about fighters, either the major motion pictures invariably promised (and to which admission ought, by right, to be by major credit card only) or the minor motion pictures (minor credit cards should be all right for these) nobody acknowledges making, it is impossible for any fight to go the distance. There is always a fast-moving montage of opponents collapsing into the ropes, thudding into the canvas, or being escorted, helpless, to their corners by the referee while the hero dances about, waving his gloved hands, and the sound track carries the thunderous roar of the crowd. The hero may also smirk a little, if it is the sort of movie in which he is to get his comeuppance later on.

This murderous progress was not for Aubrey. Despite his knockout of McGrath, he was not, as he himself acknowledged, that hard a hitter. He pinked with his left and crossed occasionally with his right and didn't get much body into his punches. Not that his body looked as though it would have added anything.

Yet the knockout of McGrath led to learned analyses of how he had cleverly pretended to be only a boxer and had insisted that he had no Sunday punch when in reality he was saving the big right hand as a surprise. One columnist headed a piece, "The Thinking Man's Fighter." Another headed his, "Philpott-Grimes Fills the Bill." *Time* magazine, commenting on Aubrey's distaste for being called a Limey, gave its readers some advice on pronunciation placed in parentheses immediately after his name — "Rhymes," *Time* pointed out, "with ill-got limes."

The McGrath fight was followed by a decision over Palmer, who fought with his shoulders hunched most of the night, protecting his jaw, and who found Aubrey a disconcertingly narrow target when he did throw punches. This put Aubrey in a position where a few more victories would make him a logical, if cadaverous, contender. The principal obstacle now became John-John McKenzie, the Trinidad Tornado.

McKenzie was pitting against Aubrey's killer right, which had again gone into hibernation during the Palmer fight, his own specialty, which he called the rum punch. "My country has the bes' rum," he said, "an' we make the bes' rum punch. But it ain' jus' rum. It has to be mix'. It's rum an' sugar an' bitters an' lime juice, an' you shake she and you pour she over crush' ice. Or you froth she up with a swizzle stick. I do both, swizzle and shake. An' when she in the glass, I sprinkle she with nutmeg. It a combine. My rum punch in the ring — that a combine, too. Is a jab an' a hook an' a uppercut an' a bolo an' a straight right. An' I shake she up an' add whatever take my fancy. But too much rum punch ain' good, man. Put you to sleep. Aubrey find that out."

On the day before the fight, Fogbound and I came upon Aubrey with his head in his hands, staring at the office wall.

"I'm uncomfortable about beating McKenzie," he said. "He's a likable chap."

"You'll feel better if he beats you?"

"It isn't that, Sam. It's simply that he personifies the developing countries of the Third World. They're like children leaving home for the first time, fledglings leaving the nest."

"Aubrey," I said, "Trinidad left the nest seventeen years ago. And it has oil, asphalt, teak, copra, sugar, cocoa, coffee, bananas, citrus fruit, tourism, and some manufacturing. By the way," I went on, noticing a gap in the conversation, "Trinidad became a British colony in 1802, having been ceded as a spoil of war by Spain, for which it had been claimed by Columbus on one of his later voyages. The capital is Port of Spain. Population a hundred twenty thousand."

Fogbound closed the gap. "Aubrey, sometimes I know another manager. We play cards together. His wife knows my wife. He has, let's say, a nervous stomach, which can make a wreck out of him. I remember once a manager had a duodental ulcer. I sent him a card in the hospital. But should I tell my boy, Broadback Simmons it was, not to hit his boy when he's open?"

Looking as though he might get down on his knees at any moment, Fogbound paused to let the message get through. Aubrey still was troubled.

"As I recall," I pitched in, "Broadback was known for always giving his best."

"Always," said Fogbound. "Like me. You think I enjoyed beating a boy, his manager had an ulcer? But I did it. You think McKenzie will leave his rummy punch home? You think he's saying, 'That Aubrey, I can't beat. He's too nice'?" Fogbound now employed sarcasm. "Or maybe I should only get you fights with communists."

Aubrey walked over to the window, which gave him a view of an outside wall rather than the inside wall he had been staring at. I handed Fogbound a newspaper opened to the sports section and pointed to an interview with John-John. The reporter had rendered McKenzie's speech phonetically. Strained through Fogbound's accent, it was even more exotic.

" 'At home they got men who are plenty robus,' but I the most robus' of all. Ask my wife, Dorotee. Anybody bunks up John-John McKenzie gung be hit va-dam!' " Fogbound read. " 'I give he licks like fire, he bound to surrender.' "

McKenzie had been asked what his strategy would be and had replied, "I hit he va-dam! Make he fall down bup! on the floor." He had also alleged that after he finished serving his rum punch, Aubrey would be "basoodee." This was translated as "thoroughly confused." Finally, McKenzie said that he expected eventually to fight the champion, Irish Mike Turner. "I hit he va-dam! I t'ief his title."

Aubrey listened to this with no change of expression. "If needs must," he said. "He's a diverting fellow. I wish it were otherwise. I'm gung — I mean going — home, Sam. There's some reading I want to do. A history of the Caribbean."

Aubrey's departure did not mean that the staring in Fogbound's office was at an end. As I left, there was no reply to my "So long, Sam." Fogbound had his head in his hands and was intent on the wall. Inside. The outside wall was in reserve.

Given Aubrey's ambiguous mood, I more or less expected complications. They came, announced on the telephone by Fogbound. "He's disappeared," he said. He had called Aubrey at home to read him McKenzie's latest interview, in which John-John had proclaimed himself no pacootee fighter, but rather so famous at home that a calypso had been written about him — "When the Tornado Strike, Everyone Run for Cover," which included the couplet, "Aubrey's hopes of victory can only be truly absurd, / Against the Tornado from Land of the Hummingbird." The writer had translated "pa-cootee" as "tenth class." McKenzie had gone on to say that Aubrey might run for cover, but to no avail. "He run," said the Tornado, "but he cannot hide."

There had been no reply when Fogbound called. Nor was Aubrey with Fredda; he had checked there; she wanted to be informed at once of developments.

It occurred to me on the way up that if shaking the ingredients helped a rum punch, the elevator in Fogbound's office building would be an ideal place to prepare one. Because he looked desolate, I spared him this observation; but I did suggest that perhaps Aubrey had been unable to sleep and, not knowing that Vincent Van Gogh had fought off insomnia by dousing his pillow and sheets with camphor, had gone out for a walk.

"Some walk. Two hours."

"Sam," I said, "this is not a time to rush wildly into the streets, searching at random."

Fogbound grunted.

"It is a time for thought."

"Who's arguing?"

"I think," I said, sounding as much like a fictional detective as I could, "that we may safely assume that Aubrey's absence has something to do with the fight tomorrow night. We may assume further that it has nothing to do with fear of his opponent or fear that he will lose."

"To tell me this," Fogbound said, "you could have stayed home."

"Rather," I went on, "it is fear — or more properly, apprehension — that he will win. As an Englishman, beneficiary of the colonial system, he feels a residual guilt. He wonders whether the British played fair."

"You said think, not talk," said Fogbound.

I stood up and paced the floor, to see whether it would help. It didn't. I sat down again.

"He wondered whether the British played fair," I said musingly, which I enjoyed almost as much as I did saying something tartly. I would have gone on with it had I not seen Fogbound's tortured expression. I thought heroically. I pictured myself at an editorial page meeting, and pulled out my pipe, lit it, and felt ill. At that moment, it came to me. "Aubrey needs reassurance about Britain's role in the world. He must find a justification for victory tomorrow. There is your answer, Sam. He has gone to seek reassurance."

"That's an *answer*? That's an answer to what question?" Fogbound turned his eyes toward heaven.

"Sam," I said, "I believe that if my deductions are correct, we will find Aubrey at a British shrine. Fetch me" — I felt myself falling into Sherlock Holmesian diction — "the telephone directory."

Fogbound glared and dumped the directory on the desk in front of me. While I found the page I wanted, he took the telephone off the hook and raised his finger over the dial.

"Ten East Fortieth Street," I said.

Fogbound replaced the phone. "Who can dial that?"

"One fifty-three East Seventy-eighth," I said, writing it down. "Six thirty Fifth Avenue. Eight forty-five Third Avenue. One fifty East Fifty-eighth. Six eighty Fifth Avenue. Right. Let's go."

"Where?"

"Sam, come on. I'll explain."

In the taxi, while Fogbound peered from side to side, just in case Aubrey should be somewhere around, I set out my theory. Aubrey needed to commune with the British spirit and regain his sense of purpose. I knew of no British establishment that I would call a shrine, but Aubrey might see things differently. Ergo, we were heading for 10 East Fortieth Street, the British-American Chamber of Commerce.

"It's almost midnight," Fogbound said. "It's closed."

"Closed in the physical sense," I said, "but to someone like Aubrey, it may be sending out emanations. We shall see."

At 10 East Fortieth, there was no sign of Aubrey.

"Six thirty Fifth Avenue," I told the driver.

At the building that houses the offices of the British Broadcasting Corporation, there was no sign of Aubrey.

"Crazy," Fogbound said. "He's crazy, you're crazy, and I'm crazy to have anything to do with two crazy people."

"We'll get out here," I said.

"Why?"

"We'll walk to Six eighty Fifth Avenue."

"Why?"

"The British Tourist Authority is there."

There were strollers outside the building. None of them was Aubrey. I consulted my list. "One fifty East Fifty-eighth Street," I said.

"I won't ask," said Fogbound. "I humor Aubrey. I'll humor you."

As we approached our next destination, Fogbound cried out, "It's him! It's Aubrey!"

Maddening assurance was the note I was searching for. "Of course it is," I said.

There, walking slowly and calmly, back and forth, in front

of the building, was Aubrey. Fogbound galloped up to him.

"Hello, Sam. What brings you here?"

"Why should we be here? We just happened to be out for a walk."

"We'd like to take you home, Aubrey," I said. "Sam thinks you ought to get some rest."

"I intend to do exactly that," Aubrey said. "I was on the point of leaving."

"Aubrey," Fogbound asked fearfully, "you're all right? You know what I mean?"

"I'm perfectly splendid," said Aubrey. "This has done the trick. We must put the past behind us and press on."

After we had deposited Aubrey at home, Fogbound telephoned Mrs. Franklin and I called Fredda.

"You say he was communing with the exterior of a building?"

"I wouldn't put it in quite that way. I'd say he was coming as close as he could to a meaningful British environment."

"I've heard of actors who imagined themselves to be the characters they were playing. This is the first time I've heard of anybody getting inspiration from an office building. He did look normal to you?"

"Oh, yes. Entirely."

"You think the spell the building cast will last through the fight?"

I said I did.

"I thank you," she said, "and I bid you good night."

At Hanrahan's Bar, Fogbound asked why I had expected to find Aubrey at 150 East Fifty-eighth Street.

"Because it is the headquarters of the British Trade Development Office and the Export Credits Guarantee Department. Nothing is closer to Aubrey's heart than that."

"So why did you lead me on a wild goose chase to those other places?"

I was about to tell Fogbound that he had been privileged to witness a truly astonishing exhibition of ratiocination when I saw that he was smiling and that there were tears in his eyes.

"I'm happy for Aubrey," he said. "I only hope that to-morrow night he won't be tired."

Aubrey was not tired. He danced around the ring for ten rounds, the picture of determination and serenity, popping the Tornado's head back with his left, putting in a right hand to head or body every so often, and slipping and picking off punches as though the Tornado was a novice. With Aubrey in top form, it was sad to watch McKenzie. He entered the ring, lithe and handsome, bouncing and skipping lightly, with a gleaming smile, and wearing a purple-and-gold robe with an emblem embodying a funnel-shaped cloud with a hummingbird fluttering above it. He had explained in an interview that his robe was as beautiful as the hummingbird's plumage and that his hands moved as fast as its wings. "Aubrey find this out when I give him punishment for so," he proclaimed. "Not for nothing I called the Trinidad Tornado." During the referee's instructions, he kept a hand affectionately on Aubrey's shoulder until the referee removed it.

McKenzie's strategy was based on nonstop punching. They came from all angles. It must have seemed to Aubrey that it was raining punches. And when the cry, "Swizzle!" came from his corner, the Tornado would repeat, "Swizzle!" and punch even faster. The only defect in the strategy was that Aubrey was not there to be hit. He took some punches, but without damage. As the rounds wore on, it seemed to me that the only danger was that Aubrey might become careless. This was the expert sportswriter in me asserting itself, for after the sixth round, as I was to learn, Aubrey told Fogbound that when "Swizzle!" went up from the opposite corner, he was tempted to say, "Stick!" and ram another left in McKenzie's face. "But it wouldn't be right to humiliate him," Aubrey said, "and besides, I don't want to lose my concentration."

Measured in bloodshed and heavy hitting, it wasn't much of a fight. The Tornado was cut here and there, and near the end he was weary and taking some booing for his futility. As the bell went at the end of the tenth round, he threw his arms around Aubrey. "You sweet, Aubrey," he said. "You come Trinidad for Carnival or Christmas, you see us firing rum punches for so."

"I'd very much like to do that," Aubrey said. "And I'd like to see how your economy has changed from the colonial mode."

John-John hugged Aubrey again. "I ain't in that, man. Forget all this set of foolishness about economics and Third Worlds and that. You come Trinidad and we show you how to jump up, man, and how to live. We Trinidadians happy people, man, with we rum and we calypso."

"John-John," Aubrey said, "there is nobody in the world I wanted less to beat than you."

Some saw in Aubrey's lopsided victory an assertion of Britain's former glory, something like the invasion of Suez in 1956, but more successful. Aubrey saw it differently. "The emergent nations," he said, "though they do need help, should not be coddled. It is a hard world, and the sooner they learn that, the better."

"He's right," said Fogbound.

When Fredda came into the dressing room to collect Aubrey, she also had a comment. "The Export Credits Guarantee Department, did you say? One fifty East Fifty-eighth Street?"

I nodded.

"I'm not sure a woman can compete with it, but I'll try."

Aubrey came out, and Fredda said, as they left, "We'll go past the building. It may still be transmitting."

Fogbound waited for the door to close. "Maybe the building isn't," he said. "But she is."

6

Two days after the McKenzie fight, I dropped by Fogbound's office just in time to see him rising from his desk and going to a small refrigerator that had not been there before.

"Aubrey," he said, "time for your elevenses." He turned to me. "Every morning, Pauline calls whether Aubrey's had his snack. A snack Aubrey calls elevenses."

Aubrey grinned. "Mrs. Franklin says I need building up."

"I guess it's safe," I said. "A boxer as skinny as you are makes copy. Develop your chest, spring a muscle, and you're like all the rest. But that won't happen. Not at your age. How old are you, by the way?"

"Twenty-six. And it's only milk and cream crackers."

"You have to keep your angle," I said. "I remember an Italian heavyweight years ago. The writers called him 'The Leaning Tower of Pisa.'"

"He came from Pisa, then?" Aubrey asked.

"Naples. The most interesting thing about him as a fighter

was the distance he fell when hit. But he picked up some purses because he had an angle. And who was the most famous British heavyweight? Phil Scott. Why? Because he was always being knocked out, and the papers called him 'Phainting Phil.' With a name like that, he'll live forever."

"That was decades ago," Aubrey said, "and —"

I interrupted him. "In the annals of fistiana. Because he had an angle."

"That was decades ago, and I'd rather not be compared with Phil Scott. And if I were going to fill out, I'd have done it years ago."

"Muscles he won't get," said Fogbound. "He doesn't have that kind of a system."

Fogbound's assurance about Aubrey's metabolism was based on highly developed postulates, some of which had popped out in imperfect form when Mrs. Franklin, putting aside retirement plans for a while, took her initial interest in her husband's new fighter. After a quick glance, she had volunteered to cook for him as a means of protecting the family interest, for she considered it improbable that anyone so thin could survive, let alone be a fighter. Soon thereafter, she submitted to Fogbound a request for additional household money.

Unlike Aubrey I did not need building up, except in my confidence, which was suffering because of the fate of one of my editorials about Congress. I had ended it by writing, "It would be kindest, did not duty forbid, to draw a veil over the proceedings." The editor had ostentatiously impaled it on the spike where rejected copy wound up, and had said: "I won't tell anyone you wrote this, Mercer. I'll draw a veil over it." He shook with silent mirth over his own wit, and I made for the Franklins' as for a refuge. That evening, Mrs.

Franklin again raised the subject of the method by which Aubrey's body assimilated matter and provided energy for vital activities and processes. "Where does he put it?" she said. "It isn't natural."

Fogbound shrugged and fell back on the centerpiece of his medical learning. "It's his system."

"Maybe he's sick," Mrs. Franklin suggested. "Maybe a deficiency. *In* his system. God forbid."

Fogbound took over like a distinguished specialist grown impatient with a not-very-bright general practitioner. "Sick he's not. A deficiency he hasn't. He's *hungry*. Look at him. He's a middleweight. Somebody as skinny as that has no right to be a middleweight. Right now he should be a lightweight, maybe a featherweight. But he's a middleweight. It's simple. He eats the difference."

Mrs. Franklin, hands on hips, head over to one side, considered this diagnosis. "Tell me again," she said. "I'm not following."

"I'm not either," I said. "And it's sound medical procedure to get a second opinion. It may save a malpractice suit. I happen to have one with me."

Had Fogbound accepted this, I would have pointed out that I had increased my caloric intake since transferring to the editorial page, for it took a prodigal expenditure of energy merely to stay awake on the job. Aubrey was dealing with economics. It was surprising that he wasn't eating all the time.

But Fogbound did not choose to hear my theory. "Please," he said. "You're both in the minority in this discussion. Drop the subject."

At about the time that this conversation was going on, as I learned when I acquired the status of an almost universal confidant, Fredda was asking Aubrey a question that had long been on her mind. She had waited until she was certain that he would not misunderstand. At her picture window, they looked at the lights of the city, with the pink sky darkening to the west, and Fredda said, "Tell me, darling. Where did you learn to fight?"

"Have a dekko." Aubrey pulled his sleeve back over his wrist and revealed what appeared to be a flattened toothpick. "Makes you blanch." Fredda looked and a maternal feeling welled within her. "I've always been this thin," Aubrey said. "As a boy, I was called names and made the object of childish malice."

Fredda kissed him on the forehead. "You poor thing."

"I had to learn to protect myself, and I soon learned that my reach was my most valuable weapon. It happened by accident, really. A chap thought he'd have a go and came dashing at me. Up to that time I'd been fairly gormless about it all, but I held out my left hand to keep him off. He ran into it and I realized that he couldn't come any closer. He was cheesed-off, I can tell you."

Fredda looked at the wrist again. "Amazing. And that was all there was to it?"

"Not quite all. I didn't begin fighting in earnest until a few years later. After I'd made a few bullies look foolish, I realized how eminently gratifying it was."

"You're so clever," Fredda said.

"That reminds me," Aubrey said. "Have you read that article I gave you on money volume as a determinant of inflation?"

"I tried it under the drier. They didn't quite go together."

"What about the short piece on limited floating exchange rates?"

Fredda shook her head and her hair floated gently across her face. "Maybe tonight. In my tub."

Aubrey looked disappointed. "I'm afraid I won't be able to give you much help in the next few weeks. I'm going into training. Another fight."

Fredda pouted. "Will it be very nasty?"

"I believe I shall be the betting favorite."

"Hooray!" Fredda threw her arms in the air and bounced up and down. Settled again, she reached around painfully and rubbed her side. "Too God damned sportive," she said. She folded her legs under her, yoga-fashion, and sat quietly. "I now become the serious, attentive type. More attractive to adult males. Also less dangerous to myself. Aubrey, darling, what does Sam tell you about me?"

"Nothing."

"He must mention me."

"Oh yes, he mentions you. After all, you're not the sort of person one can ignore. I remember his telling me that you were an actress."

"Praise indeed."

"And he does say that women have ruined a lot of fighters. Then he asks something indirect — at any rate, he thinks it's indirect — like 'Fredda's all right?' or 'Fredda has a new part to learn?' "

"It's the damnedest thing," Fredda said. "Sign up with a boxing manager and he behaves as though you've taken a monkish oath." She paused. "Do monks still take monkish oaths, do you suppose? It would be a shame if they didn't. I would hate to see the monkish oath disappear. Such a rich sound. Not easy to say. It takes training." She paused again. "And such a dramatic idea. Incomprehensible. But dramatic."

Aubrey looked at her admiringly. "Tell me something about yourself, Fredda. You're so vital. Sometimes I think you embody the very spirit of America."

Fredda smiled. "What would you like to know?"

"Tell me where you were born. That's a good beginning."

"I was born in a log cabin on the Great Divide. My family were Mennonites seeking religious freedom."

"Is that so?" Aubrey was impressed. "Where is the Great Divide? I've always wanted to know."

"How the hell should I know where the Great Divide is?" Fredda asked. "Do I go around asking you unanswerable questions like that? It's out west somewhere. Look it up. I was born in New York."

"Were your people really Mennonites?"

"Mennonites and womenites."

"I was born in Steeple Bumpstead," Aubrey said, trying to redress the situation.

"How droll," Fredda said.

"It's true. Bumpstead, with a *p*. It's in Essex."

To Fredda, this seemed a cruel fate. It made her sad. "Do you really have to go into training so soon?"

"I'm afraid I do."

Fredda brightened. "We still have tonight."

"That's right."

"Come closer," Fredda said. She moved to give him room on the couch.

"Fredda," he said, "I hope that someday soon you will be able to meet my mother and father."

"Aubrey," Fredda said, "you're a dear."

They leaned against each other and Aubrey put his arm around her. Their eyes met. "It's wonderful here," Aubrey said. "I do love being with you. I still don't know why I've been so lucky."

Fredda patted his cheek and stroked his hair. "Big fighter boy. Hold me closer."

Aubrey tightened his grip with his right arm. Her left arm was around his middle. With her right hand she reached toward the chrome-and-glass coffee table in front of them and picked up a volume. "I think," she said, "we're on page eighty-eight."

Using his left hand, his face still against hers, Aubrey held the book with her and read aloud:

Propounded in this explicit fashion, the view that a given technological system will have an economic value and a cultural incidence on a community which takes it over ready-made, different from the effects it has already wrought in the community from which it is taken over and in which it has cumulatively grown to maturity in correlation with the other concomitant changes in the arts of life — when so stated as an articulate generalization this proposition may seem unfamiliar and perhaps dubious

Aubrey raised his eyes from the book and looked into Fredda's eyes. "I wish we could go on reading this way forever," he said.

Fredda smiled and kissed him softly. "Don't rush things," she said.

7

THE SENSE OF RIGHTNESS and security that Aubrey got from Fredda gave him peace of mind, but something else accounted for the unusually cheerful outlook which, on a lovely spring day, he made known to Fogbound. There had been no advance sign of it: Aubrey had begun the day's conversation unsurprisingly by asking whether Fogbound knew why the United States was stronger economically than Britain. Fogbound, to whom the question was familiar, said, "No," before ducking lower behind his paper.

"The differential in resources, of course," Aubrey said. "But it's also because Britain was the first truly mature industrial nation. We have paid the price of that pioneering. We have been left with obsolete plant."

"Maybe you would have been better off to wait," Fogbound ventured.

That closed the discussion, but a few minutes later, Fogbound heard Aubrey chuckle. "Now will you just look at that?" Then Aubrey said, "I'm a happy man today, Sam."

"I'm glad," Fogbound said. "Some reason?"

"I've just made my income tax return."

"That makes you happy?"

"Very. I'll be paying a tremendous tax."

"Aubrey," Fogbound said, "people don't realize. They think you're English, there's no sense of humor. I'm glad to hear you joking."

"I'm not joking, Sam. I'll pay a tremendous tax and I'll be delighted to do so."

Fogbound looked at Aubrey, realized he was serious, and put up his hand like a policeman directing traffic. "Wait a minute." He looked at his watch. "Wait fifteen minutes. Joe is coming over. He can be a witness."

Aubrey said, "Righto." He sang softly, "There'll Always Be an England" and "Rule, Britannia."

Fogbound leaped to his feet as I arrived. "Joe," he shouted. "I want you as a witness. You hear Aubrey. He's *singing*."

"I don't hear it," I said.

"He stopped when you came in. But he's been singing now for fifteen minutes, maybe more."

"He must be happy."

"That's it," Fogbound cried. "He's happy. Ask me why." He sat still, looking like a child waiting for the teacher to call on him.

"Why?" I said.

"Because he just heard his income tax and it was big."

"Tremendous," Aubrey said.

"Tremendous," Fogbound repeated. "And that makes him happy. So I said don't tell me anything until you're here, as a witness."

"I'm here," I said.

"Already first he doesn't want to hit McKenzie, he's from a small country. Now he pays a big tax, he's happy." He turned to Aubrey. "Tell."

The explanation proved to be simple. Britain, a manufacturing country shy of natural resources and obliged to import raw materials, needed large amounts of foreign currency, including dollars, if it was to make its way. Thanks to Fogbound, he had been making bags of dollars. Through the income tax, the British government was able to acquire most of them and use them where it felt they would do the most good. In this way, he was helping his country to build a sound economic future. "Paying taxes in good heart is necessary to the well-being of the polity," he said. "One does one's part."

"What will you pay?"

"Between Britain and the United States," Aubrey said, "about eighty per cent. Maybe a little more."

"That's twenty per cent left?" Fogbound asked.

Aubrey agreed that it was.

"If you paid that, too, I could hear you singing all the time. When you wanted to come here," Fogbound continued, "you told them you liked paying taxes?"

Aubrey had not.

"A mistake," Fogbound said. "They're looking for tax-payers. They don't have enough."

I did not join Fogbound in this raillery. Instead, I embarked on a short speech. It was an established editorial practice to appeal to the public-spirited citizen. I myself, though I should not have run dry so soon, already had chalked up a fair number of editorials that told readers that they were in one way or another, behooved. Now, here was Aubrey, behooved before the editorial writers could get at him. He was self-behooved, and among the few self-behoovers extant.

I paused, while Fogbound sighed. From Aubrey, thanks to

his perfect courtesy, there was no sound. "But, Aubrey," I went on, "the entire edifice of newspaper editorializing rests on the assumption that what we write is ignored. Suppose people in numbers began following our suggestions. Editorial writers would go about weighed down by care and worry. More than that, civilization would be unlikely to survive for a week. It behooves you to think of that."

I shook my head, pleased with my performance. "Aubrey," I said, "this development, if replicated elsewhere — and note the word *replicated*, a comer in government, the social sciences, and editorial writing — this development, if replicated elsewhere and on a sufficiently large scale, may have incalculable consequences."

"I am accustomed to unthinking reactions like yours, Sam," Aubrey said. "I expect them. And I am accustomed to attempts to be funny about my attitude to taxes. I've put up with them for years. They're really awfully dim."

As Aubrey said this, Fogbound's face lit up, for he realized, so he told me later, that this meant that Aubrey's delight in paying taxes was not a recent thing, caused by blows to the head. He had been paying taxes happily before. Now, blushing under Aubrey's reprimand, he said, "I'm thinking."

"About what?" I asked.

"Publicity. Another angle besides Aubrey is skinny."

"You mean something like, 'He fights for the Exchequer'?"

"For what?"

"The British Treasury."

"Speak English," Fogbound snapped. "Life is complicated enough."

"What good will publicity do?" I asked. "The British government gets most of the money anyway."

"Pardon me," Fogbound said. "I have a family, too." He

turned to Aubrey. "Aubrey, speak frankly. Maybe we can work something out. I don't like to think of you fighting for nothing."

Aubrey smiled. "Don't worry about me, Sam. I've never been happier. I like things just as they are."

I took a silent vow never again to twist the lion's tail editorially and said that I would arrange for a feature writer from the paper to get the entire story from Aubrey next day.

Then Aubrey asked us to watch our television sets that night. He was appearing on a late night talk show and hoped to be able to work in an explanation of the need for a more effective attack on structural unemployment in the west. He hoped some good would come of it. There was a fee attached to his appearance, of which Fogbound would get his usual share.

Fogbound would not hear of this. He did not manage that side of Aubrey.

"That is most generous," Aubrey said. "It means that I will be able to turn over the entire fee."

"Turn it over where?"

"To a British task force studying United States sales possibilities for tinned trifle."

Fogbound looked puzzled.

"It's a sweet."

"A cake," I said. "A dessert."

Recognition swept over Fogbound's face. "I had some. Save the money."

"We won't ask you for an endorsement, Sam," Aubrey said. "Or you, Joe. There wouldn't be space enough on the label."

Aubrey left and Fogbound followed him into the corridor. I heard him saying that he was sorry and that he hoped Aubrey wasn't angry, and I heard the sound of a slap on the

back and Aubrey saying, "Good old Foggers. Of course not."
Then, as the elevator shuddered downward, we heard Aubrey
singing. It was possible to pick out a few words: "Wider
still and wider shall thy bounds be set; / God, who made
thee mighty, make thee mightier yet."

" 'Land of Hope and Glory,' " I said.

Fogbound looked around. "Where?" he asked.

AUBREY NOW FOUND HIMSELF the object of the interest of one Frankie Barbetta, who arrived at Fogbound's office unannounced and stood inside the door with his head thrust slightly forward in an appraising way, and on his face either an insolent smile or a contemptuous leer. A drama critic might have been able to tell the difference; coming from the coarse world of sports and the remote world of editorial writing, I could not. Barbetta was a young man of medium build. The most striking thing about him was his dress. His suit was black, his shoes were black, his shirt was black, and so was his hat, a fedora with a brim wide enough for the rest of us to shelter under. His tie was white, and I thought of saying that it shone like a good deed in a naughty world; but our visitor, standing there, saying nothing, with his body bent forward in pursuit of his head, had a chilling effect on such observations. He looked at Fogbound, then flicked his eyes to Aubrey, then to me, then back to Fogbound, where they remained.

After this tableau had lasted several unnerving minutes, Fogbound spoke. "You're selling something?"

The visitor shook his head once over a span of perhaps a half inch, his hat casting a shadow as he did so.

"You're lost? You need directions?"

Again the head moved half an inch to the right, then back.

"Maybe you need the key to the men's room?"

This time, as the head moved, Barbetta's eyes closed for a moment. Even without experience as a drama critic, I interpreted this as a sign of impatience.

Fogbound opened his mouth and pointed toward his throat. "You can't speak?"

"I can talk," the visitor said. His voice sounded like the crushing device of a residential refuse collection and compaction vehicle, or garbage truck. "Something worth talking about, I talk."

"Are you quite sure you're in the right office?" It was Aubrey.

The visitor kept his emotionless gaze fixed on Fogbound. "What office you think I want?"

"I don't know," Fogbound said. "A mindreader I'm not."

The visitor continued to stare at Fogbound. "I ain't in the wrong office."

"No? So who are you?"

"Barbetta. Frankie Barbetta."

"What can I do for you?"

Barbetta nodded toward Aubrey. "Your boy. I like to buy in."

"This is a joke?"

"No joke. I like a good clean fighter with brains. I'm ready to go high. Not crazy high. But high."

"How high?" There didn't seem to be any harm in asking,

and it was the only conversation under way at the time.

"How high?" Barbetta thought for a moment. "High."

I withdrew.

Barbetta still had not moved from the position he had taken just inside the door. Fogbound got up from his chair and approached him, apparently to get a better look. Because of the circumference of Barbetta's hat, this was not easy to do.

"Somebody told you I wanted to sell? Wrong."

"I don't say you want to. I say I like to buy in."

"The answer is no."

Barbetta shifted his smile from insolence to indulgence. "Maybe you don't know who I am."

"Okay," Fogbound said. "Who are you?"

Barbetta threw the line away. "You heard of the Mafia? I'm in organized crime."

"I've seen men like you in the films," Aubrey said, with conviction.

"Yeah, they're like me. Only I'm real."

"Why should I sell? Give me a reason."

Barbetta laughed and the compaction gears ground again. "Look." His hand went to a jacket pocket and outlined a bulge. "A reason."

"You'll *shoot* me if I don't sell?"

Barbetta shrugged. It was his most expansive motion so far. "I don't say that. I say maybe you don't get the fights you want. We got a little influence. Or maybe something happens, like you say." His hand went to the bulge again.

"Is that what they call a 'roscoe'?" Aubrey asked.

Barbetta laughed again, and I could hear tin cans being mangled. "Maybe a long time ago a roscoe. Not now."

"What do they call it now?"

"Lots of names. We call it lots of names. Artillery, maybe. Hardware." He stressed the "we."

"I should have thought that a genuine gangster, quite possibly suspected by the police, would hesitate to carry a gun around so openly."

"Don't you believe it," Barbetta said. "I'm a gangster and I'm here, ain't I? And — which I already said and I'm tired repeating — I like to buy in." He turned back to Fogbound.

Fogbound called on the arts of persuasion. "Barbetta," he said, "you're the kind of fellow I like on sight. But Aubrey I can't sell. We don't even have a contract."

"That makes it easier." Barbetta swung around and faced me. "Who are you, Jack?"

"Take off your hat," I said, determined to be as brave as Fogbound. "Your keeping it on makes it awfully dark in here."

Barbetta ran his tongue over his upper teeth. I was to learn that he did that when trying to control his temper. "I ask you who are you, Jack."

"I'm a journalist."

"In the media?"

"Some would put it that way."

"Then you know me, Jack. Tell them who I am."

"I never heard of you."

"Then you can't be much of a mediaman, Jack," Barbetta said with contempt.

"I'll test you," I said. "What's your nickname?"

"Nickname?"

"What do they call you in the trade? Don't you have a name like Frankie the Barb or Three-Hand Jake or Schenectady Louie or something like that?"

Barbetta shook his head.

"I conclude that you are not a gangster. I'm sorry. Nothing personal."

Barbetta reached out with his left hand and grabbed my lapel. With a sudden motion, he drew his gun from his pocket with his right hand and held it in front of me. It gleamed metallically as in detective novels, which I found gratifying, but I had no time to think about this. "You're a wise guy," he said. "With some people that's dangerous, you know what I mean? I ain't here for jokes."

"Suppose we give you the benefit of the doubt." I was speaking directly into the gun and the brim of Barbetta's hat. "We all like to help young people. But Mr. Franklin does not wish to sell, and I believe that Mr. Philpott-Grimes does not wish to be sold."

"Spot on," Aubrey said.

"Look." Barbetta released me, and pocketed the gun. "Do I have to kill somebody before you believe me? You never heard of organized crime moving into legitimate business?" He answered his own question. "You heard. So you know. You play rough, we play rough. Then somebody gets hurt. Think it over. I'm in the phone book."

"The Yellow Pages?" I said. "Under organized crime?"

Barbetta walked close to me. "Mediaman," he said, "don't push your luck. I already make allowances because I like that Frankie the Barb. I think I use that. Thanks, Jack." He spun around, patted the bulge in his pocket, and walked out.

Aubrey recovered first and said that such brazenness astonished him, and that London's police, unarmed as they were, kept things under better control. Their ethos, he said, might profitably be studied by those in authority in the United States.

"You saw that gun?" Fogbound asked.

"I couldn't miss it," I said. "I was breathing through it."

"Then why did you go on as you did?" Aubrey asked.

"I was displaying sheer bravado. Besides, I didn't think he'd shoot. If he shoots you, he loses his fighter. If he shoots Sam, he antagonizes his fighter."

"And you?"

"He'd never shoot an editorial writer. It's frowned on."

"Who frowns?" Fogbound asked.

"Other editorial writers. There would be a storm of criticism. That acts as a deterrent. Though for a moment there, I had doubts. I think, by the way, that we'll be hearing from Mr. Barbetta again."

Fogbound raised his hands and let them hit his sides. Aubrey walked over and patted him on the back. "Don't fret, Sam," he said. "I'm not for sale. And in economic terms, it's a good sign. I'm in demand. But I do wish we could call in Scotland Yard."

A MEMBER OF CONGRESS with nothing to investigate cuts a forlorn figure in Washington. He runs the risk that time will pass him by and leave him vulnerable to defeat, lurking in the shadows, and wearing a hangdog look. None of this — the shadows, the look, the forlorn-figure cutting, which tend to go together — is much fun, so almost every Congressman will search for at least a small investigation to demonstrate that his heart is in the right place and to tide him over until he gets onto something big. Otherwise, he will be placed in the Smithsonian Institution with other relics, or consigned to limbo, which has more space available.

It was the quest for an investigation that brought Representative Webster Bindle (D.–Mo.) to New York. It occurred to Bindle that an investigation of television might be in order, and he wanted authoritative advice on its depravity from Fredda. They had met during his last investigation of television, some thirty-six months before, when she had been a witness. Now he was her guest at dinner. So was Aubrey. So were a dozen or so others, most of them from the theater. So, having apparently reached the point where I went with the franchise, was I.

Fredda had the kind of apartment interior decorators describe as dramatic. It was heavy on sconces, most of them bearing acting trophies she had won. There were marble floors, a terrace stacked with ferns, a room lined with theater posters, most of them with FREDDA PLANTAGENET near the top in large letters, an arched hallway, a portrait of Fredda as Lady Macbeth — "She must have been mesmerizing," Aubrey said when he pointed it out to me — and a dining room in American colonial style. "Ordered before I knew Aubrey," Fredda told me. "It's risky reminding him of what the Empire once was."

There was also a drawing room two stories high, with a gallery and a winding stairway, down which Fredda made a number of descents. She made no ascents that I could see, and I thought that perhaps she levitated until I came on another stairway, near the kitchen, which she evidently used for going up. She must have known that she was not impressive climbing stairs, but was at her best descending. It's a strain, being a public person.

It was a buffet dinner, and the guests broke into small groups. I sat down with Fredda and Bindle and struck what I hoped was a properly federal note by remarking that William Jennings Bryan committed a classic diplomatic boner when, as Secretary of State, he invited Switzerland to send its navy to the opening of the Panama Canal. Bindle appeared not to welcome the instruction; he continued with what he had been saying, which was an explanation of why he had to clean up something. "It's been a long time for me, honey," he said. "I have my career to think about."

Fredda, though she appreciated Bindle's need, was inclined to vote nay. It seemed to her that congressional investigators asked questions that were so long, and had so many parts, that when they got to the end, you could not remember where they had begun, or what the question was. Also that they were extraordinarily slow about understanding anything. If congressional investigations charged admission, she said, they'd close in a week. "And," she asked, "isn't there a limit on the number of times something can be investigated? It must be in the Constitution somewhere? Everything else is."

"There's nothing personal in this," Bindle said. "Just part of my job."

"Why don't you clean up crime?"

"Been done. And it's dangerous. You don't know where it may lead."

"What about Wall Street?"

"Old stuff. Anyway, that's a different committee."

"Monopoly?" I suggested.

"In what?"

"Anything. Sports."

"That's a different committee, too. I don't have unlimited jurisdiction." He looked at me with what could have been called ill-concealed displeasure were it not for the fact that he made no attempt to conceal it. "You're a newspaperman. You ought to know that."

"Drugs?" It was Fredda again.

"The public wants something new," Bindle said.

"Then give them something new. Television's been done, too. You did it."

"I only scratched the surface," Bindle said. "Never got to all the undressing on television these days."

"It seems popular," Fredda said.

"I don't want to be misunderstood. I'm on record that the American woman's bust is the finest in the world. But you have to think about our boys and girls."

Fredda said that the term *boys and girls*, if it carried any hint of innocence, applied to fewer and fewer young people. There was almost nobody left to protect.

Bindle was unmoved. "Just my point," he said. "That's how far corruption has gone."

Fredda tried another tack. She moved closer to Bindle and took his hand in hers to show her sympathy for him. "Webster," she asked, "didn't you just have an election?"

"You might say that. Four months back."

"And you're already worried about the next one, twenty months off?"

"Not worried. Just far-sighted. Never hurts to plan ahead."

"Poor boy," Fredda looked down at his hand, and put it, still in her two hands, in her lap. "Well, look. It's like the theater. No one cares about last season's plays. Put on your investigation next year and there probably won't be anybody brave enough to run against you."

"My dear," said Bindle, "I do enjoy hearing you speak."

"I haven't finished." Fredda released his hand and shifted around so that she was staring at his profile and he had to turn his head to meet her eyes. "Put off your investigation and you can spend more time at home, finding out what your constituents want. What do they want, by the way?"

"That kind of activity can be overdone," Bindle said. "I can't be an unthinking puppet. The country is entitled to my best judgment."

"I think that voters value the personal touch," I said. "They want direct contact with their representatives. Evidence accumulates almost daily that the people feel Washington is remote. That was what one of my first editorials was about."

"If I were you, boy," Bindle replied, "I'd study committee jurisdiction in the Congress. Bring a little reality to your writing."

"I am not trying to hurt you, Webster," Fredda assured him. "I want you in the House. The country needs your level head."

Bindle was not deflected. "Suppose somebody else does it while I hold off?"

"Can't you reserve the subject? Take an option on it?"

"Fredda," Bindle said, "the argument is not worthy of you. I will think the matter over. But I can see that you are not on my side."

"How about waste in foreign aid?"

"Fredda," Bindle said severely.

"The failure of the Model Cities Program?"

Bindle did not bother to reply.

"It's easy to turn down other people's ideas," Fredda said. "Give me time. I lead a fairly despicable life. Something's bound to turn up."

"Enough," Bindle said. "I will take the matter under advisement. I come now to a more pleasant subject. I am here as the personal emissary of Simco Savory."

There were people in whom the mere mention of Simco Savory inspired respect, awe, and longing. For Simco Savory gave parties in Washington at which, it was widely assumed, matters of high importance were talked about in a witty manner, indiscretions were committed, and spies might be among those present. It was further assumed that all of this had some bearing on the well-being of the nation and the fate of the world by bringing together people evidently unserved by the telephone, postal system, and modern wheeled vehicle. When these persons expressly did not want to see each other, a hostess, by cleverly inviting them to the same party, gave them an unavoidable opportunity to compose their differences, or in some cases compound them.

To Fredda's mind, as it happened, Savory's name brought a blank. Bindle found this hard to believe. Savory's photograph had, after all, often appeared in the public prints. *People* magazine had shown him, sleek and neatly made, his thin hair combed forward, the strands deployed like sentries covering more of a military perimeter than they should, cuddling his two Persian cats, Smokey and Moky.

"You've never heard of Simco Savory?"

"Never."

He spelled it. "S–i–m–c–o S–a–v–o–r–y?"

"I am barely able to face my friends because of it," Fredda said, "but never."

"Allow me to explain," Bindle said. "You are of course aware of celebrated Washington hostesses?"

Fredda was. She remembered a musical comedy about one of them. Not a bad show, and it had provided some theatrical employment.

"Thank you," Bindle said. "But note that it was about a woman. Simco Savory is a man." He paused, apparently expecting Fredda to smite her head in disbelief. She didn't.

"He is, as I say, a man," Bindle continued. "This alone would be enough to annoy the ladies with whom he competes. But in addition, his parties are every bit as good as theirs. I speak as something of an expert here." He paused again, hoping, perhaps, that there would be questions and an opportunity to elucidate. None came.

"On the distaff side," he now said, "this has created some anger." He smiled in a way that implied that Fredda should join him in enjoying the cream of the jest.

"Very interesting," Fredda said, "to exaggerate wildly. And what has all this to do with me?"

"Simco Savory is inviting you, through me, to a party next weekend."

Bindle revealed this with great solemnity. He was chagrined when Fredda managed to keep her composure and said that it was kind of Simco Savory but that she did not think she could make it.

"Honey," Bindle said, "people who go to Simco's parties are part of the living history of this nation."

To Fredda, Bindle's words opened vistas of oafishness rampant. From occasional glances at television news programs, as she was to explain to me, she knew that the high point of Washington parties came when someone's aide, at the moment not busy aiding, looked down the dress of the Iraqi minister's wife and commented on the Hanging Gardens of Babylon. Or peered down the front of a female judge and asked a question about double jeopardy. Fredda was certainly not going to have some overpaid publicity-seeking yokel attempt a witticism about her frontage. Then, when she was about to reject the invitation with finality, her mind clicked and her mood softened.

"Would you like me to come, Webster?"

Bindle said he would.

"You would consider it a personal favor?"

Bindle said he would.

"You would feel obligated to me?"

Bindle said he would.

"Then I shall come. Those are terms I like. What about Aubrey?"

"That English fighter you have been seeing?"

"The same."

"The one the papers call 'The Happy Taxpayer'? Haven't I met him tonight?"

"He's here."

"Bring him along. I'll tell Simco you're both coming."

"There's no danger that they'll stuff and mount Aubrey and put him on display at the Internal Revenue Service?"

"We'll get you both out alive," Bindle said.

10

IF YOU HAVE SOCIAL AMBITIONS in Washington and cannot use a mansion, the house to occupy is one in Georgetown, of the type described by real estate agents as bijou. The ideal house looks weathered on the outside in a way that suggests age rather than disrepair; inside, it is unostentatious and crowded, but suggests solid wealth. Pictures of ancestors — anybody's ancestors — on the walls will help; so will an old family retainer or two, real or simulated.

All these things Simco Savory had, and a patrician appearance, meaning that he was tall, gray-haired, neat, sometimes wore a bow tie, and looked as though he might be connected with the administration of the Boston Symphony Orchestra. With them he enjoyed social success. But it took more than these material things to explain his success. There was behind it, it seemed, an unconscious master plan, a small piece of destiny. Exactly what had made Savory a giver of parties was not known, even to him. It was not politics; he had no political interests. It was not a socially ambitious wife; he had no wife. It was not social ambitions of his own; he had none of those. An inner voice said to him, "Simco Savory, give parties in Washington." Other men, receiving such a message, might have submitted to a series of tests and treatments aimed at clearing things up once and for all. Simco Savory obeyed the voice, and found the reason later on.

To continue flourishing in his chosen field, Savory did not need Fredda's presence. He had already made his mark. Nevertheless, he was delighted when she appeared in answer to the invitation extended through Bindle. Aubrey was to meet her there, so she showed up with me in tow. I thought that my continuing education as an editorial writer required some knowledge of Washington parties, which I might want someday to deplore, praise as a unique bit of Americana, or accept with reservations and a caution against excess. I had arranged, through our Washington bureau, to attend.

"*Enchanté*," Savory said to Fredda as he kissed her hand. "You will give my *petite fête* beauty. I am most grateful."

Fredda, who had decided to be gracious for the evening, murmured, "Not at all."

He addressed himself to me. "You will give my *petite fête* distinction. You are most welcome."

Unable to blush prettily, I merely thanked him. "But I hope," he went on, "that you will consider yourself a guest and not a reporter. My other guests may be self-conscious if they see someone taking notes. I'm sure I can rely on you."

"Indeed you can," I said stoutly. I looked around to see whether Fredda or Savory had noticed that I was speaking in that manner. Neither had.

Later, in the manner of the lemming going willy-nilly to its doom, or the willy-nilly going lemming to its, Fredda asked Savory to explain why he gave parties. He wound up genteelly and let go.

"My dear," he said, "there is far more art required in being a host than in being a hostess. Here in Washington, who are the political leaders? Men. One spots the token female now and then, and one is gratified to see the number increasing, but it is still a man's world." He looked at Fredda to see whether she was following him. "This gives the hostess an advantage — her own feminine charm. Simply being a woman gives her a head start. Obviously, in such a world, the host cannot compete on the same terms. What then can he do? He must have something else — and the something is art. Of what, you are asking yourself, of what does this art consist?"

Fredda, who was not selfless on stage and who tended to bustle about and engage in extraneous business while other performers were speaking, suppressed an urge to testify that this question was not one of her preoccupations, and Savory continued. "The answer again is simple: It consists of knowing what men want. And what do men want? Yet another simple answer — the company of women."

"The way you answer those questions so quickly," Fredda said. "You're awfully clever."

"So," Savory continued, "the art of the host is to have at his parties the women men most want to see. And, my dear, your being here is beyond my fondest. I have felt for ever so long that my *petites fêtes* should have some of the enchantment that only New York can supply. It has a different quality from Washington's own, a gemlike brilliance. I am ever so to you for coming."

"Ever so?"

Savory beamed. "Ever so." He rubbed his hands together. "I confess that I hoped you would ask me why I give parties. I do it for the universal male." He paused for effect. "Why should Washington parties be given only by women? Can you think of a valid reason? I can't. So I am extending the scope of man's activities. It is, if you like, a retaliatory encroachment. And do you know?" He squirmed with pleasure. "The women are up in arms about it. Simply *up in*."

Fredda detached herself from her host and walked about to see what the retaliatory encroachment looked like. So did I. Among the guests were a Supreme Court Justice, three Senators, a number of Representatives, two generals — one with three stars and one with two — a rear admiral, some diplomats (mostly junior), an undersecretary who arrived early and left almost immediately, and a smattering of newspaper and television people. There were numerous women not so easily classified.

Also present was a Hollywood western star, Cal Buck Buck, once known as Cal "Buck" Buck. He was wearing a string tie, boots and a seamy face, and a cowboy hat that remained on his head throughout the evening, even when he joined the dancing that occasionally burst out, and he seemed to me to say "Ma'am?" to Savory's sirens more often than necessary. I did not want to call him "Mr. Buck," because he might think that a strange use of his middle name, and I did not want to call him "Cal," because that might be only half of what he should be called, and I did not want to call him "Buck," because he might think that a peremptory use of his last name. Eventually, I worked it out.

"Tell me, Cal Buck," I said, "why did you drop the quotation marks from the first Buck?"

"Wasn't my doing," he said. "My press agent got the idea. He thought the name worked better that way."

"Does it?"

"Career took right off," he said cheerfully. "Quotation marks in your name sound sort of frisky, if you take my meaning. Once we dropped them, I could do more serious parts. Like the one I'm doing now."

"What's that?"

"Well," Cal Buck said, "that's why I'm in Washington. We're shooting here." He gestured me closer, leaned forward earnestly, and, as he spoke, banged one hand into the other for emphasis. I realized that except for a shy expression and one in which he drew his lips tightly together in emergencies, I was watching his entire acting range. "You see," he said, "I play a United States marshal trying to help some illegal immigrants. 'But it's your job to arrest people like that and deport them.' That's what the townsfolk say. Then I say, 'I know, but they're hard-working, good people. They're just looking to give their children better lives. And without them, the crops would rot. Americans won't do stoop labor. A marshal has to do more than just make arrests. He has to help people. That's what I'm doing.'

"Now, the director — he's all right; worked with him lots of times — he wants me say, 'He has to perteck people. That's what I'm a-doin'.' The scriptwriter says, 'No, marshals these days are educated, they don't talk that way, and we have to encourage young people to stay in school.' I'm with the writer. I'd be pleased to have your opinion."

"I'm with the writer, too," I said. "Not that I've ever met a marshal."

I rejoined Fredda as she approached a group in which a tall man with a large jaw was holding forth. He was plainly an experienced broadcaster.

"I had lunch with the Secretary the other day," he said. "Just a few of us there." He looked around to see whether he had the group's rapt attention. "The Secretary told us that the next two years are likely to be the most critical so far." He stopped again. On most faces there was a mixture of gravity, awe, and expectation. But the man with the large jaw said no more. He left his audience hanging.

"Cheap," I advised Fredda. "Where's the body of the piece? In his place, I'd be ashamed."

"All the fun of the *fête*," Fredda said.

As the evening progressed, it became clear that the lines spoken by the broadcaster set the tone of the evening. The only guest who seemed to be actively enjoying things was a woman who laughed uproariously at everything said by any of three white-haired men in her group. I learned, by questioning other newspeople, that she was a lobbyist for hire, whose success owed much to her attending Washington parties to laugh at Senators' jokes. When unable to find Senators, she laughed at Representatives' jokes. If they did not joke but showed the other side of their personalities and were profound, she nodded soberly and looked impressed. She had, I was told, created good will for, among other things, olives, printed circuits, cold rolled steel, mass transit, and the idea of a national flower.

Fredda watched the woman bend almost double in a paroxysm of laughter at a remark from one of three men around her. He laughed only slightly less heartily than she did. "It sounds like the laughter you get when you paper the house on opening night," Fredda said. "Maybe they should hire themselves out to a laugh-track producer."

She now gestured toward the group still clustered around the broadcaster. "Isn't he in television?"

I affirmed that he was John J. Leary, and that he could be seen on the screen of an evening, standing in front of a government building and saying that only time would tell, or that it was certain that things would never be the same again, and that the administration did not underestimate the difficulties that lay ahead."

"I think you're wrong," Fredda said. "He doesn't stand in front of buildings. He did, once. Now he's in a studio, with rows of books behind him and busts of Plato and Socrates on his desk. If he does stand in front of a building, the building is highly flattered."

"I see," I said. "May I remind you of something?"

"As long as it isn't my obligations as a citizen," Fredda said. "Or can't you control yourself at any time?"

"Why did Savory invite you?"

"He said that I had been imported from New York to lend enchantment to the evening."

"Then why don't you go where the men can see you?"

"I did," Fredda said. "I spent fifteen minutes with a member of what I am sure is an unnecessary commission and fifteen singing western songs around the piano with someone who claimed to be one of the most promising young lawyers in Washington."

"Did anyone remark, 'Yes, he's promising every girl in town'?"

"Nobody."

"Remarkable."

Aubrey now appeared, and it developed that he had first taken a nap and had then had difficulty with his tie.

"You took a nap?"

"Part of the training routine. I missed it earlier in the day, so I made up for it. Very important."

"A fighter must get his rest," I said.

"What do you know about it?" Fredda asked.

"I am a many-sided journalist. I remember these things from my sportswriting days."

Just as an argument was about to develop, we were joined by a woman who towered almost as high as Aubrey and looked as though she took her baths in a floating drydock. "Aren't I lucky to find the two of you together?" she bleated, beaming at Fredda and Aubrey. "Now sit down and be interviewed. It won't hurt a bit. And thank you for coming to Washington. Washington's glad to have you."

She glanced at me but I stood my ground so that I could find out who she was and listen to her interviewing technique.

"We are sitting down," Fredda said.

The woman perched on a chair next to them. "Now tell me everything," she said. "How did it happen?"

Fredda looked at her from under lowered eyebrows. "Who are you, the housemother?"

The woman giggled. "I declare that's a good question. You do have a right to know, don't you?" She giggled again. "I'm Bobby Lou Bridewell." She extended a hand. "And I'm very happy to know you."

Fredda took the hand and examined it. "It's real," she announced. "What does it do for a living?"

The woman took her hand away from Fredda and extended it to Aubrey. "I'm just a little old newspaperwoman."

"Which paper?"

"Not just one," Bobby Lou giggled. "Heavens. Dozens of them. They take my column." She inched closer and lowered her voice. "I think it's because I haven't changed. I'm really just the same girl I was when I came to Washington." She smiled coyly at Aubrey. "I won't tell you how many years ago that was, but I'm still just me." She lowered her voice again and Fredda and I strained forward to hear. "I really truly shouldn't interview you here. Simco doesn't like it. He says he wants his parties to be fun, not work."

Fredda did not forgive easily. "Something slipped up to-night," she said.

"But he'll never know," Bobby Lou went on. "I'll just keep everything you say in my head and then, when I go out to fix my hair and powder my nose" — she smiled at Aubrey once more — "I'll write it all down in my little book."

"How'd you get to be so damned vivacious?" Fredda asked.

Bobby Lou laughed. "Isn't it bizarre? I've always been this way. As long as I can remember, people have said, 'Bobby Lou is good for you.' I think that's cute. It means I cheer people up."

"All right," Fredda said. "Let's get on with it. What do you want to know?"

"Everything," Bobby Lou said, "just everything."

In the course of telling everything to Bobby Lou Bridewell, it was also possible to find out everything about her. It was difficult not to. When Aubrey made the mistake of asking whether she was Miss or Mrs. Bridewell, she told him that it was Miss, that it was sweet of him to ask, that she had been married, but life did not always work out as people would like, and it was her philosophy that it was best to take things as they came. Only last Sunday, the minister at her church had given a sermon about the slings and arrows of outrageous fortune. They had to be accepted, the minister felt, and she felt that when it could be put as beautifully as that — her minister should have been a writer, with his gift for words — it was easier to face our troubles. Besides, everyone was called to his or her station in life. That was her philosophy.

When Miss Bridewell resumed the questioning and confirmed from Aubrey's own lips that he was English, she told him that she loved the English. They were courageous and well-mannered and, contrary to general belief, they were not cold. She had been there herself and she knew. They had taken her to their hearts, and she had taken London to hers.

Now she learned that the first words Aubrey had spoken to Fredda were "How do you do?"

"I declare that's wonderful," Miss Bridewell said. "So natural."

This brought silence and Miss Bridewell thrust ahead. "Now I want to know just everything. What is your manager's name?"

"Franklin," Aubrey said. "Sam Franklin. Most people call him Fogbound."

"I think people in the fight game — they do call it that, don't they? — people in the fight game have the most wonderful names. And was it love at first sight?"

"We are just good friends," Fredda said.

Miss Bridewell turned her gaze to Aubrey. In his dinner jacket, he looked like a white-streaked thermometer case. "But Mr. Philpott-Grimes, aren't you rather slender to be a prize fighter?"

"Philp'tt," Aubrey said. "You pronounce it with just the suggestion of an *o*. Philp'tt."

"I'd never be able to say that," Bobby Lou said.

"It's like the p't of gold at the end of the rainbow," Fredda explained.

"I do admire the way the English speak. But I declare I can't do it. I'll just have to say Aubrey."

"Good," Fredda said. "That is his handle, as Cal Buck Buck might put it. Why don't we get back to the question, which was whether Aubrey wasn't thin for a fighter. The answer is self-evidently yes."

"Aren't you afraid you might be hurt?"

"No," said Aubrey, "I am not."

"I think that's wonderful." Miss Bridewell switched to Fredda. "Don't you worry terribly when he's in the ring?"

Fredda said that Aubrey knew how to look after himself.

"I have this little trick." Bobby Lou switched back to Aubrey. "I ask famous people to give me a message for my readers. It makes it all more friendly."

"Very well," said Aubrey. "Tell them that although the United States is no longer as dominant as it once was, it remains the linchpin of the economies of the west. It isn't only you who want a strong America. We want a strong America, too. Partnership, cooperation, coordination, we must have all of these. And a steady grip on the money supply."

"My goodness," Miss Bridewell exclaimed, "are you really a fighter? I never heard of a fighter talking like that before. Have you studied these things?"

Aubrey said he had, and that a knowledge of economics was indispensable to sound political judgment.

"My goodness. That's marvelous. I just love the English." She lowered her voice. "I'll never be able to keep all that about the money supply in my little head. Would you write it down for me?"

Aubrey looked concerned. "But if Mr. Savory sees us, won't he be suspicious?"

"You're right. I tell you what. You go into your room" — Bobby Lou giggled — "and I'll go into mine." She looked around to see whether Savory was watching them, then reached into her pocketbook and pulled out a piece of paper and gave it to Aubrey. "We meet here in five minutes."

After Aubrey returned the paper, now bearing his message, and Bobby Lou, oozing good cheer, took herself off, he reproached Fredda.

"Why did you say we were just good friends?"

Fredda shook her head. "My God, you're innocent. No other phrase in the English language excites evil thoughts as quickly as 'We are just good friends.' Gargantua will squirm all night thinking about it, and then she'll pass it on to her readers. The result will be something called publicity."

Aubrey looked at her admiringly. "Your brain. Like a steel trap. I wish we could get you working for Britain."

"Everybody can't work for Britain. You do. That ought to be enough for one *petite fête*." Fredda indicated the laughing woman. "Or would you like me to go on as she does?"

Aubrey asked for an explanation and, on receiving it, looked disapproving. "When one devalues the people's delegates, one devalues the people themselves," he said. "To do so is thoroughly misguided."

Miss Bridewell was not the last treat of the evening. It was a standing rule of Savory's that as each guest left, he said his good-bye into a tape recorder so that there should be a lasting record of each party in his tape library. When the time came, Fredda and Aubrey took their places in the line for this chore. Most of the guests said, "Thank you for a wonderful evening," and added their names; and a few said, "See you again, hopefully." Leary commentated, "Thank you, Simco. This is John J. Leary in Washington." He might have made a longer speech, but Smokey and Moky had appeared and were attracting attention. Leary did not like being upstaged. He also found it difficult to broadcast except in conditions of perfect order.

Fredda was correct and no more. She said, "Many thanks. Fredda Plantagenet." Aubrey said, "You are most kind. Aubrey Philpott-Grimes." As for me, I saw this as an opportunity to jab at television correspondents and as an opportunity, even rarer, to opine. "Only time will tell," I opined, and "Whether things will work out as envisaged remains to be seen," added "Mercer, *Star-Telegram*," in as rough and ready a tone as I could, and strode out into the night.

11

THE NORMAL COURSE OF EVENTS when a fighter begins to achieve fame and importance outside the ring, as Aubrey was doing, is that his work inside it suffers. His mind wanders to his next recording session with his newly organized musical group, The Running Sores, or to his work as a member of the Board of the Foundation for Participatory Democracy at the Preschool Level, and along comes a left hook that provides a rude awakening, or its rude opposite.

In spite of Fogbound's anxiety, and mine, Aubrey's mind did not wander, for he looked on boxing as a heaven-sent means to further his life's work, paying taxes and helping the British economy. That meant that he had to go on winning. He was able to see the connection.

Not that he found winning difficult. Fogbound kept him slogging past second and third raters, and he managed to pepper them with enough lengthy rights and lefts to keep his record clean. In one fight, it is true, he gave Fogbound a scare. Fogbound had begun to look on Aubrey's stomach as a freak of nature benevolently given to their side, for there was no plausible explanation of his being able to take a punch there. From waist to rib cage, Aubrey appeared to have the resilience of vanilla yogurt. On this night, in the third round, Aubrey took what seemed an ordinary belt in the body and folded to the canvas like a dropped necktie.

"What happened?" Fogbound asked when Aubrey came to the corner.

"Tactics."

"What?"

"I have an odd feeling in my chin tonight. I can't quite explain it. But I want him to keep after my body. He won't hurt me there."

"What's the matter with your chin all of a sudden?"

"Nothing that I know of," Aubrey said. "It just feels wonky. You know how your ankle feels when you've sprained it? That's how my chin feels."

Through the rest of the fight, Fogbound watched Aubrey's chin as though it were unconnected with the rest of him and wondered whether the problem might be Aubrey's incessant talk about economics — "All that abracadaver," Fogbound muttered to me — but Aubrey's opponent couldn't get a clean shot at it and his early success against the stomach persuaded him to concentrate his fire there. Then, with about fifteen seconds to go in the last round, when Aubrey had a clear lead, a wild swipe landed flush on his chin. Aubrey stopped in his tracks, shook his head, and carried on as though nothing had happened. He came to his corner smiling.

"I've been a bit of a twit tonight," he said. "There's nothing in the slightest degree wrong with my chin. It was pure imagination."

Aubrey won the fight, but the episode almost prostrated

Fogbound. He told me that this nuttiness, coming on top of Aubrey's dedication to paying taxes and the John-John McKenzie affair, plus Barbetta, made him wonder whether there was not something to be said for early retirement, after all. "I've handled some oddball eggcentrics in my time," he said. "You remember Rudyard Diebendorf? And that LaBrea?" His face became haggard as he thought of them.

Neither had made a profound impression on me, so he forced himself to tell me their grim stories. Diebendorf had somewhere read about John L. Sullivan's habit of slapping his right glove against his hip while waiting for an opening. Diebendorf had chosen the wrong opponent to confuse with this tactic and was slapping himself on the hip at the precise moment an urgent blow reached his chin. His career was blighted by the incident and Fogbound was strengthened in his view that fighters read anything at grave risk to themselves and those around them. He of course suppressed this opinion around Aubrey.

Then came Eric LaBrea, who scored each round himself and gauged his efforts in the later rounds according to whether he placed himself ahead or behind, and by how much. "On the five-point-must system," he would tell Fogbound as he came to his corner, "I give myself five in that round and him four," and "I am so far ahead that I cannot lose, except by a knockout." One night after having been knocked down twice and saved by the bell, LaBrea pronounced the round even, and Fogbound knew the end was near. In his next fight, LaBrea decided in the last round that he needed a knockout to win, went in swinging, left himself open, and was flattened. After learning that he was well ahead on all three cards up to that point. LaBrea retired from the ring.

"This is no place for me," he said. "The judges and referees don't understand my style. And no wonder. Did you ever meet anybody who wanted to be a referee or a judge? I never did. They're just men who can't find other jobs. They're misfits."

Fogbound watched him go without regret. "He gave me a headache," he said.

There had been others, but Fogbound found Aubrey the most perplexing of all. Aubrey believed, for instance, that one of the difficulties in the Middle East was that the Arabs did not have enough arable land. That puzzled Fogbound — after all, if the Arabs didn't have enough arable land, who did? — but he did not press the point. He filed it away as another piece of evidence.

I had a theory and I put it forward after reminding Fogbound that there was a distinction to be drawn between Aubrey and such combatants as Diebendorf and LaBrea: Aubrey won his fights.

"That I can confirm," Fobgound said. "A reason to stay. No retirement."

My theory was that Aubrey was not unhinged but that he did require treatment different from other fighters. This was because he was an intellectual and was always analyzing things. Just what he had analyzed that led him to believe that his chin was weak, I did not know. "He's no Steamboat Johnson," I said, recalling an unfortunate heavyweight who had been briefly under Fogbound's wing. As Johnson's name passed my lips, the haggard look returned to Fogbound's face and he threw up his arm as though warding off a blow. I reminded him that Johnson had once rested his chin on his hand to think, and the impact had put him out of commission for minutes.

The next of Aubrey's vagaries took the form of a request for a jam roly-poly pudding with custard. Aubrey said that it was full of homely goodness, and as much the staff of British life as ever bread was. "After jam roly-poly," he said, "I'm ready to get cracking. And it's value for money. That's important. We operate on narrower margins than you do."

Mrs. Franklin had never heard of jam roly-poly and could find no recipe for it. Even when Aubrey, from memory, produced one, as he had earlier produced one for cabbage pie which began with the recommendation that the cabbage be inspected for grubs, she doubted the existence of such a dish. She was particularly distressed by the suet pastry on which the jam was to be spread. "It's fat," she said. "To you, it's suet. To me, it's fat." Nevertheless, she made it, Aubrey ate what he called lashings of it, and Fogbound remarked contentedly that Aubrey's hands were as fast at the table as they were in the ring. Then Aubrey's appetite for jam roly-poly disappeared as abruptly as it had arrived. Fogbound attributed the incident to the difficulties of adjusting to a new country, though it seemed to Mrs. Franklin that the absence of jam roly-poly should have made the adjustment process easier.

But after these aberrations, Aubrey's progress was serene, almost majestic. Moreover, his television dissertation on structural unemployment moved Fredda to tears and brought $34.67 in anonymous contributions from Americans to the British Treasury, and his preoccupation with economic affairs made further newspaper copy. He was referred to as "Britain's Human Deficit," and "The Asparagus Spear That Walks Like A Man." A photograph of him reading *The Economist* was printed all over the United States.

All of this Aubrey welcomed. "Who could ever have imagined," he said, "that I should be an instrument by which Americans would be brought to an understanding of economic realities? Or that I should have the privilege of helping to make my country sound again? I am made humble by the thought of it."

"Suppose they lower taxes in Britain," I said. "What then?"

Aubrey spoke with certainty. "They'll never do that."

I tiptoed out.

Aubrey's popularity was also welcome to Fredda, but she sometimes felt that his devotion to duty was excessive. She raised the subject one day as the three of us walked from Fogbound's office to the studio at Cosmic Television where she was rehearsing.

"You're off to the nation's capital again?" she asked.

Aubrey paused to acknowledge a greeting — "How ya doin', Norbrey?" — and to say that he was doing very well, thank you, and waited for her to respond to the greeting, "How ya doin', Frieda?" Aubrey then said yes, he would be going, not so much for the social activity as for the chance to learn something of Washington.

Fredda turned to me, waved in the direction of somebody who had announced, "It's Friedanorbrey," and asked, "You, faithful amanuensis, will be going along?"

"All the world's a stage," I riposted. "I watch the action."

"All the world is not a stage," Fredda declared. "Or if it is, it's a lousy production. About Savory's *petites fêtes:* I think your going encourages Aubrey."

"I'd go even if Joe didn't," Aubrey said. "In a broad sense, I'm doing it to make the pound sterling stronger."

"I can't imagine why," Fredda said. "You don't keep the pounds long enough to find out what their physical condition is."

As Fredda said this, we reached the studio. She looked at Aubrey, smiled, kissed him, and smiled again. "See you tomorrow, darling. Have ever so a time."

Savory, now in a sense Aubrey's Washington proprietor, had been interviewed a few days before the party by Bobby Lou Bridewell.

"One wants to have a number of arrows in one's quiver," he said. "I have Aubrey Philpott-Grimes." She then told her readers that it was wonderful to hear Savory's pronunciation of the name. "I can't manage his last name the way he likes," she wrote. "I call him Aubrey."

"Not that I could not get along without him," Savory went on. "I pride myself that I did for a long time. One is appreciated for oneself. My *petite fête* is not in his hands."

"At first, I did not see the joke," Bobby Lou wrote. "When I did see it, I just laughed and laughed. Washington is brimming with wit and humor."

Bobby Lou asked why Aubrey never appeared at parties given by Savory's rivals, and reported that he smiled inscrutably when he answered: "One can gad about Washington. There are doors swinging open every night. But should one go through them? Whom would one meet? On what level would one find oneself? One does not want to become the common currency of Washington's social life."

"I could think of no more questions," Bobby Lou wrote. "I just felt privileged to have a front row seat at the spectacle that is Washington."

I also had a front row seat at the spectacle that was Washington at Savory's party. I therefore was able to watch Representative Webster Bindle, upright and bulky, his hair crew-cut, as it had been in the Marines decades before, but now gray, his brow permanently furrowed, in keeping with his belief that holders of political office should be seen to be thoughtful and concerned. He was still searching for something to investigate, when the sight of Aubrey excited his questing mind. He strode over, and Aubrey felt his hand being surrounded by Bindle's two-handed grasp, then felt Bindle's left hand on his elbow and moving up his arm and grabbing his shoulder, while Bindle's eye engaged his, this being the standard congressional method of greeting constituents and others in whom members of Congress wish to incite friendly feelings. Bindle was accustomed to encountering flesh when he applied these grips, and his failure to do so on Aubrey, so it seemed to me, led him to relax his hold and look away sooner than he otherwise would have.

"Son," Bindle said, "I am considering investigating professional pugilism. I think it may be necessary to save it from itself." He held up a large hand. "I know that you must feel as I do. You may feel it even more strongly. It has needed cleaning up for a long time. Trouble is, people look to the government for everything. If something needs cleaning up, they look to the government to do it."

Aubrey agreed that that was so.

"I don't like it," Bindle went on. "It saps the country's moral fiber. It is a symptom of the time we live in. But that will not stay my hand. And I'll tell you something else. If I investigate professional pugilism, there will be no ifs, ands, or buts about it. It will be an investigation in depth. Son, you're a credit to the sport. If it comes to a showdown, I hope that you will be on my side."

"What you say is extremely gratifying," Aubrey said. "I should like to think that I deserve it."

"Son," Bindle said, "I'm a man who measures his words. If they were all like you, fighting would be welcomed in every home."

"Thank you very much, sir."

"I'm only speaking the truth."

"Everyone in the United States has been so friendly."

"Finest country in the world," Bindle said. "You have a good one, too."

12

DESPITE THEIR DIFFERENCES over Savory's galas, the affair be‑ tween Fredda and Aubrey showed every sign of being a per‑ fect, if incongruous, match. It went along swimmingly. All the same, there were occasional disturbances.

For example, it is not convenient for a man having an affair with Fredda Plantagenet — or with almost anyone else — to be pursued by a determined young woman who behaves as though he were guilty of an unspeakable crime. This hap‑ pened to Aubrey.

Doreen Morden had come from London to confront Au‑ brey and, if necessary, Fredda. This she considered she had some right to do for she was, as she described it, "Aubrey's real girl friend." She also considered it her mandate, for to her Aubrey plainly was in need of rescue, high life in New York having corrupted him beyond his power to resist. The immediate cause of her arrival was an item in the New York column of a London newspaper which read:

Best-known Englishman at the moment in unpredictable New York is middleweight boxer Aubrey Philpott-Grimes, whose spare build has led American sportswriters to tag him "The Asparagus Spear That Walks Like a Man." He has yet to lose a fight, and his canny manager, Mr. Fogbound Franklin, is steering him carefully to the top.

But Philpott-Grimes is as well known here for his views on economics as for his left jab, and his learned concern about the British economy and his avowed delight in handing over large chunks of his purses to the British and American governments have brought him another nickname — "The Happy Taxpayer." He is as likely to speak about the difficulty of capital formation in labour-intensive industries as he is about his tactics in the ring.

To the side, there was a photograph of Aubrey, smiling and pointing to two checkbooks, one American, the other British. He was about to sign a check to the Internal Revenue Service and another to Her Majesty's Collector of Taxes. The check with which he was meeting his income tax obligation to the state and city of New York had been judged not worthy to be in this company. Under the photograph, he was quoted as having said, "I do not wish to make a stunt of this. But it is not a solemn occasion, either. We should pay our taxes willingly. It is a mark of responsible participation in the nation's affairs."

The newspaper story had one more sentence: "And the Latin-quoting Englishman is having one of New York's big affairs of the year with fiery TV star — former star of stage and screen — Fredda Plantagenet."

It was the last sentence that convinced Doreen that her presence was urgently required in New York. She went to the United States embassy in London, got a tourist's visa, having first sworn not to overthrow the government while on American soil, and the next thing Aubrey knew, Doreen was standing in front of him, in the manner of Micaela trying to save Don José from Carmen, except that Micaela does not come on stage carrying two suitcases and a shopping bag that holds three bars of chocolate, an apple, a jar of orange marmalade, a bottle of lemon squash, a jar of malt, a tin of Golden Syrup, and a copy of the magazine *Woman's Own*.

She looked reproachful, which was easy for her to do, because the face under her light brown hair and atop her somewhat gawky build, though friendly, seemed to wear permanently a sad and slightly indignant expression. Doreen was also not impressed with the immediate neighborhood of Fogbound's office or with the building in which it was located. The taxi driver, to her surprise, had carried her luggage into the building's dark lobby, where the ravaged surface of the walls suggested that they had recently withstood — but barely — a flood, and the tiled floor seemed more appropriate to a bathroom. She had ample time to reflect on this as the elevator shuddered upward, and as she stood in the sullen corridor, knocking on Fogbound's door, she said aloud, "Scruffy, terribly scruffy."

Her reproachfulness thus reinforced, she set out for the astonished Aubrey the reason for her journey, wondered how he could have brought this on himself, and on her, and asked him what his mum would say. He had no ready answer. He was, so he told me later, when trying to "put the Doreen matter in perspective," busy wishing that he could call back the picture postcards he had sent her, and the single letter on which he had incautiously given Fogbound's office as his return address. In it, unable to resist the teaching impulse, he had tried to explain the United States: "Very different from our beloved England, Doreen, with a certain gruff quality, and given to using Englishmen and -women as authority figures in television advertising, yet friendly withal, and very large, with vast resources toward which it has a profligate attitude. No wonder the motto *Annuit Coeptis*, 'God has smiled on our undertakings,' appears on the reverse side of the Great Seal of the United States."

Doreen asked again what his mum would say.

"About what?"

"About you and this woman." Doreen was forthright and, when she came to the phrase, "this woman," full of contempt.

"What is there to say?"

"That," said Doreen, "is what I am waiting to hear."

"I don't understand," Aubrey said. "My name has been coupled in the public prints with that of an American woman. What has this to do with you?"

At this point, Fogbound and I had the good grace to be embarrassed. "You know each other?" Fogbound said.

Aubrey, who looked stern when facing Doreen and sheepish when facing us, performed strained introductions. "Mr. Franklin, my manager," he said. "My friend, Mr. Mercer, who is a journalist. He writes leaders for the New York *Star-Telegram*."

"I shouldn't wonder," Doreen said. "Living on other people's troubles." She plainly regarded us as proximate causes of Aubrey's unpardonable behavior, and barely nodded.

"We'll wait outside," Fogbound said. "Three's a crowd." He remembered me. "Also four." We went into the corridor. It *was* scruffy.

Doreen had hoped to overwhelm Aubrey with the force of her accusation. From the words that now came floating through the door, it was possible to deduce that this was not to be.

"But Aubrey, I thought that you and I had an understanding."

"I never said anything to lead you to believe that."

"You didn't have to say anything. I knew how you felt."

"That," Aubrey responded, "is where you were wrong. You did not know how I felt, for the very good reason that I did not say anything." Here I thought he must be crossing his arms. "For you to have known how I felt, I would have had to say something."

"Sam," I said, "I think we ought to go down."

"I can't," Fogbound replied. "I'm expecting a call. Important."

"A fight?"

"If Aubrey has time." He nodded toward the door. "And he doesn't mind. I know it interferes."

By this point, the tone of the voices coming from the office would have told us the outcome of the conversation even without the words. Aubrey's was cool and unyielding, Doreen's broken and teary.

"But Aubrey, we went together for so long."

"You made an unwarranted assumption." Aubrey was decisive. "Unwarranted assumptions are at the bottom of much of the trouble in the world today. That is why budget deficits appear where surpluses are recklessly forecast."

Doreen must have realized that she had lost. Aubrey's use of an analogy from economics showed that, although he had been shaken at first, he had gone back to being imperturbable. She cried, "I hardly know you, that woman has changed you so. And after all I've been through for you."

Aubrey became even more distant. "And what, pray, do you mean by that?"

The words came out through sobs. "You know perfectly well what I mean."

"I am afraid that I do not."

"I went out with you — when no other girl would so much — as look at you — because you were so thin. Don't think I didn't know it."

"My dear Doreen," Aubrey said, "you seek to play on my sympathy merely because you were not guilty of the same boorish behavior as those of whom you speak. That is unworthy of you."

"And what you are doing now is unworthy of you. Crikey! What would your mum say?"

"Who's this 'mum'?" Fogbound wanted to know.

"His mother."

"He should ask his mother? At his age?"

"Doreen," Aubrey said, more loftily than before, "I have no intention of asking my mother's opinion. I value her opinion on matters on which a mother might be expected to speak with authority. This is not one of them." There was silence, and I pictured Aubrey looking thoroughly peeved. "If you persist in this attitude, I really shall not know what to do with you."

Again there was silence. Then the door opened and revealed Doreen standing with her suitcases and shopping bag. "If you want to be rid of me," she said, "I am not the sort to hang about where I am not wanted." She put down the suitcases and shopping bag and, sniffling, held a handkerchief to her nose. "And you can make quite sure by paying some American official or other to deport me. I understand that bribery is a common practice here."

Aubrey smiled, a little sadly, I thought, and placed himself between Doreen and the door. "I haven't bribed anyone since I arrived. And now that you are here *in partibus infidelium,* it would be silly to leave so soon. You should see something of the country. *Utile dulci*, the useful with the agreeable."

"Thank you, Aubrey," Doreen said humbly.

"Not at all. And if you'll just be sensible, I'll try to help you. Always glad to do what I can for a compatriot in distress." He handed her the shopping bag and picked up the suitcases. "We'd better find you a bed-sitter somewhere."

They came out into the corridor and Fogbound tipped his hat, although he was not wearing one, and I said, "Hello again." Doreen must have been recovering for, from inside the office, we heard her say, "It *is* scruffy, Aubrey. This lift would never have passed our building inspectors. I thought the Americans were so up-to-date. They do boast about it." Aubrey's reply was lost in the elevator's groaning descent.

When I saw Aubrey the next day, I offered, as tactfully as I could, my plaudits on his handling of the Doreen crisis. I thought that kudos might be in order, as well, but concluded that plaudits and kudos jointly would be excessive. Fredda, I gathered, had no such poser to resolve.

"Aubrey," she asked, "can I trust you?"

"Implicitly. But I do feel an obligation to Doreen. I did squire her about a bit in London and I can't let her go back at once. It would be frightfully embarrassing for her. Nor can I fail to make some provision for her while she is here. There is no one else to do it."

"What about the British Consul? He must have some of those dollars you've been giving the Exchequer."

"Oh, Fredda, you're too harsh. Have pity on a poor, impressionable girl. She means no harm."

"The hell she doesn't," Fredda said.

Fogbound was as wary as Fredda. Although it was his opinion that fighters should fight, with a minimum of outside interests, he had known fighters who were successful in spite of involvement with one woman. One woman properly handled could sometimes even be a help. Never had he heard of success won in the face of involvement with two women. When an almost obsessive concern with Britain's aging industrial plant was thrown in ("I can't feel sorry for old factories," he had once told Aubrey. "It happens to everybody.") the odds against success seemed to him crushingly heavy.

"You misunderstand, Sam," Aubrey said. "I'm merely helping Doreen until she's ready to go home. There's nothing between us, honestly."

"Wait till she meets Fredda," Fogbound said, and thinking of this prospect, he brought into effect his mental torment curriculum number one. Curriculum number two was reserved for times when things looked bad and three for when they were hopeless. Number one, which now went into operation, expressed itself in much shaking of the head, exhalations, which came out as sighs or as grunts, and a tendency to raise the head and open the mouth to say something, only to think better of it and fall back into silence.

From long experience, Mrs. Franklin was able to tell at once when any of the curricula had been invoked. She could tell which it was by the amount of food she took back to the kitchen. With number three, in which Fogbound sometimes called for his robe and sat up all night, resulting in his proclaiming that he had a headache and then sleeping during the day, she knew that she might as well stop preparing meals at all. The onset of curriculum number one therefore disquieted her. She advised her husband that worry had deleterious effects on the health. He replied that he was sorry but he did not worry because he enjoyed it. He worried for cause.

"A doleful mien, Sam," I said, on coming upon him in

this mood. "It may interest you to know that Lord Chester-
field, who was equally celebrated for the piece of furniture
and the overcoat that were named for him, and for his letters
to his son, once said that from the time he had full use of
his reason, nobody ever saw him laugh."

"What age?"

"Seven."

"I can understand it," Fogbound said.

13

AUBREY WAS, I had by this time concluded, a good guy, in spite of his being so self-assured. He was courteous and considerate, he wished no man ill, and his smile was uncompromisingly honest and retained a trace of shyness. He was too thin to be handsome, but he was winningly boyish. In only one particular was Aubrey objectionable — he did not mind the heat. In recognition of the advent of summer, he made a minimal change in his clerklike costume of black coat, waistcoat, and trousers, white shirt with stiff collar, gray tie, and black rolled umbrella. He removed the waistcoat.

Aubrey was in Fogbound's office, where he had suggested turning off the air conditioner, a veteran and noisy, and had been overruled. I was working on a theory that someone as thin as Aubrey was metabolically unable to perspire, and a companion theory that it was Britons on the order of Aubrey who had secured the Empire. Britons who perspired freely could not have commanded the respect of the lower orders at home or the lesser breeds abroad. Aubrey had accepted

Fogbound's decision with his usual good grace, when Doreen staggered in. Her dress was clotted with perspiration and her hair was stringy. By her count, communicated to us as she collapsed into a chair held by Aubrey, forty-seven complete strangers had asked whether it was hot enough for her.

"Such heat," she gasped. "It's frightful. I've never known anything like it."

"It is a question of attitude," Aubrey said. "Where have you been?"

"Grant's Tomb," Doreen panted. "It's a bit cool, really. If I die in New York this summer, I'd like to be buried there."

Aubrey had ambitious plans for her self-improvement. "Only Grant's Tomb?"

"Only Grant's Tomb?" Doreen repeated angrily. "I wish it were only Grant's Tomb. I've also been to Central Park."

"A far cry from Kensington Gardens," Aubrey said, "don't you think?"

"You needn't perform your usual cross-examination," Doreen said. "I can prove that I was there."

She dug into her handbag and brought out a large button which she pinned on Aubrey's jacket. The button bore the legend WHEN I'M FULL, TAKE ME HOME. She pinned one which said FOR LADIES ONLY on Fogbound's sodden shirtfront. Then she pinned on her dress a third button which said OUT FOR A GOOD TIME. There were three others, saying TELL ME WHEN, I'M LOOKING FOR MY THRILL, and IF YOU LIKE SEX, SMILE. These she spread on Fogbound's desk.

"May I?" I pointed to I'M LOOKING FOR MY THRILL.

"Please," Doreen said. "All bought at the Central Park carousel."

Aubrey disregarded the buttons. He was standing in the

middle of the office, fresh and unrumpled. It was as though he controlled the space immediately around him, took it with him when he moved, and told the heat to stay out. "Where to now?" he asked cheerfully.

"Nowhere," Doreen said. "Nowhere at all. I've run out of places to see."

"Oh, surely not," Aubrey protested. "What about City Hall?"

"I've seen it."

"The Battery?"

"I've seen it."

"Chinatown, then."

"I've seen it," Doreen said. "Also Times Square, Macy's, Fifth Avenue, the Bowery, the Empire State, Chrysler, RCA, Woolworth, and Citicorp buildings, the museums of Modern Art, Natural History, City of New York, and Non-Objective Art; Little Italy; the Triborough Bridge, the underground, Broadway, the World Trade Center, the Jumel Mansion — "

"Hold enow," I said, "which you will recognize as a quotation from a play about life in Scotland in the eleventh century. Which mansion?"

"The Jumel. Something to do with your George Washington." She turned to Aubrey. "Wherever did you hear of that?"

"It's an historic place," Aubrey testified. "It had an important role in the loss of the American colonies."

"I can do very nicely without the reminder, thank you," Doreen said.

Aubrey paused for reflection. "Let's see now. Where else can you go?"

Doreen ignored him. "You don't mind if I stay here, do you, Mr. Franklin?"

Fogbound, who had barely escaped asking "Hot enough for you?" when Doreen came in and had been a silent onlooker up to this point, shook his head. For others this would have settled matters, but Aubrey, a tireless seeker after knowledge, was trying to convince Doreen that a visit to the Prospect Park Zoo would be rewarding when Barbetta entered without knocking.

"Ho, Barbetta," Fogbound said, and still having the phrase unused and available, he added, "hot enough for you?"

"Yeah." Barbetta was once again all in black except for the white tie. "Enough. How about you?"

"For me, too," Fogbound said.

"I show you something," Barbetta looked around, spotted the air conditioning unit heaving away, strolled over, and flipped it off. "Why I do that?" he asked.

Nobody said anything.

"Why you think I do it?"

There was silence.

"I put the heat on you. You know what I mean. It's maybe a warning." He flipped the air conditioner back on. "If you don't do like I say." He leaned against the air conditioner with his hand on the on-off switch.

Fogbound played for time. "So what brings you here?"

"I come to give you another chance."

"A chance for what?"

"I like to buy in. I told you."

Fogbound looked at Aubrey, looked at me, and said, a little desperately, "Listen, Barbetta. I like you. From the first minute I saw you, I liked you. But I told you already Aubrey is not for sale."

Barbetta's smile remained fixed but he allowed his glance to wander to the air conditioner. "You like me? I like you.

That's good. But I tell you what I like more. I like to buy in. You don't sell, I take. So, better you sell."

Aubrey rose to his feet, his arms at his side, almost as though he were standing at attention as a member of the Brigade of Guards. In a way, he was, and opposing the probity and sobriety of his black costume to the gangster black of Barbetta. "Barbetta," he said, "there are still forces of decency in this country. I refuse to believe that American society is utterly degenerate. It rests on traditions of common law as surely as our own. I am, in any case, a freeborn Englishman. I am not a chattel to be bought or sold at whim. I shall speak to you plainly. Sod off."

Barbetta tapped the right pocket of his tropical worsted. "I like to do this friendly. I ask you in a friendly way. I don't want trouble. I just like to buy in."

"In any proper transaction," Aubrey said, "there must be a willing buyer and a willing seller. In this instance, half of the equation, as you can surely see, is missing. Now be on your way."

I mustered my courage. "He means they don't want to sell."

Barbetta permitted displeasure to flit across his face. "I know what he means. I don't need no lessons. Who needs lessons around here ain't me." He smiled indulgently, shrugged, then tapped his right pocket again. "Some days I'm very sad. I try to do business with people I think got smarts and I'm wrong. No smarts. Today, I'm very sad. You think we play games in organized crime? You think maybe it's only air conditioners turned off?"

He reached toward the switch and was stopped by Doreen's voice. "Please don't do that. It's perfectly loathsome in here when you do."

Barbetta looked around and noticed Doreen for the first time. "Who's that?"

"None of your business," Fogbound said. "Why don't you be nice and leave?"

"I'm a visitor," Doreen said. "And I think you can make whatever point you want to without turning off the air conditioning."

Barbetta walked close to Doreen and looked her over. "I know *you're* here, I don't turn it off." He continued his appraisal, rocking back and forth slightly, and looking over at us from time to time. His grin became wider and he seemed to be considering a line of conduct.

"I'm not looking my best," Doreen said, "and your turning off the air conditioning doesn't help."

"You look good to me, baby," Barbetta smirked. "Open your mouth." Doreen did. "Nice teeth," he said. "Nice teeth. I like a girl with nice teeth." As Doreen came to and clamped her mouth shut, he turned to face us. "I take her for my moll."

"Your what?" Aubrey asked.

Barbetta turned back to Doreen. "Always I'm looking for nice teeth. You got nice teeth. I take you for my moll."

Fogbound walked over to Barbetta and tapped him on the shoulder. "Listen, my friend, you got a gun, you're tough, that I know. But the girl is not interested."

"I don't hear her say so," Barbetta said.

"Interested in what?" Doreen asked.

"In being my moll. I like you for my moll."

"And what, may I ask, is a moll?"

Barbetta whistled. "Don't you go to the movies? Don't you read no books? The way American kids brought up these day." He shook his head.

"I'm not American. I'm English. A Londoner."

"I thought you talked funny," Barbetta said. "Hey, I like you even more for my moll. An English moll. Frankie the Barb goes way ahead with that." He walked to the window, glanced out, and turned back.

"I thought the word *moll* went out some time ago in your circles," Aubrey said. "I haven't heard it in the cinema in years."

"I don't go for this changing fashions every day. Some of us still use it."

"You still haven't told me what a moll is," Doreen complained.

"It's a girl," Fogbound shouted. "A moll's a girl. He wants you for his girl."

I realized that I had made almost no contribution to the conversation. "A moll is a female companion of a thief or gangster," I said. "The word is derived from the name *Moll*, which is a pet form of *Mary*."

Barbetta puffed up. "That's right. A thief or a gangster. I'm a gangster."

"I thought you said you were an organized criminal," Doreen said.

Barbetta smiled and put his arm around her shoulder. "You got a lot to learn, baby. I take you for my moll, I teach you."

"But what have my teeth to do with it?"

Barbetta blushed. "Some like one thing, some like something else. Legs, maybe. Other parts." He looked uncomfortable. "You know what I mean. Some words you don't say. With me, teeth are very important."

There was a pause. "Teeth?" Aubrey and I exclaimed together.

Fogbound muttered, "That I never heard."

"Lots of things you never heard." Barbetta faced Doreen again. "I show you a good time." Her face brightened. "I show you the town." Her face fell.

"I've seen the town," she said.

"What you see?"

"Everything." She wearily rattled off her list, adding the Soldiers and Sailors Monument, Trinity Church, and the George Washington Bridge.

"Half those places I never heard of," Barbetta said. "I show you the town. I show you a good time. What I mean, the *town?* I mean the clubs, the discos. I think we go good together, baby."

"Do you make lots of lovely lolly?"

"What's that, *lolly?*"

"Money."

Barbetta walked to the window and pointed down.

Fogbound, Aubrey, and I got up to look, and Barbetta pointed imperiously to the chairs we had just vacated. "I like you there better. You I don't remember asking." The outline of the gun in his right jacket pocket was easy to make out. We sat down. He nodded to Doreen and pointed down once more.

"Is it yours?" Doreen asked.

Barbetta threw an arm in our direction. "It ain't theirs."

Doreen pointed down. "Who's that?"

"He works for me. You my moll, he works for you."

"Smashing," Doreen said.

"Also it's cool. Not like this." He pointed to the air conditioner, which seemed to me to have had a bad day and to deserve no further disparagement. "New. The latest."

"Well," Doreen said, looking out of the window again and then at Fogbound's office, "I know I've had enough of *this.*"

She indicated with a wave of her hand the world to which Aubrey had consigned her, then turned to Barbetta. "What would happen to me if you went to prison?"

Barbetta laughed and I heard chicken bones and jam jars being ground up. "I look to you like I spend time in the joint? I don't spend no time in the joint. That's for losers. I look to you like a loser?"

"No," Doreen said, "you certainly don't. All right, I think I'll have a go. I'm your moll — on trial. Where to first?"

"Forgive me for breaking in," Aubrey interjected. "I should think twice about this if I were you. I'm sure the National Health Service would be pleased to hear that Mr. Barbetta admires your teeth. But if an old friend may say this, you're taking an awful risk."

"Thank you for your advice," Doreen said haughtily. "You've been perfectly foul to me, Aubrey."

Barbetta, though he was not following the conversation entirely, understood that Doreen was throwing in with him. "You make the right decision, baby. Okay, we go." As he moved toward the door, his eye caught her button, which said, OUT FOR A GOOD TIME. It puzzled him for a moment, then he smiled. "You got a sense of humor. I like a girl's got a sense of humor." He swung around slowly, as though expecting an argument on this point from us, and noticed our buttons. "What's this, a party or something?"

"This is no party," Doreen said emphatically. "I got them in Central Park. Sightseeing."

"You got one for me?"

Doreen took the one that said TELL ME WHEN from Fogbound's desk and pinned it on Barbetta's neatly tailored lapel.

"Okay," Barbetta said. "First we get you some new clothes. Then some place cool."

Fogbound broke his long silence. "I never heard such a

thing," he shouted. "A young lady like you. You can't do such a thing."

"Oh, can't I just," Doreen retorted. "Watch me." She linked her arm with Barbetta's. "Come along, Mr. — " She paused. "What did you say your name was?"

"Barbetta. My friends call me Frankie."

"Mine call me Doreen."

"I like it," Barbetta said. "Classy. Like you, baby."

As they left, Doreen threw a last remark over her shoulder to Aubrey: "See you at the Prospect Park Zoo."

Barbetta stopped at the door. "Remember. You don't sell, I take."

When we heard the elevator chugging downward, we went to the window. Below us was a large black car with a man in a chauffeur's uniform hovering nearby. As we watched, he took off his cap, grabbed a revolver that had been resting under it, slipped the gun into his pocket, mopped his head, brought the gun back out, and replaced it and the cap on his head.

"You saw that?" Fogbound gasped.

Now Doreen and Barbetta came out of the building, and Barbetta spoke briefly to the chauffeur. Doreen got in, then Barbetta removed his hat, a virtual parasol, for the first time showing us his hair, which was slick and shiny, and followed her. The car pulled away.

"For the like of me, I never expected to see such a thing," Fogbound said. "A girl goes with a gangster. In my office. We should have stopped her."

"My dear Sam," Aubrey said, "her mind was made up. My own intervention was purely pro forma. Nor am I certain that we should have stopped her even if we could have." He was standing now and orating. "Doreen has gone into the unknown. She has acted with courage and daring. She has shown the spirit which, could it be again brought forth from our workers and managers, would make British industry a model for the world."

"You overlook something, Aubrey," I said. "Doreen has not gone into the export trade. She has run off with a member of the Mafia."

"Thank you," Fogbound said. "Already he makes it sound like going with Barbetta is good for England."

Aubrey was orating again. "We must take the world as we find it. Doreen is getting to know New York. In New York, there are many gangsters. I had not imagined that they were so shameless, but now she will know something of this gangster aspect of our city. One cannot say that some knowledge is good and some bad. Knowledge is desirable in itself. Doreen will return a wiser woman."

"Maybe also sadder," Fogbound said. "If she returns."

"There is no such thing as a riskless existence," Aubrey said. "Nor should we want there to be. Excuse me, Sam. I have some research to do at the English-Speaking Union."

Aubrey's final words did, for a while, drive Doreen's fate out of Fogbound's mind. He was puzzled. "I don't always agree with them. But the other unions, they don't speak English?"

14

AUBREY HAD SEEN many British programs on public television; in fact, his first impression of the New York station was that it was part of the British Broadcasting Corporation's overseas operations. "Extremely resourceful of the BBC," he said. "This gives the lie to those who say that British zeal is no more. Slumbering it may be, but it needs only to be awakened."

His satisfaction was only slightly reduced when he was told that it was simply that British programs were being sold here — he thought that a sign of "British gumption" — and so when he was asked to contribute something personal that could be sold at auction during one of public television's money-raising campaigns, he readily agreed.

Mrs. Franklin decided what he should contribute. She knew that celebrities sometimes helped various causes by donating lunches or dinners with themselves. "Aubrey can do it, too," she said. "I'll cook."

Fogbound had doubts about the undertaking. It seemed to him to introduce yet another unknown quantity into Aubrey's affairs, which he thought complicated enough. As for Fredda, she was pleased by the existence of public television, a possible employer some day if she lost out in commercial television, but her contract with Cosmic made it impolitic for her to join in. "I am," she said, "remaining aloof."

Dinner with Aubrey was auctioned off between an Egyptian artifact and an album of Gregorian chants, and the sale was conducted by one of the station announcers. "He should have been told it was Philp'tt," Aubrey said. "Though I should have thought a compère would know that."

The bidding was not spirited and Aubrey was plainly uncomfortable each time the announcer said, "Come on, folks. Dinner with the one and only Aubrey Philpott-Grimes. You'll see why they call him 'The Asparagus Spear That Walks Like a Man.' You won't be served that asparagus, because then there'd be no more Aubrey Philpott-Grimes. But there'll be lots to eat and lots to talk about."

"They're awfully arch," Aubrey said. "A license fee would obviate all of this."

Eventually, the dinner was sold for $74.50. Aubrey tried unsuccessfully to calculate how much of the money might go for British programs. Mrs. Franklin knew that the price was not an appraisal of her cooking but thought it sufficient to bring out her best.

The high bidder was identified only as Rainbow Light. Fogbound at once pronounced this an alias. "Who's named Rainbow Light? A horse, maybe. Not a person. Anyway, I don't like it. We should know who's coming to our house. That's manners."

Fogbound did not go so far as to suggest that the dinner

be canceled, and at the time agreed, arrangements having been made by the television station, Rainbow Light rang the bell at the Franklins' Riverside Drive apartment. With me behind him as a strategic reserve, Fogbound approached the door as though Attila the Hun might be on the other side. He opened it to reveal a brown-haired woman in her early thirties, about thirty pounds above her best fighting weight, with a friendly face, and wearing sandals, a caftan, and a substantial display of beads.

"Good evening," she said, in a tiny voice. "I'm Rainbow Light."

"That I guessed," Fogbound gallantly responded.

Mrs. Franklin and Aubrey, who had been helping her, came out of the kitchen and were introduced. Then we all went into the small, crowded living room and sat down. Rainbow Light refused a drink but added quickly that she wouldn't want to spoil anyone else's fun. "I'm laid back about it," she said. There was a long silence, during which Rainbow Light tried to look interested in the bibelots on the Franklins' sideboard, among them a tea set, souvenir of the London silver vaults, and a pottery representation of Ann Hathaway's cottage.

"You don't mind my asking," Fogbound said. "Rainbow Light is your real name?"

"Yes."

"That's the name you were born with?"

"No, but that name was not my real name. I mean it was given to me by, like, a corrupt society. When human unfoldment and accelerated personal growth came, I knew what my real name was. It was Rainbow Light."

"When what came?" I asked.

"Human unfoldment and accelerated personal growth. Y'know?"

That set the tone of the evening. Not that Rainbow Light was not a cheerful guest. She had entered the Franklin's apartment smiling beatifically and did not stop doing so even while eating, which, Mrs. Franklin noted, she did sparingly.

"You don't like roast beef, Miss Light?"

"It isn't that. I'm not into meat. I'm into natural food."

"You'll go back to that tomorrow," Mrs. Franklin said. "Take advantage. Eat."

I had run what I had so far heard of Rainbow Light's vocabulary through the analytical procedures perfected at editorial board meetings and had concluded that she was not a fight fan. "If you don't mind the question, Miss Light," I said in what I hoped was an insinuating way, "are you interested in fighting?"

"I am interested in fighting. I'm interested in it as a phenomenon that will one day vanish. Experience of higher dimensionality will lead us to more positive social interaction. Y'know? I want to dialogue with Mr. Philpott-Grimes about that."

"Philp'tt," Aubrey said. "The o is barely suggested."

"Thank you," Rainbow Light beamed. "We should all be changing and growing and blossoming. Your name is part of your wholeness. I apologize."

"Please don't," Aubrey replied mildly. "It's only a matter of pronunciation."

"And please don't call me Miss Light. Rainbow Light is one name. Just as moonglow is. Or sunshine."

"You want Aubrey to stop fighting?" Fogbound asked in a choked voice. "That's why you came to dinner?"

"Well, I guess so. Like, yes."

For a moment, I thought that Mrs. Franklin was going to dart in and snatch Rainbow Light's plate off the table, but she was too polite.

"This is how you help a *fighter?*" Fogbound asked. "By telling him not to fight?"

"It is how I help another human being. Mr. Philpott-Grimes is a teacher. But he has not integrated his inner energy with the fundamental nature of the universe. He is, like, almost seeking his identity through external validation. You see, he is part of a monoculture whose members must posture themselves as winners. But where I'm at, we have, like, a whole new belief system."

I made what I intended to be taken as an involuntary remark, an operation that involves blurting. "Imagine," I blurted. "A guru." Miss Light looked surprised, so I added, "A term that comes from Hindi and means venerable one. Which in turn comes from the Sanskrit *guruh*, meaning heavy or venerable."

Rainbow Light allowed her countenance to shine upon me. "Oh, but we're not heavy. We're like, therapists. It's a whole gestalt process."

"What makes you think that Mr. Philpott-Grimes will be interested in this?"

Quoth the guru: "Vibes."

Except for his objection to the egregious *o* in Philpott, Aubrey had been silent to this point. He often sat silent at gatherings, looking something like a cogitating giraffe. Now he spoke:

"Do you read?"

"Read?" Rainbow Light squeaked.

"Yes, read."

"Of course I read. Why do you, like, ask?"

"I have heard that some members of sects like yours don't. They say it dilutes the vibrations they receive."

"It doesn't dilute mine. And we're not a sect. We operate under assumptions rooted in the major philosophical transformation that is going on at this point in historical time."

Mrs. Franklin called to mind what she had heard about people who dressed as Rainbow Light did. "You have men and women living together not married?"

"We don't advocate a permissive situation ethic, if that's what you mean."

Eventually, the dinner ended. Aubrey said that if he wanted to learn more about human unfoldment, he would be in touch with Rainbow Light. He had, he said, a certain sympathy with her point of view. He did regard himself as a teacher, but fighting made it easier for him to get his point across.

"But it can be done in, like, other ways," Rainbow Light piped up.

Moreover, Aubrey continued, fighting itself, as he did it, was a form of teaching. There was harmony between the means at his disposal as a fighter and the manner in which he used them. It was a useful lesson for those prepared to take it in.

Rainbow Light thanked us all warmly, particularly Mrs. Franklin, placed on the sideboard some leaflets on getting in touch with one's insides, said she hoped that this would be be for all of us the beginning of a process of integrating personal myth with the complexities of civilized survival, and left.

"A strange episode," I said, "the Sanskrit for which phrase I do not know. I wonder whether it was somebody's idea of a practical joke."

"Oh, surely not," Aubrey said. "There are so many strange beliefs in this country and, thanks to the prodigality of your resources, so many people with nothing to do but propagate them, one is bound to run into a votary from time to time."

"She's a Rotary?" Fogbound asked.

"Votary. Someone devoted to a religion, or to an ideal."

Fogbound grunted.

"A nice lady," Mrs. Franklin said. "I could see she didn't like the dinner, but she tried. Her taste in clothes, I don't know about. And my insides I don't have to get in touch with. The food that's sold these days, I hear from them enough."

15

THERE COMES A TIME in the career of every successful fighter when he reaches a point just below the top flight, when another step will take him into the upper brackets of his class and he will be, as Fogbound explained one day to Aubrey, promulgated into the rank of logical contender. Some champions prefer to take on illogical contenders, but that is another matter. In any case, Aubrey reached this point not long after Doreen's arrival, and Fogbound did what all managers with fighters in such a position do — with a certain amount of trepidation he booked his man into a tough one, against a pugilist from Harlem whose real name was Lawrence Hoskins but who, for professional reasons, fought under the name of Frosty Sirkowitz.

Aubrey had heard of Sirkowitz and his reputation as a spoiler. "He is an all-too-typical American fighter," he said. "He discovered his right-hand hitting power before mastering the use of the left, and there his development stopped. I shall trounce him."

"I wish it was all so cooked and dried," Fogbound told me, but he now felt that he was in the grip of a power greater than himself, and he settled into his usual pre-fight pattern. In this, he was able to force a smile in his fighter's presence but otherwise, as he explained to me, he was premeditated. For Fogbound, the state of premeditation was something like that which came upon him when he ate something that was not quite right. "It's in me," he would say. "My whole system is poisoned."

For Simco Savory, exploiting his connection with Aubrey, the Sirkowitz fight provided an opportunity: He would branch out into New York. He hired a ballroom at a New York hotel, though not before calling me with an inquiry:

"Can Aubrey lose this fight?"

"Oh sure, he can lose."

"Will he lose it?"

"I don't think so. He has to beat Sirkowitz to be taken seriously."

"Sirkowitz is an Israelite?" asked Savory, who had his quaint aspects.

"I imagine he's a Baptist if he's anything, but I don't know."

"It's ever so odd a name for a Baptist."

"I believe it is a *nom de guerre.*"

"How captivating," Savory said. "And I thank you for the reassurance. I would not have wanted to arrange a gala affair for Aubrey and then have him suffer a defeat. It would have been ever so awkward for him. I shall move ahead with confidence."

Sirkowitz, for his part, announced that he had a strategy that would be revealed once the fight began. "I see something," he said.

These were the words Max Schmeling had used before his first fight with Joe Louis in 1936, and since he had knocked Louis out, they caused Fogbound to worry, or more accurately, enabled him to do so. With Fogbound, it was never a matter of whether he would, but rather what it would be about.

I had seen Sirkowitz a few times and could not imagine what his strategy might be. He was a certified glowerer and had been cut sufficiently over the years so that anyone covering his fights could write, "Sirkowitz glowered menacingly from under scarred brows," but otherwise he was a fighter who went straight ahead, both hands working, trying to get inside, and being almost as dangerous with his lowered head as he was with his hands.

What Schmeling had seen was that Louis feinted a left jab before he threw it. He therefore threw his own right whenever he saw Louis prepare to lead and knocked his man out in the twelfth. Sirkowitz had spotted no such technical fault in Aubrey. What he had noticed was the thinness of Aubrey's arms. So had everyone else, but Sirkowitz used what he saw, and the first time they got into a clinch, he dropped his right hand heavily on Aubrey's left bicep, which he somehow managed to locate without the help of radar. It seemed unimportant at the time, but as the fight wore on, with Aubrey proceeding in his methodical way, moving aside as Sirkowitz lumbered in, and piling up a lead with point-scoring lefts and an occasional right, it became clear that Sirkowitz's apparently aimless punching was, on the contrary, aimful. He only looked as though he was swinging for the head and body and missing. His target was Aubrey's upper arms. By the end of the fourth round, they were black and blue, and Fogbound was complaining to the referee, who said that he would watch but had not seen anything illegal.

After the fifth round, Aubrey's arms had to be sponged with cold water to ease the pain. In the sixth, thanks to Sirkowitz's well-planned strategy, Aubrey was carrying his hands dangerous low and hardly punching at all. He caught a good right near the end of the round and came to the corner murmuring that the failure to count fringe benefits in the cost of a wage settlement leads to underestimating the settlement's inflationary effect. It took thirty seconds to get him back to business.

On Fogbound's instructions, he bicycled around the ring in the seventh, but that is no way to win a fight, and Fogbound knew that Aubrey had to get his hands up where they belonged. "Aubrey, my boy," he said. "I know it hurts. But the hands have to be high. And you have to punch. It's only three rounds."

"Sam," Aubrey croaked, "I shall do it somehow. We have come too far to be turned back by blunderbuss tactics."

In round eight, Aubrey was again holding his hands high. I winced when his left banged against Sirkowitz's head but he bravely managed not to. After about a minute of this, Sirkowitz became convinced that his strategy had failed. Aubrey's attenuated arms had taken punishment and were still at work. Sirkowitz stopped hitting them and went instead for the head. Aubrey was back in control.

During the last round, Sirkowitz, in the sort of act that will cause a fighter to be called a wily veteran, dropped his hands and, with a movement of his head, indicated that he would like Aubrey to mix it up, not box. Aubrey kept his hands up. "I think not," he said. "I'll just go on this way" — he stuck a left in Sirkowitz's face — "thank you."

Brought to the television microphone as he left the ring, Aubrey said with some difficulty, "I am happy to have won.

I hope that my victory will help to direct attention to a number of pressing questions, among them whether devoting a large section of industry to defense production, where considerations of cost are secondary, must render that industry less efficient and so place it under a handicap in selling its nondefense products in competition with countries that carry a smaller defense burden, and if so, how shall the problem be met? There are, I know, different sets of plausible assumptions about this question, but on any one of them, the industrial nations must go forward together. Thank you very much."

Savory's guests gathered in the Piazza Navona room of the Midtown Spires hotel. Bobby Lou Bridewell was visible above most of the others. She had come to New York because she never missed one of Savory's functions, but considered herself too softly feminine to stomach a prize fight. Savory himself had not seen the battle but had remained at the hotel, making certain that everything would be in order. It wasn't. He had asked for trout and glazed ham served with mousse and truffles, capon with chaudfroid sauce and adorned with chicken liver pâté, tiered cakes decorated to represent the seasons of the year — "Light mauve for spring," he had specified — and much more. Instead, the waiters had wheeled in fresh fruit protein shake, zucchini quiche, whole grain bread, a salad of mustard greens, yogurt pie, and multivitamin pills, one per head.

Savory had angrily demanded that things be put right and had told one of the hotel's assistant managers that he was upset and disappointed and that he thought that what had happened was quite out of the. The assistant manager had said that he would do what he could, and that Savory would be charged no more for the natural foods than he would have been for those he ordered, but good staff was hard to come by these days and perhaps the problem could be solved by an exchange of populations, Savory's guests overtaking their food in the Grotta Azzurra, and the long-life regimen people coming to join theirs. Savory ruled this out on hearing that this would have meant spreading his guests over a number of rooms rather than the single ballroom he had rented. "Not a *fête*, you see," he said. "Simply not a *fête*. Not a *fête* at all."

In the event, nothing was done, and Savory was obliged to tell his guests as they arrived, "I'm so very sorry about the food. The caterers brought the wrong order. Do forgive me. But the drinks are just as dangerous to your health as we can make them."

When Aubrey's party arrived, Savory threw his arms wide and said to Fogbound, "*Ah, mon vieux, comme vous êtes le bienvenu.*" Fogbound replied that he and his wife had always liked French food. Then Savory called the room to order. "Good brave Aubrey is here." There were cheers. "With another victory." More cheers. "When we see Aubrey among us, we are reminded that the British and American people are not only allies; they are friends. Hands across the, of course. In a troubled world, that connection is ever so. And Aubrey, you are, too. Just ever so."

Nobody denied this, and Savory raised his glass. "To Aubrey." There were shouts of "Hear, hear," and more applause. Then Fredda, who had preceded Aubrey from the Sportitorium, gave him a big kiss and an even bigger hug. On another night, she might have played her dewy-eyed ingenue role, hanging on Aubrey's arm and emitting sounds of pride and joy. Because of the painful and bluish state of that arm, she chose instead the part of prince's consort — lively, gregarious, on center stage.

For all his self-possession, Aubrey had a way of effacing himself, and after the opening ceremonies, except that Bobby Lou Bridewell swiveled around constantly to keep her awe-filled eyes on him, he was allowed to go his own way.

I had noticed that he was barely able to raise his glass when Savory proposed the toast. "A hard fight," I said.

"Jolly hard. It shouldn't have been. Sirkowitz is rather like a bulldozer — good against stationary objects but a bit clueless if you keep moving. But I had not run into these tactics before. Made it a bit dicey for a while."

A little later, Fogbound and Mrs. Franklin and I found ourselves in conversation with a young couple, he an English instructor whose field of concentration was class-consciousness in Elizabethan drama, she a sociologist doing research on authority, power, dominance, legitimacy, aggression, and deference in the skateboard generation. They had, on marriage, abandoned their own names and taken the name Wetlands to demonstrate their solidarity with the environment and particularly with the marshes and swamps endangered by property developers. "We're sometimes called the threatened Wetlands," Mrs. Wetlands remarked.

This drew no response, though I thought it clever enough and did not laugh solely because I liked to be recognized as the only amusing person at any gathering. Oppressed by the silence, the Wetlands offered Fogbound congratulations on Aubrey's victory and guessed that the Franklins must be enjoying the party.

"Every minute," Mrs. Franklin said.

"I could feel just as good without a party," Fogbound said. "I keep thinking how Aubrey won that fight. In his career, a mildstone."

"Such a boy," Mrs. Franklin said. "A genius."

"Let me get you a drink, Mrs. Franklin," Wetlands said.

"All right." Mrs. Franklin gave him her most dazzling smile. "Soda water."

"Only that?"

"Soda water."

Wetlands took his wife's order, Fogbound's, and mine, and was off.

Mrs. Franklin lowered her voice. "Some party. I don't count the food. It can happen."

"The yogurt pie is delicious," Mrs. Wetlands said. "Have you tried it?"

Mrs. Franklin looked at her with pity, then continued. "What does he do, this Mr. Savory?"

"He gives parties."

"That's all? A gorgeous-looking man like that?"

"So far as I know."

"He has a reason," I said. "He does it to give the male party-giver equality with the female."

"I don't say no, but that's a life?"

"He seems happy with it, and it's more benign ecologically than some other occupations," Mrs. Wetlands said.

Mrs. Franklin closed her eyes and nodded eloquently. "Some country, when a man can give parties and that's all." She spied Wetlands coming toward her. "Your husband," she said. "Such manners." She spoke to Fogbound. "Learn something."

Fogbound was about to make a cutting retort when his eye fell on two figures entering the room. One was Doreen. The other was Barbetta, who was immediately recognizable even without a hat that preceded him by eighteen inches: He was wearing a black shirt and a white tie with his dinner jacket. Fogbound groaned.

Mrs. Franklin, hearing the groan, thought that her butcher

must have given her something not quite right. "Sam," she said, "what is it?"

"It's that gangster," Fogbound groaned again, "that Frankie."

"A gangster? Here?" Wetlands exclaimed. "Hey, I'd like to see him."

"Look and you'll see him. By the door, with the girl, taking off her coat."

They all looked. "That's a gangster?" Mrs. Franklin sniffed. "That's somebody to be scared of? To me he doesn't look so tough."

"So arrest him," Fogbound said.

"Who's the girl?" Mrs. Wetlands asked.

"His moll, from England," Fogbound said.

"His what?"

"His moll."

"Doll?"

Fogbound's voice rose. He was feeling the strain of Barbetta's presence. "A woman went with a gangster, she was called a moll." He spelled it for emphasis: "M–o–l. Moll."

Mrs. Franklin sniffed again. "Some gangster. To me, that's no gangster. A sissy, maybe. But no gangster." She waited for the inevitable argument from her husband and, getting none, turned anxiously toward him. He was leaning forward, eyes narrowed, peering at Barbetta. Mrs. Franklin nudged him. "Enough staring. Be polite."

Fogbound regarded her peevishly. "If you don't mind, I'm trying to see his gun. If you don't mind."

"His gun?" Wetlands asked.

Fogbound nodded. "Look at his coat pocket. On the right side."

Wetlands moved forward for a closer look, then returned

with the report that the pocket of Barbetta's dinner jacket was perfectly flat.

Fogbound breathed more easily, and the Wetlands, disappointed, excused themselves and moved off for a better view. As they did so, Savory noticed the newcomers, approached them to find out who they were, and advised them pleasantly, even winningly, that he was afraid that he did not know them. I made myself inconspicuous, which is not difficult for an editorial writer, who lives without bylines and labors principally for the public enlightenment, and drifted over in time to hear Barbetta's reply:

"We don't know you, either, Jack."

Savory must have been upset by the mountains of zucchini quiche and nut cutlets lying unconsumed on the tables. Even if he looked up, he couldn't escape them, for the ceiling was formed of concave squares of aluminum, which reflected the scene below. He took a firm tone. He identified himself as the host and suggested that Barbetta and Doreen had better leave. Then he waited expectantly. "You are," he said, "quite *de trop.*"

Barbetta glanced coolly at the red and brown carpets, the walls covered in brown, the banner that said WELL DONE, AUBREY!, and at Savory's guests. "This a nice party," he observed. "I like a nice party. Same with Doreen. She likes a nice party. So I think we don't leave. I think we stay."

Savory looked around for some hotel employees, risking the possibility that if he found them, they would confuse things again and eject him, and said that he was afraid he would have to have them put out.

Barbetta extended his right hand, palm down. Stepping close to Savory, he spoke as from one man of the world to another. "Take my advice, Jack. You don't want no trouble.

I don't want no trouble. I and Doreen came here all decked out to congratulate the next champ," he snickered, "and his manager. Friendly. No rough stuff. I like a good, clean boy with brains."

Savory looked at Barbetta. "Would you mind telling me your name?"

"Sure. Barbetta's my name. Frankie Barbetta. You ever heard of Frankie the Barb?"

Savory had not.

"Some people." Barbetta shook his head. "Where they been?" He indicated Doreen. "And this here's Miss Morden."

Savory bowed, then murmured, "*Je suis ravi.*" Doreen, who was on moll patrol in a red silk blouse, cut almost to the navel and tied at the waist, and red silk trousers with bows at the ankles, inclined her head grandly. I assumed that her costume was Barbetta's choice. He was taking no chances that she would not be noticed.

"You Savory?" Barbetta asked.

Savory reluctantly acknowledged that he was.

"Thanks for having us. Now first a couple drinks and then I see my friends." He nodded to Savory, took Doreen's arm, and led her to the bar. Savory watched him indecisively, then returned to his guests.

Two drinks later, Barbetta confronted Fogbound.

"Hey," he said, "I seen your boy fight tonight. He done good."

Barbetta's enthusiasm failed to fire Fogbound. He said warily, "Thanks."

Barbetta continued full of fervent congratulations. "Very good. He done very good. Didn't he, Doreen?"

Doreen confirmed his judgment.

"I'm glad to see you again," Barbetta went on.

"Thanks," Fogbound said. "So tell me. You're out of the gangster business? You're going straight?"

"No cracks," Barbetta said. "I don't like cracks."

"He is quite serious," Doreen added. "He doesn't like cracks."

"From him," Barbetta said, hitching a shoulder in my direction, "I expect cracks. A mediaman. Always with the cracks. Not from you."

Barbetta could not have paid me a prettier compliment. In the hope of being classified as a wisecracking newspaperman, I had wearied relatives, friends, acquaintances, and strangers for years with my insouciance. But I had little time to think on these things. Fogbound was speaking again.

"I was only wondering. I didn't see a gun in your pocket."

Barbetta was scornful. "I don't carry no gun in my pocket with a tux. Spoils the shape. I carry it in a shoulder holster. Here." He patted a spot on his chest just under the left armpit.

Mrs. Franklin, an engrossed onlooker, reached forward and patted it, too. "He's got something there, all right. Something hard. A gun, maybe."

"Maybe." Barbetta shook his head wearily again. He beckoned Mrs. Franklin forward. "I unbutton this jacket quick and you look inside. But fast. Ready?"

Mrs. Franklin nodded.

"Okay. Here we go." Barbetta unbuttoned his jacket and flipped it open for a second, like an inhibited stripteaser, while Mrs. Franklin stared at the spot indicated.

"A gun," she announced. "I could see the part you hold." She nodded her head. "It's a gun," she said again, "but maybe" — she shrugged her shoulders — "maybe it isn't loaded."

"It's loaded," Barbetta grated. "You want me to show you?"

"We take your word," Fogbound said.

Mrs. Franklin shrugged again. "Well, Mr. Gangster, what do you want?"

"I like in."

"Not a chance in a million," Mrs. Franklin said firmly.

"I'm sorry to hear that. Very sorry. Ain't I, Doreen?"

Doreen confirmed it.

"For your sake, I'm sorry, too," Mrs. Franklin said. "But Aubrey's not for sale." She caught her husband's eye. "Am I right, Sam?"

Fogbound glanced at the vital spot near Barbetta's left shoulder and swallowed hard. "It's like I already told Mr. Barbetta. Aubrey's not for sale."

"I don't say anything about for sale. I warn you before. No more buying. Now I move in."

"Mercer, *Star-Telegram*," I said, thinking it would do no harm to remind Barbetta of the power of the press. "If Mr. Franklin won't sell you a percentage of his fighter, it is surely even less likely that he will give it to you."

Barbetta permitted himself a slight scowl. "That makes me sorry. Don't it, Doreen?"

Doreen said it did.

"Mercer, *Star-Telegram*," I said, picking up courage from Mrs. Franklin. "This conversation would go faster if we just took it for granted that Doreen agrees with you. And you've already said you're sorry. It's time-consuming for you to repeat yourself."

Barbetta eyed me coldly. "Mediaman," he said, "not so much talk." He turned back to Fogbound. "Because a boy can fight like that can maybe be champ. If he plays his cards right. And his manager plays his cards right. You don't do that, Sam."

Fogbound, also borrowing courage from his wife, said that was too bad.

"Too bad is right. Because this way, he never gets to be champ. He don't get close. Does he, Doreen?"

Doreen started to say, "He doesn't," but, unable to throw off the effects of education, said, "No, he won't."

"There it is again," I said. "These confirmations carry no weight. We know that Doreen has no independent positions."

"All the time cracks," Barbetta said. "Your friends better off without them. Better off without you. Which I maybe arrange." He faced Fogbound. "You like six-round prelims, Sam? That's what Aubrey fights when I'm finished. And I'm starting now. Think it over." He stared at Fogbound, bowed sardonically to Mrs. Franklin, who glared back defiantly, turned on his heel, spinning Doreen around with him, and moved off.

"Sam," Mrs. Franklin said decisively. "Call the police."

Fogbound sighed. "First I'm having a talk with Aubrey."

"Always no," said his wife. "It's in your family. A real Franklin. Some retirement you'll have. A corpse."

The party had begun to thin out when Barbetta, leering, came back. "Hey, you meet somebody named Rainbow Light lately? Where she come from?"

Mrs. Franklin took over. "Do you know? That's how I know."

"I send her. She wins the dinner with money from Frankie. Look." He extended an arm. "What you see?"

"Did I tell you?" I said. "Did I tell you? Rainbow Light was not what she seemed. You have seen the editorial mind at work. A masterly performance. Mercer, *Star-Telegram*."

"Hey!" It was Barbetta. "I'm tired holding this arm up."

"Take it down," said Fredda, who had joined the group. "It's of no interest up there. Not that I think it will gain in interest in another position. Why are you directing attention to it, anyway?"

Barbetta pointed again to his arm. "What you see?"

"An arm."

"Long?"

"So-so," said Fredda. "I've seen longer. Aubrey's are longer."

Barbetta laughed a short laugh, enough to crush a discarded six-pack. "That arm" — he pointed to it — "reach into your house, Sam. Maybe next time I don't send no Rainbow Light. I hear about this auction and I hear she wants the dinner. Too bad it goes for $74.50. I'm ready to pay more."

"Rainbow Light wasn't a real guru?" Fogbound asked.

"I send you a real guru. I send you a reminder. Maybe next time I send you something else. Not so nice."

He glanced up as Doreen, full of wrath, bore down on us, with Mrs. Franklin, flushed and distressed, a few paces behind. There had been an altercation. Doreen had become convinced that Mrs. Franklin was engaged in covert intelligence work.

"I do not skulk about powder rooms," she shouted, " — a name, I may say, I never heard of before I came to your country — spying on people. It is inexcusable."

"From a gun moll," Mrs. Franklin said, "I don't need lectures. And if I'm quiet, am I spying? Should I make announcements? What could I learn in a powder room, anyway?"

"I'd like to hear," Doreen said. "I'd like very much to hear."

"What a guest list," Fredda said. "She sees spies in the

ladies' room and he wants us to spend our time looking at his arm. On top of all this, nothing to eat but sunflower seeds. And Aubrey's off somewhere, talking, I have no reason to doubt, economics. A glorious night's entertainment."

I intervened. Barbetta was being let off the hook. "You sent a guru to talk Aubrey out of being a fighter?"

Barbetta was puzzled. "What you mean?"

"That's what she did. She tried to get Aubrey to give up fighting."

"She don't tell me that."

"What did she tell you?"

"Something about — " He turned to Doreen.

"About the vital life force, dear. She wanted to open channels for its expression."

"That's it," Barbetta said. "Nothing about not fighting."

"Barbetta, you funded an attempt to make a pacifist out of the fighter you want to own. It is to laugh." I emitted a series of one-syllable chuckles. It was tiring.

Barbetta was trying to recover his bluster and, while he was at it, his aplomb. He looked at Doreen. "That Rainbow Light." He tapped his head with his forefinger. "I'm too easy on her. I remember this. No more gurus."

Fredda fixed an eye on Barbetta. "Barbetta, I know something about the theater. It's time for you to exit, muttering threats. Your presence here has become anticlimactic."

"Too many cracks," Barbetta said, "all around. You live to regret them. Don't they, Doreen?"

"I'd like to predict an affirmative answer," I said.

Doreen hesitated because of the tense. "They do."

Barbetta now sought out his host to say goodnight and to thank him. "Maybe I do something for you sometime," he said. "A favor for a favor. That's how I like to work."

"It is hardly."

"I know it ain't hardly. But I like to do it. So you got problems, let me know."

"It's generous of you," Savory said. "But I fear I would not know what sort of help to request."

"I'm a gangster."

Savory decided to be charmingly humorous. "Aren't we all?" he said. "Each and every one of?"

"No, we ain't all, each and every one of," Barbetta said unpleasantly. "But I am. Ain't I, Doreen?"

Doreen said he was, and I considered saying, "That reply came as no surprise to this correspondent," but decided not to intervene in the conversation.

Savory smiled indulgently. It was not the sort of smile Barbetta liked to have smiled at him.

"What's the matter with people?" he complained. "A plumber says he's a plumber, people believe him. A fireman says he's a fireman, nobody laughs. But a gangster says he's a gangster, everybody acts like it's a big joke. What's the matter, I don't look like a gangster? I don't sound like one? You want I should say stick 'em up?"

It was a difficult moment for Savory. If Barbetta really was a gangster — and his cry from the heart had an authentic enough ring — he would be a notable catch. Barbetta might well be the year's lion, bigger than Aubrey. Savory came to a decision. He would be honored if they would attend one of his Washington galas. He hoped they would permit him to send them an invitation.

Barbetta thought for a while. "You get better food in Washington?"

"Oh, indeed. Tonight's was simply beyond the."

"You want me to come, write me a letter," Barbetta said. He glanced at Doreen. "Give him my address."

Doreen wrote it in a small notebook which she took from

her handbag, tore out the page and handed it to Savory. She also made a mental note to get Frankie some calling cards. Savory looked at the paper, then folded it carefully into his wallet and, affirming that meeting them had given him great, shook hands.

Later that night, Savory thought about having a gangster at his parties, and smiled. The ladies would go perfectly berserk. So would Webster Bindle. When he fell asleep, Savory was smiling still.

16

AUBREY HAD BEEN ENGROSSED in explaining to a bewildered party guest the theory of analogous advantage in international trade, when he noticed Barbetta's approach to Fogbound. That is, he saw Barbetta and Doreen talking to Fogbound, but with so motherly a soul as Mrs. Franklin apparently getting along famously with Barbetta, he concluded that Frankie was not pursuing his peculiar line of business. He noticed that Fredda was present for some of the conversation, and that I was, too, and he thought that if his help was needed, it would be asked for. He did not bother to ask himself what Barbetta was doing there at all, and he was in any case reluctant to interrupt his remarks on how benefits from trade arise.

When Fogbound told him what had happened and passed along, with his endorsement, Mrs. Franklin's suggestion that they go to the police, Aubrey pointed out that this might get Doreen into trouble. Fogbound replied that she had brought it on herself and that she had egged Barbetta on. Nor was he pleased by the charge of espionage she had lodged against

Mrs. Franklin. "A well-oiled team," he said. He did, however, accept the proposal that Aubrey go and talk to Doreen first.

Doreen had, somewhat presumptuously, all things considered, left her address and telephone number in Fogbound's office in case any mail should come for her from England. Aubrey telephoned ahead to be sure that Frankie was not there, and, if he were, prepared to disguise his voice and to pretend to be a public opinion pollster seeking data on attitudes to solar energy.

Doreen lived in a building of the class denominated "luxury." It was called the Lac de Genève, apparently because there was a small fountain in the lobby, and its corridors were so narrow that anyone much wider than Aubrey would have had to go through them sideways. Doreen's living room was small, and it was shrunk further by the low ceiling and by the decor, which included a number of white statuettes of cockatoos and shepherdesses, and a wall decoration with flashing neon lights. The small aquarium, Doreen advised him, held water flown from the Indian Ocean, and there was also sand from the Sahara Desert flown to New York and made into a botanical garden by an expensive florist. Aubrey, in his report on his expedition, said that he had remarked, "It's ghastly," and that Doreen had replied, "I know, but that's the way he likes it."

I had been fascinated by Doreen's get-up at Savory's party, for although she was attractive in an unglamorous way, she had in her red silk overreached herself, like a singer who tries for a high note and fails. Her alliance with Frankie had introduced Doreen to a new world of *basse couture*. I therefore asked Aubrey to take note of what she was wearing. From his description, and with the help of the paper's fashion editor, I deduced that it was TV-jamas, a costume made especially for watching television during the day, with slim, tapering silk shantung harem pants topped by a matching scooped neck and sleeveless blouse in navy blue, and over the blouse a reversible coolie coat combining silk honan in pink and chartreuse, the front dotted with sparkling rhinestone and gilt buttons.

Aubrey was a careful observer, and of what followed he gave an adequate account, though at times it lacked authenticating detail. I have therefore enriched the ambiance in places. He was able to tell us that on the couch next to Doreen lay a magazine featuring the article, "Six Million Frigid Women Can't Be Right," and another splashing on its cover, "I Gave a $3,000,000 Fortune to Charity — Anonymously." The television set showed a baseball game which Doreen switched off with reluctance. She explained that Frankie like baseball, especially the maneuvers called the stolen base and the hit-and-run, and he wanted her to understand them.

This remark enabled Aubrey to introduce his subject. "Sounds rather dictatorial to me, if you don't mind my saying so."

"I do mind. Frankie is the most considerate chap in the world. He wouldn't ask me to do a thing I didn't want to."

"Where is he now?"

"He isn't here, if that's what you mean. He isn't hiding in the cupboard."

Then came a long silence, Aubrey told us, during which Doreen switched the ball game back on, only to have Aubrey announce that he was ready. He regretted having to tell her that he and Fogbound were going to the police about Barbetta. Their patience was at an end. They deemed it only right to warn her.

Doreen was stunned. "The police? Whatever for?"

"What would you do if you were confronted by a gangster who insisted that he was, in that awful phrase, moving in? And who continually threatened you? He does carry a gun. *Abeunt studia in mores.* Practices zealously pursued pass into habits. What are we to do if it goes off?"

"Don't flap, Aubrey. Let him, in that dreadful phrase, move in."

"Really, Doreen, does one simply deliver oneself, neatly wrapped and tied with a ribbon, to any brigand who comes through the door? If one benefits by the rule of law, one has an obligation to uphold it."

Doreen shrugged. "This is not our own dear England, Aubrey. One adapts. The Mafia moves in. Isn't that routine practice here?"

"The Mafia has virtually set itself up as an extragovernmental taxing authority. I cannot go along with that."

"I thought you were concerned about your safety. If Frankie moved in, wouldn't that guarantee it?"

"No doubt. But I should then be as culpable in my own eyes as your Barbetta. In any case, the police would guarantee my safety, too. And rather more economically."

"Aubrey, don't go to the police. It's such a stuffy thing to do. And probably wouldn't work. If gangsters go about so openly . . ." She did not finish the sentence. "At least give it a little more time. Anyway, for all the brouhaha, damn-all's happened. And perhaps the Mafia will change its mind."

Aubrey hesitated, and Doreen beckoned him onto the couch next to her. It was not much of a walk from his chair. "Please?" she said. "For me? In a way, it's your doing that I'm here."

Aubrey glanced at her hands on his. "I've always liked you, Doreen, you know that."

The language of the magazines she had been reading must have affected Doreen's speech. "We are both British in a strange country. Don't dash my hopes for happiness."

Doreen went into the kitchen to brew tea, evidently to reinforce her plea for outlanders' solidarity on foreign strands. When she came out, Aubrey resumed his questioning. This time he learned that Doreen had never heard Frankie mention his family, and that he had not introduced her to any of his fellows in organized crime.

"You are his moll. Shouldn't you have met them?"

"He says security is tight and that molls have a probationary period. I'm still in mine. It's a rule."

"Have you any influence with him?"

"He'd rumble that. He'd think I was your agent."

"Quite so." Aubrey made a small joke. "What the intelligence chaps call a mole. Not a moll."

"Very funny." Doreen looked up. "You won't go to the police, will you?"

Aubrey frowned. "No. Not for the present. But I would like to be relieved of this foolishness. *Aeque servare mentum.* Preserve a calm mind. For a fighter, too many distractions can be harmful."

Doreen seized the opportunity to move to the offense. How many distractions would too many distractions be?

Aubrey would set no specific limit. Statesmanlike, he said only that a fighter should have as few as possible. He himself had two, Fredda and paying taxes, and he found that they took all the time he could spare, sometimes even more.

"You've always been so honest."

"Well, I always think that honesty is the best policy."

Doreen waited for the Latin translation, but there was none, and it was clear that this was the end of the interview.

Aubrey rose to go and graciously minimized the debt Doreen said she owed his generous nature. When she expressed certainty that he was taking the proper course, he said, "We shall see. Good luck," and Doreen said, "Cheers. And the best of British luck to you."

In the lobby, near the Lac de Genève fountain now illuminated for the evening hours, Aubrey ran into Barbetta, who was in his usual ensemble and was looking menacing in a casual way.

"You backdooring me?" Barbetta asked.

"What was that?"

"You backdooring me?"

"I can't make you out. Why don't we get away from the fountain?"

They moved to a corner where Aubrey found himself facing Barbetta and, above Barbetta's titanic fedora, a painting of the Cathedral of Notre Dame in Paris. Aubrey was wondering whether the landlord thought that it stood on the shores of the Lac de Genève when he heard Barbetta ask again, "You backdooring me?"

Aubrey thought for a moment. "Ah. I get it. No, I am not backdooring you. I am not backdooring anybody. I came to see Doreen. We're chums."

"Yeah. I know."

"We had a chat and a cup of tea and a biscuit. I hope you don't object."

"I don't object. As long as you keep it clean."

"That's an offensive comment. Swinish, really."

"I'm a gangster."

"That reminds me," Aubrey said. "I've been meaning to ask you this. You say you're a gangster. Have you a gang?"

"I tell you I'm a Mafioso. You ever hear of a Mafioso alone? Mafia — that's a big organization."

"Why don't I ever see any of your mates? It isn't as though you were making a whacking great success of this project. Why don't they send in somebody higher up?"

"This goes on, maybe they will. Then they rearrange your looks, or something falls on you from a prominent height. You're better off dealing with me."

"Thank you."

"Don't mention it."

They parted, and here Aubrey's account ended. When Frankie reached the apartment, as I was to learn in the fullness of time, Doreen had the ball game back on and was watching closely. She was chewing gum, because Frankie thought that becoming. It was sugarless, to preclude decay and cavities in the teeth he loved so well. She was also wondering, though she did not mention this to Frankie, why the players expectorated so often. She thought it might have something to do with the American diet, or poor upbringing.

"I seen Aubrey," Frankie greeted her.

"Yes, he was here."

"What he want?"

"He came over for a chat. For old times' sake. And a cup of tea and a biscuit."

He sat beside her on the couch and kissed her. "What you talk about?"

"England, mostly."

"We go someday. Maybe I do some business there. He say anything about I move in?"

"You know I leave those things to you."

"Who's winning?"

"The Yankees. They always win, it seems to me."

"They play heads up. What's the score?"

"Three–nothing in the top of the fifth."

"Who's pitching?"

"'That new fellow. The left-hander.'"

Barbetta patted her on the back and squeezed her arm. "Hey, you learning this game good. How they score?"

"I don't know. I had it off when Aubrey was here and that was when they scored. Now be quiet and let me watch."

"Okay, baby." He sat quietly, watching the screen, but only for a moment. Then he put his arm around her. "Gee," he said, "I like a girl catches on fast. You watch out, we make you an American before you know it."

Doreen turned her head toward him, away from the screen, and smiled. They kissed, then settled back, eyes glued to the set. An inning went by before Doreen asked what he'd had for lunch. Frankie believed in being adventurous at the table and liked to talk about it. On this occasion, he replied, "Lapin."

Doreen said that she had never heard of it, which gratified Frankie, and when she asked what it was, he explained. He had been in a restaurant and had asked the waiter for advice. The waiter had pointed to an item on the menu, and Frankie had agreed, eaten it, and liked it. "Comes in a stew," he said.

"What's it like?" Doreen asked.

"Kinda like chicken," Frankie said, "or maybe frog's legs. Only not so much."

"Tell me the name again."

"Lapin."

Doreen, her mind on the evening's television, particularly a film about an uprising of zombies, scheduled to begin at 2:30 A.M., at last found her way through Frankie's pronunciation and remarked that she had often had rabbit in England.

"What's that got to do?" Frankie asked.

"That's what you were eating, dear."

"I don't eat no rabbit. I eat lapin. This guy tells me it's an animal called lapin."

Doreen favored him with the proper pronunciation. "French for rabbit," she added.

At Doreen's words, so casually spoken, Frankie cried out, "It can't be." He fell to moaning weakly, and Doreen, puzzled, was on her way to the kitchen to brew some tea — for she could see that he badly needed it — when it dawned on her that Frankie's seizure had been brought on by the eating of rabbit. She hurried back, remembering that she had always believed that menus should be printed in French in French-speaking countries only, and watched as Frankie sank into a chair, sweat pouring from his forehead. He buried his face in his hands and from time to time his body was racked by great shudders. He did not range widely during his autocritical attack. "Ate a rabbit," he said over and over again, fighting back the tears. "A little white fluffy thing that never hurt nobody."

Doreen tried to comfort him, wondering the while whether all Mafiosi were so emotional, but Frankie continued to punish himself.

"No defense," he said, "it had no defense. Not a chance in the world." Then he turned sarcastic. "My old man, he hears this, he's proud of Frankie. I know what he says. He says, 'Go it, Frankie boy, go it.'"

Eventually, it ended. Frankie yielded to the argument that gangsters could not be expected to know French, unless they were French gangsters, and if restaurants printed their menus in French, they were responsible for the consequences, to both the rabbits and those who ate them.

"Maybe I get some spieler and sue them," Frankie said. "They put me through a lot."

Doreen advised against it.

"That restaurant don't see me again," Frankie said. "Next time they're more careful who they serve rabbit."

17

Aubrey loved Fredda with a deep passion coupled, he liked to think, with the calm that comes with maturity. True, he was not as old as she was — as a matter of fact, he did not know how old she was, for he had never asked her and she had never volunteered the information — but he did not feel the difference in age keenly. If anything, he reveled in it. It was proof of his sagacity, he told me. Before this, he had known only girls. Fredda was a woman.

In spite of the depth of his feeling for Fredda, however, Aubrey occasionally asked himself where their romance was going. The usual result of this stocktaking was that he was able to answer only for himself — he wanted to get married — and one day he put the point to Fredda.

"Marry me? How utterly unsordid of you, Aubrey," Fredda said. "If I had no other reason to like you, I would like you for that alone. It is such an endearing quality."

Aubrey pursed his lips. "I know you like me. Do you love me?"

"Of course I love you. You're so nice." She leaned over and kissed his straight blond hair.

"Very well. Now what happens?"

"It depends on the time, really. What time is it?"

"I didn't mean that. What I mean is, what's going to happen in the future? I want you to marry me."

Fredda smiled. She always smiled at compliments. "What a charming idea," she said.

Aubrey took heart, but Fredda did not stop there. "Aubrey," she said, "I've been married from time to time. I now have what Sam would call mixed givings about the institution. I can't put them aside overnight. It would make it pointless to have had them in the first place."

"Will you never marry, Fredda?"

"I never said that. I might even marry you. There's a very good chance that I will marry you. It's just something I cannot do — do with anybody, I mean — in cold blood. I guess it's because I'm a hot-blooded southern belle."

"You're not from the south."

"Come on, Aubrey. There's never been a hot-blooded northern belle. You know that. How long have you been in this country?"

This conversation took place in Fredda's apartment, where Aubrey had gone to collect her and take her to dinner. His insistence on maintaining a residence in Steeple Bumpstead so that he could go on paying United Kingdom taxes did not always leave him with enough money to take her to the sort of restaurant she preferred, but she accepted that, even to the extent of sitting quietly when a wine waiter, asked for a recommendation, replied that he did not drink wine himself because it gave him acid. "I wouldn't want the British government to go short," she said.

Nor did Aubrey live in grand style. He had an apartment in a building a cut above the Lac de Genève. It was called the Ile-de-France Towers and — this was the cut above — it had two sections opening off the lobby and so two fountains and, in the lobby, a concierge who did not speak French and did not speak English, either. Aubrey's apartment was barely larger than Doreen's, but it was less stuffed with bric-a-brac and so appeared somewhat more spacious. Aubrey did not complain, but he tended to go around the apartment hunched over because of its modest dimensions.

Aubrey had this night gone beyond his means and, to please Fredda, chosen a restaurant called The Prologue. It happened that Barbetta had, too, and as Aubrey and Fredda made their way in, they found Barbetta and Doreen near the entrance.

"Take off your hat, Barbella," Fredda said, "and stay awhile."

"Barbetta. First a table, then I take the hat off."

"Hadn't you better warn the checkroom it's coming? They'll have to make room for it."

Frankie scowled but did not reply. Doreen stared straight ahead; Fredda made her uncomfortable. Aubrey, faintly embarrassed, as he later told me, tried to move toward the table he had reserved but was held back by Fredda.

"I'm surprised," she said to Barbetta, "that someone with your connections would have to wait for a table. Especially with that hat on. You look like an unlit lamp. I should think the proprietor would give you a table just to get the hat stored away and under control."

Barbetta defended his reputation. "We wait for a special table. A table against the wall, I see everybody. I don't like nobody behind me."

"A normal precaution," Fredda said. "In case of gang warfare, you'd rather be shot from the front." She started to move away, then came back. "I know Aubrey has been unreasonable in not sharing his purses with you. Though you'd be surprised how little is left after he enjoys himself paying taxes. You don't plan to rub him out tonight? Or are you off duty?"

"Never off duty. I take it easy with Aubrey. I blast him, I think Doreen cries. But the organization don't like to wait. Already I get complaints. It ain't healthy to get complaints."

"You chose your metier," Fredda replied. "I don't suppose you went to auditions with other aspiring mobsters, but there must have been something like that. You must have known about the risks."

Aubrey thought that Fredda deserved his support. "Quite," he said. "It's hardly our responsibility. Nor the responsibility of your government's Occupational Safety and Health Administration, come to that. You must be sporting about it."

He took Fredda's arm, and this time she went with him, saying as she did, "There's no need to pull. I'd had enough of the present tense. I'm coming."

She picked up the theme a few minutes later. "Why would anyone want to spend time with Barbella? Doreen excepted, of course. A girl has to live. But what a pair! His conversation, when it exists at all, is inert. His dress is grotesque. And that bovine moll. Probably one of those Englishwomen who call drinks *drinkies*. Which reminds me. I'd like one."

There was a delay while the drink orders were being filled. Aubrey asked for pale ale served at room temperature, and the waiter went away to find out whether the restaurant had it. It didn't, and while the waiter was gone again, Fredda complained. "Why do you ask for the stuff? You know they don't have it. They never have it. Can't you let the British export drive shift for itself this once?"

"I like pale ale. If enough people ask for it, maybe they'll stock it."

"You're a lone voice. Anyway, you've got the room temperature. Settle for that and we can get on."

Aubrey made do with tonic water. Fredda did not return to the subject of Barbetta and Doreen until the meal had ended. "I don't know what's happening these days," she said. "There was a time when there were standards that meant something. There was professional pride. When a woman was a gun moll, she was a woman to respect. Now anybody can be anything."

Aubrey said he thought she was being unnecessarily harsh about Doreen.

"For God's sake, Aubrey, you sound like Albert Schweitzer. Stop being so damned humane. If gun molling is to be revived, it should have something better than this. And the gangster business is going to pot, too, judging by that Barbella."

"Barbetta."

Fredda shook her head. "I never thought I'd say this. I don't think it's age. You've got to have traditions. Ours just haven't lasted."

"I didn't know you felt so strongly about it."

"It is the curse of our time," Fredda said. "Falling standards. Wasn't it Veblen who wrote about the instinct of workmanship? You have it. I have it. But look around you. It's almost gone."

Aubrey reached across the table and took her hand. "I think that's your first quotation. Oh, I am a lucky man."

18

Because Barbetta eventually was led to a table in a different part of the restaurant from theirs, Aubrey and Fredda were not aware of the drama that was now enacted. None of us was until Doreen passed the story along in a more peaceful epoch.

At the table, Barbetta's anger knew no bounds. It also knew limited English. He sat there, with his back to the wall, making unkind remarks about the proprietor, to whom he had said, "About time, Jack," when a table became available, and Fredda. "Too many needles from her. Frankie don't forget that."

My impression from Doreen's account was that he was venting his ire, which is an activity practiced much less widely than it once was. I was sorry to have missed it.

When Doreen got him quiet, Barbetta gave his attention to the restaurant and their dinner. The Prologue's claim to fame was that some of its working help sang operatic arias to piano accompaniment, evidently to take the patrons' minds off the food and the prices. The headwaiter might, as he took your order, pour out Rigoletto's tortured ravings against the vile courtiers who aided and abetted the Duke of Mantua. As Doreen and Barbetta went to their table, they brushed past a man who wore a kind of usher's uniform and who was singing a duet from *Don Giovanni* with a stout woman who appeared to have some vague supervisory function.

"I think this is fun," Doreen said after they were seated. "So original."

"Yeah," said Barbetta.

They ordered drinks and listened for a few moments. Doreen tried again. "They sing well, don't they? I wish I could sing. It must give one such a feeling of satisfaction."

"You don't have to sing good," Barbetta said. He put his hand on his heart. "Here. There's where it counts."

A tall girl in an evening dress came swinging past their table from the kitchen. Leaning on the piano and holding the ends of a scarf around her shoulders, she navigated carefully through an aria they did not know. Tossing off the final high note, she smiled at the patrons and bowed out.

"I wonder who she is," Doreen said.

"Nobody," Barbetta said. "A broad. She sings for her supper.

Doreen smiled. "Frightfully well put."

It was while they were working their way through the antipasto that a pensive look came over Barbetta's face. "My mother. She sing that."

"What is it?"

"What they call a lullaby."

"It's lovely," Doreen said. "Your mother must have had a good voice."

"Yeah. Nice. I see you, sometimes I think of my mother."

Doreen was touched. "Frankie, that's the darlingest thing you've ever said to me. Thank you." She dabbed a tiny handkerchief at her moist eyes. "Was your dad musical, too?"

"The old man? That's a joke." Frankie's laugh chewed up some eggshells and apple cores to show how risible the idea was. "Hey. Sometimes he jokes. 'I marry you for your voice,' he says, 'and your money.' That's his joke. And they both laugh."

"Was he very humorous?"

"Oh, he's pretty funny when he wants. When he's not too busy giving me a turndown. But Frankie can take it."

"Of course you can take it, Frankie. Everyone knows that."

"What they got?" He picked up a menu and examined it. "Veal cacciatore. I like veal cacciatore. What about you?" Frankie motioned to the waiter. "Two veal cacciatore."

The waiter looked surprised. "You already ordered steak pizzaiola. You want both?"

Doreen blushed. "That's right. So we did."

"I say veal cacciatore," Barbetta said evenly. "I mean veal cacciatore. I don't mean steak pizzaiola. And I don't like arguments."

"I'll see if they can hold the steak." The waiter turned to go.

Barbetta caught him by the jacket. "They hold the steak, Jack," he said, "because I say hold the steak. And don't try to pull no fast ones. I don't like nobody tries to pull fast ones."

The waiter had seen fellow members of his union leave for other occupations after shooting incidents in New York restaurants. The young man he was dealing with looked as though he might be a gangster, and made him nervous. "No sir," he said, "I won't, sir."

There were no further incidents until the waiter came to take away the dishes. "You liked the veal cacciatore, sir?"

"It was lousy," Frankie said.

The waiter said he was sorry.

"It ain't your fault," Frankie said magnanimously. "You don't do the cooking. You don't even sing. How come you don't sing?"

The waiter smiled uncomfortably. "No voice, I'm afraid, sir."

"I like to hear you sing, anyway," Frankie said.

"Oh no, sir." The waiter smiled weakly. "Singing isn't part of my job. That is for the others. What dessert would you and madam like, sir?"

"She ain't madam and we like cherries jubilee. And don't sing. Be a waiter all your life."

"Yes, sir. Thank you, sir."

As the waiter drew off, Barbetta sank back in his chair, looking grim. Doreen, her face flushed, rose, hesitated, sat down, and told him that she did not like his treatment of the waiter, who could not reply in kind, that there was such a thing as fair play, and that she would not sit idly by if he persisted in abusing workingmen. Her father was a member of the National Union of Boot and Shoe Operatives and a member of the Labour Party. Her grandfather had taken part in the General Strike of 1926. "I am my father's daughter," she said. "I just won't have it. You deserve a good ticking-off. I want you to apologize to that waiter."

Barbetta said that he did not apologize to jerk waiters and Doreen reached across the table and slapped him. "I don't like bullies," she said. "England has never liked bullies. And now I daresay you'll give me my marching orders."

Barbetta smiled. "I don't leave my moll. I like a girl

stands up. Hey, your right hand better than Aubrey's. Now, where those cherries jubilee?" He looked around for the waiter, glared when he saw the other diners watching, and then slowly changed expression. "My mother."

"Yes?"

"She sing that. 'The Last Rose of Summer,' they call it."

"It's pretty."

Frankie nodded. "*She's* pretty. Like you. Sometimes I see you, I think of my mother."

"Frankie," Doreen said again, "that's the darlingest thing you've ever said to me. Thank you."

The waiter tiptoed up and served the cherries jubilee. "I hope that you and your lady will like them, sir."

"Why not?" Frankie said. "Everything else okay. And we take two espresso."

The waiter, mystified by the gentleness of the request, hurried off and returned with the coffee. Fifteen minutes later, after sipping the coffee and leaning back, eyes closed, to listen to the singing, Barbetta tipped the waiter handsomely, said, "Good meal, Jack. Thanks," took Doreen on his arm, and left.

Outside the restaurant, Barbetta's car was waiting, with the driver pacing alongside, on the lookout. He had just been to the corner to peer furtively around, when he spotted them and dashed back. "Not too long in one place, boss," he said. "It ain't safe."

"Yeah, yeah, I know," Barbetta said. Inside the car, he shook his head. "That food. No good. But I don't tell them that. Long ago, I learn that. You don't like a place, you keep quiet, you don't go back. No big deal."

Doreen said he was absolutely right.

*

One evening, soon after the incident at The Prologue, Barbetta made an announcement. It was delivered at his apartment, the decor of which was the same as Doreen's, but writ large. There was a stereo outlet in every room, and the living room featured a bar with fake beer spigots and a mirror bearing the legend THIS ESTABLISHMENT DOES NOT EXTEND CREDIT. He also had a sauna, and a dining room table and chairs in a style known to Fogbound as French prudential. He was particularly proud of a niche containing an aluminum cube called "Mother." "I keep up with the art game," he said.

The announcement was that Aubrey and his chump manager expected to get a title fight, but that they wouldn't. They might get a curtain raiser in Hoboken, but only if they were lucky.

"What have you done?"

Frankie laughed. "No much yet. These things take time. But soon I'm sitting pretty and they're looking for any fight they can get."

It was a painful moment for Doreen. She loved Frankie, but she had shared some months of her life with Aubrey, and he had done her the favor of not going to the police.

"Tell me what you did, Frankie. I'd like to know."

Barbetta smiled tolerantly, then slowly poured himself a drink. "You understand these things or you don't." He reached into his inside jacket pocket and brought out a pen and a small memorandum book. "Look." Turning to a blank page, he drew two dots, one at each end of the page, then drew a line between them. "See that? That's a straight line."

"The shortest distance between two points," Doreen murmured.

"Okay, the shortest. But for me, not the best." He crossed out the dots and the line and turned to a new page. Again he drew dots at opposite ends of the sheet, and then, starting from one end, he drew a line toward the other. He took it a fraction of an inch, then turned sharply to the right, then to the left, then forward again. As he progressed slowly toward the other dot, he went backward with the pen twice. "That's how I work," he said. "I'm hard to find. I maybe go here" — he pointed to one corner of the room — "to get there" — he pointed to another. "But when I finish, Aubrey and that lunkhead manager don't know what hit them."

"Frankie." Doreen bit her lip. "There's something you must know."

"What's that?"

"You shouldn't do that to Aubrey. He doesn't deserve it. You don't know it, but he has been rather decent to you."

"How's that?"

"Do you remember meeting him downstairs the other day?" Barbetta did.

"He came to warn me. He came here to tell me that he and Mr. Franklin were on the verge of nipping down to the police about you. I talked him out of it. He hasn't gone to the police, so I think you should leave him alone."

As Doreen waited anxiously for his reply, Barbetta smiled and shook his head, as he would over an errant child. "They finger me to the cops? They can't touch me." He snorted with contempt. "I told them I like to buy in. How many times I told them? They're smart. They won't sell." He spread his arms to show that some things were out of his control. "Okay. They don't play ball, I don't play ball."

"But, Frankie, does that mean Aubrey will never get a title fight?"

Once more Barbetta shook his head and smiled. "Today you're not so smart," he said. "It only goes to show you got to be here longer. Sure he gets a title fight — after I move in. Like this." He reached out, grabbed Doreen's wrist, and pulled her to him. "You care about that Aubrey or you care about me?"

"It isn't that. It just didn't seem fair. But so long as he gets the title fight sometime, I don't mind."

"He gets it. I see to that." He pulled her closer and held her there, then kissed her. When the long kiss ended, he held her at arm's length. "Lots of fun tonight, baby. All kinds of good stuff on TV. And I order dinner from that restaurant. We give them another chance."

"What shall we have?"

"Steak pizzaiola. We make up for last time."

"And for afters?"

"Cherries jubilee, like always."

Doreen's eyes were starry. "Oh, my good, kind Frankie. You are a poppet."

"What's that, a poppet?"

"A little angel."

Barbetta grinned. "I'm glad some others don't hear this. I all the time see that word, image. I got one, too."

19

THE CHAIN OF EVENTS that led Fogbound and Aubrey to join me in a three-man delegation to Washington, there to petition Congress for redress of grievances, began with a visit by Fogbound to Promoter Jack Smith of the Sportitorium.

Fogbound was never one to hide his emotions. He explained to me once, in a rare literary flight, "I like to think in broad brush." Consequently, when he left his office and set off to see Smith, he was chirping like a well-fed bird. The cause of his ecstasy was the conviction that he was about to sign for a title fight. On his return, he sank into a chair and shook his head slowly, uncomprehendingly, his eyes full of misery, as Aubrey and I waited for a clue.

Some people, after passing through a horrible experience, find relief in speaking about it. Others find that mentioning it at all is like reliving the horror. On this day, Fogbound was of the latter school. Only under severe pressure did he agree to speak. "We are," he said, "in the throngs of a crisis." This was not much help, but eventually he made a supreme effort and revealed that Smith had told him that he would keep Aubrey in mind if the right sort of opening against some-body not too tough happened to present itself. "I hate to talk about it," Fogbound said "It gives me a headache."

Aubrey immediately produced a comforting theory — that the champion, out of fear of being separated from his title, was trying to avoid him. But only Aubrey found this plausi-ble, though Fogbound would have loved to believe it. After joining Fogbound in its tactful rejection, I advanced another idea — that we were seeing a deliberate run-around by Smith. This gained more general acceptance, but automatically raised the question of Smith's motives.

After a lengthy, lugubrious silence, Fogbound produced the answer. He was almost reclining in his chair, with his arms folded across his chest, and he was nodding his head, heavy with grief and premonitions of early retirement, as vigorously as his position allowed.

"What's the matter?" Aubrey asked.

Fogbound continued to nod for a few moments before an-nouncing that inspiration had come to him in a flash and had whispered the name Barbetta. Then he resumed nodding.

"What influence has he with Smith?"

Fogbound's reply was pithy and revealed his wife's semantic influence. "Do you know? That's how I know."

"Then what makes you so sure?"

"Listen," Fogbound said. "First, he said he would keep Aubrey from getting a title fight. Second, lately he's not around saying he's moving in. Maybe he got tired of saying he's moving in and went to work like he said he would. Third, I can't think of any other reason. So my finger points at Bar-betta." He looked around for contradiction but got none. "And another thing. I don't like the name Jack Smith. To me, it sounds fishy. A man with the name Jack Smith, he's got an underworld connection, it wouldn't surprise me at all."

I told Fogbound that it was unsafe to draw conclusions from names. For example, I said, Cleopatra, though probably the most famous Queen of Egypt, was actually Greek and was only one of a line of seven Queens of Egypt who bore that name. That failed to spark a discussion, and it was soon after this that our appeal to Congress became inevitable, although it was the fourth suggestion put forward. The first came from Fogbound. In addition to everything else, he was under pressure at home. His wife had told him again that if something was not done about Barbetta, he, Fogbound, "stubborn, a real Franklin," would find himself "floating in the river like a corpse," or possibly, suitably weighted, dropped in the river and not floating. He therefore proposed that we go to the police. He was seconded by Aubrey, who said that he would regret any unfortunate consequences for Doreen but that the fat was in the fire and there was nothing else for it. On hearing the reference to fat, Fogbound thought that under the stress of events Aubrey was returning to his earlier preoccupation with suet pudding, but I cut him off by saying that going to the police would be naive and a mistake.

After frowning and then looking wise, Fogbound proposed that we try the Boxing Commission. Aubrey again was in support but I said it would be a waste of time.

"You're here to help?"

I submitted that I was.

"Let me ask you another issue," Fogbound. "Maybe we could go to court and get a decease and desist order."

"Devoutly to be wished," I said. "But I doubt it."

This brought an injured shout from Fogbound. He accused me of wanting him to betray the trusting Aubrey, who depended on him for taxes for his government, and food, clothing, shelter, and boxing championships for himself. I smiled patiently — a repellent act, but few among us are strong enough to refrain — certain that my explanation would disarm Fogbound. It did. It was that the effectiveness of the police and courts and boxing commissions in such matters had diminished. Times had changed. In situations of this kind, the thing to do was to enlist the help of a member of Congress.

In this field, Fogbound's competence was so limited that he felt unable to be for or against the idea. Aubrey, however, remembered meeting Representative Bindle (D.–Mo.), at Simco Savory's party.

"Webster Bindle?"

"I think so."

"The veteran legislator from the show-me state?"

"That's your department."

"He could do it easily. Just the man you want."

"You'll come with us, Joe?" Fogbound asked, anxiously.

"You'll have to wait for my day off," I said.

"We'll wait. Only make it snappy."

"I'll tell the editor what you said."

As it worked out, the editor spotted in all of this something that I had not — a story. "You could not see the forest for the trees, Mercer," he smirked, demonstrating the phrase-making ability that had sent him to the top. "Too close to the story, very likely."

I got out of smirking range as soon as I could and fixed the appointment with Bindle. Even at a distance, Washington awed Fogbound, and when he got there — having learned from me en route that President James A. Garfield could write Latin with one hand and Greek with the other simultaneously, an accomplishment of limited value in what we of the Fourth Estate call the hurly-burly of politics — he felt out of his depth, as though he were moving among people from another world. He walked on tiptoe in the corridors of the

Capitol, although he trod more normally in the House Office Building. He was unable to take any kind of initiative in Washington; he had so much veneration for the place and those he called the foundling fathers that he felt it improper to do business there. Nonetheless, once arrived, he wanted to get on with the job, for he regarded it, he said, as a chance to be heard right at the horse's mouth, and he was annoyed when Aubrey expressed the hope that the talk with Bindle would not take too long because he wanted to get to the British Embassy to see whether they had any new British Treasury Publications that might be useful to him.

"Be respectful first the Congressman," Fogbound said. "His time, I can assure you, is worth more than yours. Books you can always get. Title fights are harder."

Fogbound's fears that his affairs were too trivial for a Congressman's attention proved unfounded. Bindle greeted us cordially, sat back in a leather swivel chair, and thoughtfully smoked a cigar as I set out the complaint and Fogbound gazed reverently at the autographed photographs on the walls. Fogbound was not quite sure just what Bindle did but he knew it was important, and he called the Congressman "Sir." Aubrey, regarding Bindle, who wore a checked sport jacket and orange slacks, reflected that the clothes worn in the House of Commons, if not more expensive, at any rate were more dignified.

"You're from New York, I believe, Mr. Franklin?" Bindle said.

Fogbound confirmed this. "I was born and raised in New York fifty-two years ago."

"Should you perhaps have gone to your own Representative, my esteemed colleague, Horatia von Furstenberg, about this matter?"

Fogbound looked at me. I shook my head.

"We wanted the best, sir," Fogbound said.

Bindle got down to the business at hand. Thanks to numberless committee meetings attended and witnesses listened to, he was able to ponder in full public view and in any circumstance. As I spoke, he pondered, occasionally interjecting a question and puffing cigar smoke toward the ceiling. This restrained behavior disappointed me, for I had read many Washington dispatches about congressional hearings and I expected to be cunningly questioned and harassed, and possibly harangued, as well. It is any American's birthright. When I had finished, Bindle satisfied himself that Fogbound and Aubrey supported the story.

This done, he rose, took the cigar out of his mouth, and joined his hands behind his back. "I see," he said. He turned and paced back and forth across five yards of carpet. "Gentlemen," he said, "I confess myself pleased that you have seen fit to place this confidence in me. I shall try to deserve it." He paused and looked each of us in the eye. "From your description, I believe that I saw this Barbetta at the party Simco gave for Mr. Philpott-Grimes." Bindle pondered further, then said, "Right. I think the way to go about this is to make a speech on the floor of the House."

There being no disagreement with this judgment, Bindle said he would let us know in advance so that we could expect the speech, accepted from me a typed statement of what already had been set out orally, and, thanking us, showed us out. One of his secretaries gave us passes to the House visitors' gallery, and, while Aubrey took a taxi to the British Embassy, Fogbound and I sat in on a debate.

"These are all Senators?" Fogbound asked.

"Representatives."

"That's different?"

"There are four hundred thirty-five Representatives. They

are in the House of Representatives. There are a hundred Senators. They are in the Senate. This is the House of Representatives."

"Who can keep up with these things?" Fogbound asked.

Toward the front of the large auditorium a man was speaking into a microphone, gesturing expansively, and occasionally smiting the lectern in front of him with his fist.

"Who's that?" Fogbound asked.

"A Representative."

"He's speaking?"

"It seems so."

"Why don't they listen?" Fogbound indicated the men and women on the House floor.

"Maybe they aren't interested."

"At least they could have better manners," Fogbound said.

At this point the man who was speaking finished his speech with a few vigorous shakes of the head and returned to his seat. There was a patter of applause and a man on a platform raised above the floor said that the Gentleman from Utah was recognized for five minutes.

"He was running away, this gentleman? Somebody saw him?" Fogbound asked.

I said that this was parliamentary language. It meant that he could speak for five minutes.

"Why don't they say so?"

The recognized Utahan had managed only a few sentences when a man in the front row rose and said something.

"What did he say?" Fogbound asked.

"I think he's asking some questions."

Fogbound leaned forward in his seat, straining to hear. From time to time, words floated up — "overall policy decisions," "options on key points," "flexible structure," "direct and personal control," "major functions," "common bond."

After a while, we heard a Representative tell his colleagues that the aim of the proposal before them was laudable but he did not see how it could be made to fly in the Washington atmosphere in the current climate.

We also heard a Representative, elderly, one of the pillars of the House, intervene in the debate to deliver some remarks on a subject which he said, was germane no matter what issue was before them. I took notes:

"Let me speak, if I might," he began, "about leadership, by which I don't mean just leadership but the sound leadership that is needed and necessary over a period of time, with the competence and the certainty and assurance that you can handle some of the problems of leadership. Now, let's look down the road to a longer problem. As I have said before, and have repeated since, the opportunity to participate in either the judicial branch or the legislative branch or the executive branch is a great experience and a wonderful challenge, and I hope and trust that without any hesitation or qualification, that is the aim that our young people should be shooting for."

There was applause, he sat down, and the debate picked up again.

Fogbound listened intently, then indicated the man who sat at the front of the House, at a large table, raised above the others, with a gavel in his hand. "Who's that?" he asked.

"That's the Speaker."

"Not him," Fogbound said, pointing to the man who was speaking. "*Him*." He pointed to the man with the gavel.

"He's the presiding officer of the House and its most powerful member. He's elected by the others. He's called the Speaker."

Fogbound raised his hands in a gesture of despair. "Enough," he said. "Let's go."

As we departed, a voice from the floor could be heard saying that the last year had tried the patience of the nation and that an unparallelled effort was called for.

Outside the gallery, Fogbound said, "Terrible stuff. It's always like that?"

"Not always. But most of the time."

"Then who'll hear Mr. Bindle when he talks about Aubrey?"

"Don't worry about that," I said. "You've heard of press releases, Sam. The story will get out. Besides, after that, I'll take over. When the Congressman speaks, we'll be printing the story behind it . I'm writing it now."

"You never told me."

"You don't mind, do you?"

"Why should I mind? Attention we can always use."

As we returned on the train, which he barely caught because of a discussion at the Embassy of whether the margin for error in the industrial production index did not make it a blunt instrument where scalpellike finesse was required, Aubrey was struck by remorse. It caused him to drop a British government consultative document on productivity at the coal face. "You don't think they'll do anything to Doreen, do you?"

"She's a gun moll," Fogbound said. "What should happen, a medal?"

"It is a chancy vocation," Aubrey said, "but I don't want anything to happen to her. In a manner of speaking, she is in my charge."

"The worst that can happen," I said, "is that they'll send her back to Blighty, which whatever its shortcomings is better than being with Barbetta."

"Perhaps you're right." Aubrey returned to the consultative document.

20

THE DAYS FOLLOWING the visit to Washington found Aubrey in his usual state of calm, and Fredda unsuccessfully taking a screen test for the part of Marmee in a revival of *Little Women*. For Fogbound, they were anxious days, and within seventy-two hours of his return from Washington he could be heard complaining that if we waited for Bindle, Aubrey would be past his prime, and that going to Washington had accomplished "completely nothing."

But Bindle was as good as his word. A week after we saw him, he obtained unanimous consent to speak for five minutes and to revise and extend his remarks in the *Congressional Record*. Forewarned, we trooped down to hear him. This resulted in another absence from my desk. The editor was grudgingly compliant. We were getting occasional stories that others were not. Besides, I told him, my editorials would be more earthy, more "in touch," because of my contact with real people, people with debts and broken television sets and blocked-up drains.

"Like Congressmen?" the editor asked.

"The editorial writer's office all too easily becomes an ivory tower, chief," I said.

"Go, Mercer," the editor replied. "What you're trying to tell me is that your editorials will be more grainy, more bound up with the gut issues of our time. You seem to have trouble finding the right word."

"Thanks, chief."

"There is no need to be unctuous about it," the editor said.

We had advance copies of Bindle's speech, which made it easier to know what was being said but had an unsettling effect on Fogbound, who seemed to think that he was in possession of a state secret and might be locked up by one of the Capitol policemen or abducted by a Soviet spy. He held the papers firmly and close to his body so that no unauthorized person might see them.

Bindle began by thanking the House for its courtesy in giving him the opportunity to speak. He knew, he said, how much important business there was to be done and how pressed each member was. He would not have asked for the time had he not thought that what he was going to say — and what he going to say would be heard for the first time anywhere that afternoon — was of national, perhaps international, importance.

"Mr. Speaker," Bindle went on, "there is in this country a British pugilist named Aubrey Philpott-Grimes. He is not unknown to some of the gentlemen and gentlewomen of this House who follow the fortunes of those who engage for a livelihood in the manly art of self-defense. He has also achieved some measure of fame for his interest in economic affairs, particularly those of his own country, and for his ability to explain economic problems in terms that the average man — yes, and you and I — can understand." (Next day's *Congressional Record* showed laughter at Bindle's little sally.)

"Now, Mr. Speaker," Bindle continued. "Philpott-Grimes has won his way almost to the top of his division, which is the middleweight division. The sportswriters, who will have their jokes — and who among us is not grateful for a little colorful writing now and then? — the sportswriters refer to him by such names as 'The Elongated Englishman,' 'The Minus Sign That Walks Like a Man,' and 'Britain's Walking Deficit.' This, as you will no doubt have guessed, is because of his extraordinary physique. Several inches over six feet tall, he weighs less than one hundred sixty pounds. He has, in fact, been referred to as 'The Lengthy Limey,' but because he dislikes the word 'Limey,' although I am sure it was offered in the friendliest spirit, that expression has dropped from use.

"Mr. Speaker, Philpott-Grimes, as I say, has established himself, in the opinion of the experts, as the man who should have the next chance to face the middleweight champion. Now, what is strange — and, indeed, the reason that I am speaking today — is that Philpott-Grimes is not getting that chance. The man who controls these things, Promoter Jack Smith of the Sportitorium in New York, appears to be unwilling to give it to him.

"It would be easy, Mr. Speaker, to say that Smith is afraid that the middleweight title might leave this country and wishes to prevent that happening. Some people would find that admirable. I would call it deplorable."

A figure rose a few rows back and asked whether the Gentleman from Missouri would yield for a question. Bindle said that he yielded gladly.

"Does not the Gentleman from Missouri believe it desirable that these titles should remain in the United States?"

"I believe," Bindle said, "that the heavyweight champion of the world should be the best heavyweight in the world, regardless of where he comes from. I believe the flyweight champion of the world should be the best flyweight in the world, regardless of where he comes from. I do not believe that titles should be kept in this country by artificial means. That would seem to me misguided patriotism. In my opinion, we should follow that matchless precept, which is the basis of true sportsmanship, 'May the best man win.' "

There was a burst of applause, the figure sat down, and Bindle continued. "No, Mr. Speaker, the reason that Philpott-Grimes is not getting his chance to win the world middleweight championship is not misguided patriotism. I have reason to believe that criminal elements are standing in Philpott-Grimes's way."

There was hurried scribbling in the press gallery above the Speaker's platform and several men and women who had neglected to pick up Bindle's press release were nudged awake by colleagues and made for the doors.

"I believe that the House should know these things. Philpott-Grimes is managed by a Sam Franklin. Mr. Franklin is, I am informed, a person of good repute in his profession. On several occasions, both Philpott-Grimes and Franklin have been approached by one Frankie Barbetta, who, according to their word to me, is an avowed gangster. On each occasion, Barbetta has expressed a desire to own a share of Philpott-Grimes. This, I believe, is not an uncommon practice in professional boxing. However, neither Franklin nor Philpott-Grimes wishes to have Barbetta as a partner and they have so informed him. In spite of repeated requests, they have held to that position.

"Because of the tenacity with which they have done so,

they have been subjected to threats by Barbetta. These were that he would prevent Philpott-Grimes from getting a bout with the champion and that Philpott-Grimes would be fortunate to get any fights with substantial purses at all. I am told that he threatened Philpott-Grimes and Franklin at a party in a New York hotel and to which he had not even been invited.

"It now appears — and I say this, Mr. Speaker, with all solemnity — that Barbetta has done precisely what he vowed to do. Franklin is unable to obtain a title fight for Phillpott-Grimes, however richly the British fighter deserves it. Although I should be happy to hear that there is some other explanation, it appears that in some fashion, Barbetta has been able to persuade Smith, the Sportitorium promoter, not to allow Philpott-Grimes to meet the champion for the title. In their extremity, Philpott-Grimes and Franklin, accompanied by a reputable New York newspaperman, came to me for help, for we had met through a mutual acquaintance. I thought that nothing I could do would be better than to present the matter to the ready conscience of this House and the American people."

A figure rose to Bindle's left. "Is the Gentleman from Missouri proposing that the House take some action? I know of no legislation before us to which this pertains."

Bindle shook his head. "I thank the Gentleman from Maryland for his question. I believe that the mere airing of the facts will bring results and bring them quickly. In matters of this kind, making the facts known is often enough to right any wrongs that may have been done." He glanced over his shoulder at a clock on the wall. "I see, Mr. Speaker," he said, "that my time is up. May I express my gratitude to the House for the kind attention with which I have been received."

Bindle walked to his seat, where about a dozen of his colleagues gathered about him to pat his back and shake his hand.

Bindle's analysis proved correct — that simple ventilation of the subject would be enough. Three committee chairmen barely had time to announce their intention of investigating before Smith issued a statement saying that depriving Aubrey of a title fight was the farthest thing from his mind and that, while he could not remember precisely what he had said to Mr. Franklin, he was sure that it could only have been a complete misunderstanding on Mr. Franklin's part that led him to believe that Aubrey would not get every opportunity due him. Perhaps it was something said in the spirit of levity.

"My only interest," Smith declared, "is in serving the fight-going public. Nationality plays no part with me. There is a time-honored axiom in boxing — 'May the best man win.' That is the rule by which I have always tried to guide myself."

Frankie was also reached for comment. "There's nothing to it," he said. "I never threaten nobody. After Franklin refuses to sell me a piece of Philpott-Grimes, I lose interest, and that's as far as it goes. They hold the fight, hopefully the best man wins."

The British Ambassador, a socialist who owned 15,000 acres of agricultural estates and grouse moor in Scotland, and who had inherited a title and renounced it, therefore being known as Tim Thwaites rather than the Earl of Portcullis, was asked by Washington correspondents whether he wished to comment. He replied that he was certain that Philpott-Grimes would receive fair treatment from the great American people, with their merited reputation for sportsmanship and fair play. On both sides of the Atlantic, he said, there was respect for the time-honored axiom, "May the best man win."

In private, Frankie was less restrained than he had been when questioned by newsmen. "Okay, you go to the cops. That's expected. Cops you can take care of. But running to this Congress. I got no use for people would do a thing like that."

"You did your best, dear," Doreen comforted him. "Try not to be upset."

"Something like this happens, you see who sticks with you."

"You know I will," Doreen murmured.

Frankie pressed her to him and Doreen breathed loudly. She felt it was the thing to do.

"After all I been through," Frankie groaned, "then this. You think it was easy to get to Smith? It was hard, plenty hard. I show you." He released her, pulled out his pad, and went through the now familiar diagramming while Doreen watched and tried to look interested. "And then they run to this Congress. Cops I can understand. But not this Congress."

"Not to worry, dearest."

"I don't worry, baby," Barbetta said gallantly. "I still got you. My English moll." He pressed her close again and they were happy.

Others were happy, too. Simco Savory went on a talk show to explain that it was he who had brought Aubrey and Congressman Bindle together in the first place. "Does this sound ever so conceited? Aubrey and Webster Bindle did meet on my hearth. To say how I feel is beyond my poor powers of."

Fredda's happiness was based in part on mercenary considerations. "A triumph," she said, when we were back in New York. "A triumph of right and of exploitation. Brother Aubrey here is what is known as a hot property. He should be able to make a fortune from testimonials alone."

"I don't want to advertise anything," Aubrey said.

"This is no time to put yourself first. Think of the Chancellor."

"I can't urge people to use products I know nothing about. Nor would I urge them to use products that I do know. Their needs may be quite different from mine. So far as testimonials go, *cadit quaestio*. The argument collapses. And I don't believe the Chancellor wants money that is earned by misleading the American people."

"Have you had any offers?"

Aubrey nodded. He had been offered two thousand dollars to state that he bought his neckties at a shop known — Aubrey felt this cast doubt on the intelligence of the American people — as The Ty Rak. A larger amount had been offered for testimony that he was partial to a fruit-flavored confection to be called The Au-Berry. Acceptance of this proposal would have involved his posing for a picture while holding high a partly eaten Au-Berry bar and grinning foolishly.

Another proposal had come from a wine importer. He wrote that the advertising would contain no provocative or enticing poses and no exploitation of the human form, nor would it be suggested that wine was essential to social attainment, wealth, or success. Wine would be presented as a civilizing agent, and Aubrey would come out of the commercial more dignified than he had gone in.

Aubrey's quota of dignity had remained unchanged. He declined. This was also his response when asked to say that no home is properly furnished without an electric broiler known as the Ro-tee-roaster, and that he depended for transport of his movable possessions on a limited liability company that had begun life as the Wee–Haul–U Trucking Company, Inc. When, in the spirit of the age, a more openly ethnic identification was deemed advisable, the owners had set up Lug and Shlep, Inc., as an operating division and following its success three equally ethnic branches — We Move-a You, Inc.; Hey, Man, We'll Shift You, Man, Inc.; and Begorrah, Leave It to the Boyos, Inc. To which of these Aubrey was to declare his allegiance was not stated.

He had also turned down an invitation to join a pilgrimage to the Holy Land, all expenses paid, lecturing the other pilgrims on overcoming cultural resistance to industrial takeoff among the disadvantaged along the way. But there was one proposition that did tempt Aubrey. It came from a foundation that was sponsoring a symposium on humanity.

> We feel [the organizers wrote] that your perspective as an economist and humanitarian would add a much-needed dimension, because understanding of the economically structured obstacles that need to be corrected would be an asset to all concerned persons. Discussions and workshops will focus on the grave dangers and the bright possibilities before humanity; creative action on a grassroots level will be the goal.

Aubrey was told that he would, if he spoke, be a member of a significant core group, and he twitched with delight. For a moment it seemed that a core-group membership was more attractive to Aubrey than a chance to become middleweight champion of the world. I assured him that deplete its natural resources though it might, the United States would never run short of symposia, and that he could afford to wait. Indeed, I told him, there were times when this activity rose to such a peak that perhaps half the able-bodied population was attending forums, seminars, and symposia, and that if we were ever again subjected to surprise attack, it would probably be planned for one of those peak periods. Reluctantly, he turned the symposium down.

Fredda was in the habit of swearing that her wardrobe leaned heavily on Spryngtyme dresses and that she avoided colds by wearing coats with Kold-Resisto linings, although she had never possessed either a Spryngtyme dress or a Kold-Resisto coat. Moreover, she had over the years endorsed a variety of products which she asserted were to be thanked for her glowing health, upright posture, silky eyelashes, unlined face — Hold That Line was the skin cream to which she gave the credit — cheerful outlook in the morning, zest in the evening, seductive coffee, and her knowledge of world affairs. She had also endorsed services which, she said, accounted for the well-being of her fur coat when in storage, her friendly relations with her bank manager, and her sensible choice of tax-free bonds. She therefore greeted Aubrey's attitude with a sigh. Still, she realized that his conduct was entirely in character and, though unnecessary, probably admirable.

"You have thwarted the hated Barbella," she said. "You have withstood the blandishments of American commerce, and you are as good as middleweight champion of the world. Marvelous. Though what you get out of it is more than I can see. Every time you fight, it's a benefit for Whitehall. When's Turner?"

"In about four months. I have a tune-up in Pittsburgh first."

"With whom?"

"We don't know yet. Nobody terribly good, I shouldn't think. They'll not be taking any chances now."

"The first time I saw you fight, I was sure there was a law against your being in there. If there had been a society for the prevention of somebody as skinny as you fighting, I would have called it in."

"I'm just as skinny now."

"I know, dear. I wouldn't want you any other way. It was the emaciated look that attracted me."

"You felt sorry for me?"

"I'm not sure. Maybe there's something erotic about unfleshed bones."

Aubrey smiled. "That would give me an unfair advantage."

In the presence of a distinguished journalist dinner guest, Fogbound explained it all to Mrs. Franklin. "Problems I got, I don't even know how. A manager manages, a fighter fights. But with Aubrey I got economics, moving-in gangsters, English molls, Fredda Plantagenets, Congressmen, and people from Washington who only give parties. It's the first time in living memory I can remember such a thing."

"And Aubrey? What does he say?"

"Not much," said Fogbound. "Like always. His comments are very minimum."

21

A PUGILIST named Rocky Proletariano was chosen as Aubrey's opponent for the tune-up fight in Pittsburgh. Had I still been a sportswriter, I would have described him as "a hard-swinging youngster out of New York's working-class lower East Side." Actually, he came from Wilmington, Delaware; but, although there is no written record of this, certain cities are considered not interesting enough to come from, and Wilmington, Delaware, is one of them. He was a club fighter with a moderate record who was expected to provide a good workout and nothing more. It was my opinion, delivered hard on the heels of the information that ravens and other birds have been found capable of counting up to seven, and that if progress continued, we might one day get a raven as a referee, that Proletariano would spend the night at the painful end of Aubrey's left jab. Fogbound and Aubrey saw no reason to disagree.

"Just right for Aubrey," said the doughty little manager. "The whole night he'll spend off balance."

"I expect to win," the artful ring warrior declared. "Perhaps not easily, but decisively. Then I shall go on to meet the champion."

This quiet assurance, rendered in tones appropriate to the pedestals of statues, was characteristic of Aubrey. For Fogbound, for whom pessimism was as shield and buckler, it was highly unusual. He had, however, been swept up by the fate that seemed to be carrying them toward inevitable success, and such was his light-hearted confidence, such his consciousness of destiny after the undoing of Barbetta and Smith, that he went so far as to allow Fredda to visit the training camp. Permission was not extracted without difficulty, and when Fogbound entered Fredda's apartment, at her invitation, to discuss it, he was accompanied by me as counselor. He emphasized his lingering misgivings by exacting from Fredda the promise that the visit would last for only an afternoon.

"It's plain that you never underestimate the power of a woman," she said. "What do you think would happen if I stayed overnight? Would Aubrey never be able to raise a glove again?"

"A training camp is no place for women," Fogbound said. "A fighter should keep his mind on his work. You remember what happened to Gorilla Delehanty?"

Fredda said that it was the sort of thing she normally had at her fingertips but that, for the moment, it eluded her. She glanced toward me. "Have you tried information retrieval here?"

"I yield," I said.

Fogbound shook his head sadly. "A good boy, Gorilla. Classy. A picture to watch. He's training for his fight with Ramirez, his girl shows up at camp. A blonde." He waited for the awful fact to sink in.

"A blonde," Fredda acknowledged. "Extremely serious."

"He lost the fight."

Fredda nodded thoughtfully. "There is a certain elliptical quality to your story. What happened between her appearance and the loss of the fight?"

"Gorilla lost his concentration," Fogbound explained. "He's all the time thinking about this blonde instead of the fight."

"So?"

"So she's at the training camp, Gorilla's looking over to her and smiling instead of watching his sparring partner. With sparring partners, especially the kind we had there, a three-month-old baby could push them over, it's safe. But soon, you're fighting a fighter, not a partner."

"I have heard that some fighters can't get down to business until they're hit the first time, but then they're all right," said Fredda, who was not sure about the part she was expected to play in the conversation. "It's like going on stage and speaking the first line."

Fogbound nodded vigorously. He almost bowed. "The first punch from Ramirez, Delehanty is looking over to the blonde and smiling. This is also the last punch from Ramirez. This is also the last time Delehanty sees the blonde. This is, third, the last time I allowed a woman at the training camp. My own wife stays away."

"There may be less risk with me," Fredda said. "I'm not a blonde. This week, anyway. But seriously, Sam, would you rather I didn't come?"

"Everybody knows I keep my word. I said all right for an afternoon. One to five."

Fredda's visit went off without incident. She watched Aubrey punch the light bag, shadow box, and go a few rounds with sparring partners. She smiled at the sparring partners and pointed out to Fogbound that she had done so to neutralize any effect her visit might have on Aubrey. Were the fight itself not being held in Pittsburgh, making it impossible for her to attend, she would smile as seductively as she could at Proletariano from the opening bell. After an early dinner with the rest of the camp, she left.

"A fine lady," Fogbound said. "A visit like that could do no harm."

"It's done me a world of good," Aubrey said. "Looking forward to the fight with the champion, it's rather difficult to knuckle down to this tune-up. But after Fredda's visit, I feel quite inspired."

Fogbound, having feared the worst from his foolhardiness, felt relieved. He counted his blessings, among them existence without Barbetta. "Maybe he saw he couldn't move in, he moved out," he said. He was still uneasy about the fact that Doreen and Barbetta had come together in his office, but he did not raise the subject. He thought that Aubrey might be upset.

Aubrey, however, was entertaining visions of the world championship and of the Exchequer awash in net proceeds. Moreover, Aubrey had just learned of a statement by the Financial Secretary to the Treasury in reply to a question in the House of Commons. Taxes per head in Britain, the Financial Secretary had stated, amounted to six hundred thirty-two pounds, compared to sixty-seven pounds in 1946. Even allowing for inflation, Aubrey felt, that was an impressive increase. He was almost incapable of being upset.

"I wonder how Doreen's getting along," he said to Fogbound one day.

"She's all right."

"How do you know?"

"A smart girl like that? I can tell."

"You're probably right, Sam. I think her experience with Barbetta will prove beneficial. She is being brought face to face with the realities of life. I merely wonder what she might be doing." He went off singing, "It's a Right Little, Tight Little Island," sat under a tree, and began thumbing through a treatise on trade unions and wage-pull inflation.

Fogbound now felt doubly relieved. Aubrey's physical condition always was good, and his mental condition plainly was perfect. To top it off, there came next a favorable development entirely unforeseen — a visit from a member (on secondment) of the British government's Economic Mission to the United States, Sir Giles Threave.

When Threave's letter had arrived, asking for permission to visit the camp and wish Aubrey well, Fogbound consulted me. A few days before a fight, it is not easy to tell what psychological effect any incident, however trivial, may have. Although I expected Threave to stop short of shouting "Once more unto the breach" or running up signal flags saying "England expects every man will do his duty," I suggested that his visit was bound to help. Because, after the Bindle coup, Fogbound respected any opinion of mine that dealt in any way with Washington, he agreed, on condition that I be there, as well, in case further technical assistance should be required.

At the appointed time, we stationed ourselves at the gate. Threave got out of a taxi and came striding up, pink-faced and mustached, a black rolled umbrella in his left hand, his right hand extended. He was pale and slight, with hair not quite blond and not quite brown. He looked like an English poet who had not heard that the fashion in English poets had changed, and had broadened to include large gentlemen

from the Australian outback. Fogbound saw that Threave
was dressed as Aubrey was when outside the ring and, although he did not realize that he was, in consequence, in
the presence of what anthropologists call costume echo, he
recognized Threave as an Englishman at once.

"Mr. Franklin, I presume," Threave said. "Permit me to
introduce myself. I am Giles Threave, of the British Economic Mission to Washington, on secondment from the
Cabinet office."

Fogbound — who asked me later, "What's this on secondment? He means he's a second? We don't need one. Anyway, he'd have to get a license" — introduced me, then forgot
the instruction about names he had received in what Aubrey
was pleased to call a briefing. "So, Sir Threave, you came to
see Aubrey. Believe me, you can relax."

Fogbound's tone was friendly and matter-of-fact. In truth,
he was trying to sound indulgent, because it was such a pat-
ent impossibility for Aubrey to do anything but win. Nor
did he intend to imply that the Threavian motive was pecu-
niary. As much as anything he was reassuring one Englishman about another.

The visitor, not catching the nuances of Fogbound's speech,
protested. "Philpott-Grimes has done us proud and we are
grateful. I have come to give him any encouragement I can.
But I am entitled to say that, should he lose, the esteem in
which we hold him would be in no way diminished. We
simply want him to know that we are with him."

Fogbound stuck to his set course. "This fight you can
relax."

Threave abandoned the high ground. "I take it, then, that
Proletariano is what is called a pushover."

"A pushover he's not. But for Aubrey, made to order. All

the time moving in, and telescoping his punches. For a good left hand, a setup."

"What a delightful prospect," Threave said.

"We'll take you to Aubrey."

"Oh, how most terribly kind of you."

Aubrey saw us coming and rushed over. He was dressed for the occasion in cavalry twill trousers and a green hacking jacket, a garment which puzzled Fogbound, to whom a hack was a cough, when he first heard about it. This costume seemed to Aubrey acceptable in the camp's more or less rural setting. "Sir Giles, I should have written after our last discussion in Washington. I do apologize."

"Oh yes," Threave said. "We talked about . . ." His voice trailed off.

"It was the effective coordination of macroeconomic policies."

"Of course," Threave said. "I remember it well."

Fogbound's eyebrows went up, and I heard him mutter, "Mackerel economics again. That's something to talk about."

Threave fired a big gun at once. "The Ambassador is watching your progress with close attention."

Aubrey's face looked like a traffic light that had turned red, except that the color kept deepening. It finished somewhere between scarlet and crimson.

Threave laid the tip of his rolled umbrella against Aubrey's left shoulder. Two Englishmen, far from their island, were standing sentry duty against hostile economic forces, linked by the slender shaft of a furled umbrella. "I understand that this fight should not be as testing as some of the others."

Aubrey, whose skin color was reverting shade by shade to normal, tried to say something but succeeded in producing only a gulp.

Threave lowered the umbrella. "I trust, nevertheless, that you will not fall victim to overconfidence. That has been the undoing of many men. You will not remember this case in point, but in 1947, Her Majesty's Government, then His Majesty's Government, on the basis of a large and generous loan from the United States, made the pound sterling convertible. There was no provision for further subventions. It was, I am entitled to say, premature."

"Thank you, Sir Giles." Aubrey now had a major fraction of his voice back. "I shall bear it in mind."

"I wonder whether overconfidence may not have been at the root of the troubles our British boxers have been having of late years."

Aubrey contrived a tactful dissent: "I think not, sir."

"Perhaps not." Threave paused, then fired a salvo. "Philpott-Grimes, there is nothing uncommon about an athlete's bringing glory to his country. It is one of our oldest and proudest stories. Who can forget Roger Bannister's four-minute mile, and Lord Burghley's gold medal in the 400-meter hurdles in the 1928 Olympics? And, my boy, you have done your share and more. I am perfectly entitled to say that the Union Jack flies more proudly because of you and men and women like you in many fields of sport. But — and I know that I need not explain this to you, author of a monograph on diminishing marginal utility — you are in a position to help your country in a tangible way."

Aubrey's monograph, a modest effort, had recently been privately printed and sent to selected economists with a polite letter expressing the hope that they would read it. He had sent two copies to the Mission. It seemed almost cruel of Threave to mention it, as though Aubrey were being forced to eat more of a feast than was good for him. His face was now a flashing beacon. "I finally understand, sir."

Threave continued. "We must do what we can to help ourselves. North Sea oil and gas will go on for a while. Our traditional exports will persist. Perhaps some new ones will come along. I think of reproductions of medieval chastity belts, which have found a surprising and eager clientele here in America. And you, my boy, will never rank with whiskey or gin, or Wedgwood or Royal Doulton, or even with tinned kippers. You are an adventitious asset. We cannot expect your contribution to our reserves to endure for more than a few years. But you are a considerable factor in our economic well-being, Philpott-Grimes, and I know that when you are in the ring, that thought is among those uppermost in your mind."

Another man might have considered the reference to tinned kippers gratuitous. Not Aubrey. There was a suspicious moistness in his eyes.

"But I do not want to put this only in economic terms," Threave went on. "One thinks of Rupert Brooke:

" 'Honour has come back, as a king, to earth,
    And paid his subjects with a royal wage;
    And Nobleness walks in our ways again;
    And we have come into our heritage.' "

Aubrey seemed to grow in height. "I shall not fail you, sir," he said.

"Kippers," Fogbound muttered to me. "Anyway, it's a change from mackerel."

22

BECAUSE OF AUBREY'S IMPENDING FIGHT with the champion, a number of New York sportswriters went to Pittsburgh to cover the Proletariano bout. One of them enrolled for the evening in the sardonic school of sports reporting and described it this way:

A tough, hard-swinging youngster from New York's working-class lower East Side tonight punctured the bubble of England's Aubrey Philpott-Grimes. Rocky Proletariano, a 1–5 underdog in the betting, upset the smart money and knocked said Philpott-Grimes right out of a title shot and a large amount of cold cash.

It was Proletariano's fight from the opening bell. He swarmed all over the thin man from the scepter'd isle, treated his best blows like fleabites, and belted him smartly around his bony body. When he tired of reddening Aubrey's prominent ribs, he scored with right and left chops to the head.

Philpott-Grimes, who is widely supposed to be a smart fighter, showed as much ring sense as your Aunt Tillie's Pekinese. He had no answer to Proletariano's bulling tactics and he spent most of the night pushing his left jab over Rocky's head. He had a six-inch reach advantage, but it did him no good because his principal activity was not fighting but gangling. Judging by his performance tonight, the big question is what he lists as his occupation when filling out the income tax forms of which he is so fond. After the fight, his manager, Fogbound Franklin, who looked more than a little moribund, said that his man had had an off night. Franklin understated it. Philpott-Grimes was so far off, he was never in view.

The pattern was set in the first round. Philpott-Grimes came dancing confidently out of his corner and the next thing he knew, Proletariano was thumping him around the middle. Philpott-Grimes looked surprised and grabbed the New York boy's arms. This worked only until the referee broke them. Then Proletariano did it again. He did it all night long. Only in the third round and the fifth did Philpott-Grimes give more than he took. Those were the only rounds he won on any card, with the eighth called even. He was in trouble in the second and seventh, when Proletariano suddenly shifted his attack from the body to the head, but managed to avoid being floored.

Before this match, Proletariano was strictly a journeyman. Philpott-Grimes was in line for a shot at the title. Proletariano was no world-beater tonight but he looked tough enough to give the champion a fight. Philpott-Grimes looked like a mistake. The so-called asparagus spear that walks like a man fought like one.

The contest had its fascinating personal angle. Philpott-Grimes fights to earn foreign exchange for the British Treasury. Fortunately for the British, they have other sources. He is also the current dearly beloved of Fredda Plantagenet, the robust if slightly ancient actress who is reputed to be of some importance in the television medium. Miss Plantagenet, a well-known fight fan, was not among those present tonight. She must have known something.

Aubrey's dressing room was a cheerless place after the fight. While he took a shower, and the trainer waited to help him dress, Fogbound and I, seated on chair and rubbing table, respectively, stared mournfully at the floor. A grunt escaped from Fogbound and he raised his arm and let it fall against his side. He must have been envisioning a new flood of "retirement phamphlets." It was I who first said anything with syllables. I said that these things would happen.

This well-chosen comment set off a relatively animated conversation which brought a substantial measure of agreement in a short time. Our conclusion was that Aubrey had been too high, also that he had been keyed up too far, also that the nervous letdown had come too soon, also that he slid from the peak before the fight, also that he was never able to get going. Having found five ways of saying the same thing, we added that Proletariano had fought better than anyone expected him to, and in the circumstances, Aubrey never really had a chance. The conversation ended with Fogbound, lips pursed, nodding his head knowingly while I continued my examination of the dressing room floor. As dressing room floors went, it was without interest.

When Aubrey came out and began to dress, Fogbound tried to console him. "A home town decision," he said. "By my score, you won."

"Whose home town?" I asked. "The referee's?"

"Quite," Aubrey said. "I was trounced. I felt myself rather in the position of a manufacturer whose goods never reach the marketplace. It was a poor show." He walked over to Fogbound and put his arm around his shoulders. Fogbound removed it and put his arm around Aubrey. "My job. Morals building is for the manager."

"Thank you, Sam," Aubrey said. "I've let you down" — Fogbound interrupted with a gesture with his free arm to indicate that this was not true — "and Fredda and Sir Giles and the others. Still, *nil desperandum*. Never despair. There will be other times."

Fogbound's head came up and revealed the smile that had triumphed over tears. "Maybe. Maybe there'll be other times. But you shouldn't be disappointed if there aren't."

"It is simply a question of a return match with Proletariano. After that, we'll be back just where we were before."

"A return match with Proletariano?" Fogbound gave up his selfless personnel management. "You think this Jack Smith will give us one?" He broke into mirthless laughter.

"After what we've done to him?" I asked. Then I laughed hollowly. Hollow laughter comes close to being a hoot and is unattractive, but it does have dramatic applications.

Aubrey knotted his tie and put on his jacket. "We shall carry on. I make no comment on the rum way these things are ordered here." He walked to the door. "I'll be back shortly."

Fogbound asked where he was going.

"I want to congratulate Proletariano. He was rough at times but he fought hard and he is a clean fighter, and I think that I should wish him well. *Absit invidia*. Let there be no envy or ill will."

Fogbound looked at him admiringly. "Aubrey. My boy. A lesson in sportsmanship."

"I'll go along," I said. "Aubrey may need a phrase or an elusive fact. He will be able to call on me for advice and counsel."

The corridor leading to Proletariano's dressing room was

by now largely deserted. A few men glanced curiously at Aubrey as he strode along in his City of London garb, and one said, "Hard luck, Philpott-Grimes," to which Aubrey replied, "Thank you very much." He knocked at the door of his opponent's dressing room and we were admitted by a large gentleman, friendly enough, whom we recognized as Proletariano's manager.

"I thought I would like to drop in and congratulate Rocky," Aubrey said.

The manager waved toward a corner of the dressing room where Proletariano, now dressed, was the center of a knot of excited people. He had looked up at Aubrey's knock, and he came across the room to greet him. Aubrey offered his congratulations and best wishes, and Proletariano thanked him. Aubrey expressed the hope that they would meet again. Proletariano responded, "Glad to any time," and we were turning to go when we spotted a familiar face. It was Barbetta, smiling broadly.

"I say," Aubrey said. "What brings you here?"

"I come to see you lose."

It seemed to Aubrey a good time to inquire after Doreen. "Never better," Barbetta said. "Especially after tonight."

"You think my defeat will make her happy?"

"That's right," Barbetta said.

"I should be sorry to think that true, but I suppose that in a way it was inevitable." Aubrey nodded all around, and we left.

The news that Barbetta, gloating, was in Proletariano's dressing room caused Fogbound to clap his hand to his head, sink into the dressing room's one chair, and resume staring at the floor, which had not changed since we last examined it. "He's back. I thought he moved out already." He asked

Aubrey to repeat their conversation. It offered no clues to a Barbetta-Proletariano axis, but Fogbound was convinced that there was one. "All the dressing rooms in the United States, he's in that one?" He slapped his hands against his knees to show that he had come to a decision. "Mr. Bindle. What's the name, where he belongs?"

"Congress."

"We'll go."

I agreed that Bindle was a friend. As Fogbound knew, he had just demonstrated his continuing interest in Aubrey's well-being by inserting in the *Congressional Record* a letter to the editor of *The Times* of London from Admiral Hutchison-Brewer and forwarded to me by our London correspondent. "A protean man," Bindle had called Aubrey in his introduction to the Hutchison-Brewer letter, "a renaissance man, of a kind all too rare in our time," and had then yielded to the Admiral.

Sir [Hutchison-Brewer began, as do all those who write to *The Times*], is it generally understood how bravely and well Mr. Aubrey Philpott-Grimes is bearing aloft the British standard among our American friends?

Agincourt, the Armada, Waterloo, Gordon at Khartoum, Scott at the Pole, are all behind us. Heroism no longer comes in such unmistakable garb as it did at Alamein and for The Few. Yet surely Philpott-Grimes, carrying his message of British grit and self-reliance in his fists and in his brain, arouses us all with his nobility of purpose. Patriotism, as Edith Cavell said so well, is not enough, but without it, Philpott-Grimes reminds us, we should be poor indeed.

I am, Sir, your obedient servant.

Norbert Hutchison-Brewer

"Very nice," Fogbound had said then. "But who answers such letters?" Now he repeated, "We'll go. When do they open?"

I pointed out that it would be necessary to find a connection between Barbetta and Proletariano before we saw Bindle, and Aubrey objected that the bout had been honestly fought and the decision just. Barbetta had been in the dressing room, not the ring.

"Maybe he bought a piece this Rocky," Fogbound suggested.

"I cannot see what difference that would have made tonight," Aubrey said, "but if he has, I shall have all the more incentive to thrash the chap next time."

Fogbound laughed mirthlessly. He was perfecting his technique. "Next time. I'm glad you're so cheerful. To lose isn't enough, we have to have Barbetta besides. I thought we didn't see him, maybe somebody rubbed him out already."

I ran my fingers nervously through my hair. Not that I was nervous. I think everybody should have a repertoire of gestures. It helps to pass the time. For the same reason, I scowl a good deal and narrow my eyes. In a journalist, scowling and narrowing the eyes show that he is pugnacious and hard to fool. He should also slouch. Slouching has a faintly cynical air, and shows that the sloucher doesn't care much about appearances but is concerned with what lies behind them. All of this is time-consuming, and there is no additional pay for doing it, but I accept it as part of the job.

"Gentlemen," I said, "I shall find out what Barbetta was up to. I shall give my imitation of a reporter tracking down a story. There must be some award I can get for it."

As I finished speaking, the telephone rang. It was Fredda, who had had a good deal of trouble finding us but had persevered. Fogbound and I absented ourselves from the scene until Aubrey, blushing and smiling, opened the door some minutes later and motioned us in.

"In this hour of adversity," he told us, "the knowledge that Fredda's sympathy and encouragement are with me is beyond price. *Resurgam*. I shall rise again."

"I'm glad to hear it," Fogbound grunted.

We trudged out into the cold and found a restaurant known as Les Gourmets Rendezvous, where I told the waitress, whose interest was nominal at best, that King Charles III of Spain, who ruled in the eighteenth century, dined nightly for fifty-seven years on roast veal, soup, lettuce, an egg, and a glass of wine, but that I, less demanding, would have a cheeseburger. The others gave the same order. The stoicism with which we downed our cheeseburgers might have offended any cook, but it was the best we could do.

"Aubrey," I said, "I could not help noticing that you used three Latin phrases in quick succession tonight. It's the first time I've heard you do that."

Aubrey thought before answering. "It is a time of affliction. One operates on instinct."

23

IN THE PERIOD immediately following the Proletariano fight, Aubrey turned routinely to studying boom/slump cycles, hoped for a chance to redeem himself, and was consoled by Fredda. Fogbound performed virtuoso acts of self-torment and was consoled by Mrs. Franklin, who also told him that if he brought his troubles to the table, the food would turn to poison in his stomach.

I plowed ahead. When I began my inquiry, I hoped that Barbetta had bought a piece of Proletariano. This would not have explained Proletariano's victory, but if I could have shown that he was partly owned by a gangster, sympathy would have gravitated to Aubrey for having fought against a creature of the underworld. The public might have wanted good to have another chance to conquer evil.

My research, which in an honored journalistic tradition consisted of talking to other newspeople, in this case former colleagues among the sportswriters, revealed nothing so useful. I brought the story to Fogbound and Aubrey only in the interests of truth and my reputation. Barbetta had done nothing even faintly illegal. He had not, for example, doped Aubrey or bribed the referee or judges. Nor had he bought a share of Proletariano's contract. He had helped to bring about Aubrey's downfall by using his brains. His untutored skill had far outshone the more elaborate appeal of Sir Giles Threave. He had spoken to the fighter in this vein:

1. "Rocky, you can't lose to a fighter as skinny as this Philpott-Grimes."
2. "Rocky, you can't lose to an Englishman."
3. "Rocky, think what this country done for you."
4. "Rocky, you win, the records show you're a great Italian-American fighter. You're a legend."

All of Barbetta's thrusts had landed, but my information was that the fourth was the one that really sank in. "For me to be a legend," Proletariano was telling his friends, "that motivated me. That gave me motivation."

My version of events was as disappointing to Fogbound and Aubrey as it was to me. Aubrey was embarrassed by the fact that his defeat resulted from a parochial, low-level approach, although he did agree that it had been effective. Fogbound, peaceable and law-abiding, uncharacteristically recalled a newspaper article he had read years before about an organization called Murder, Incorporated.

"It ran like clocks work," he told us. "You have these people if you beck and call, you pay them, and it's somebody's funeral. It's still in business?"

I said I thought not but that there must be some successor organizations that would take a contract on Barbetta.

Fogbound sighed. "I can't do it. All my life, I've never been in cohorts with gangsters."

By the time that Fogbound had finished these musings,

Aubrey had prepared an analysis of Barbetta's activities and the course they now made imperative. Unreasoning provincialism often defied logic and superior force and ability, he said. It was not the sort of thing that could be righted by an appeal to the police or to Congress. *Age quod agis.* Do what you are doing; to the business at hand. They must hope for a return bout and once that was obtained, thrash Proletariano decisively.

"Thrash, shmash." Fogbound had some difficulty with the variation. "First you have to get the fight."

"Have you tried?" I asked.

"My friend." Fogbound indicated me sarcastically. "You want me to try? I'll try."

Fogbound tried. Jack Smith, he reported back morosely, saw him only after a number of telephone calls and proved to be without feeling. Smith resented our appeal to Washington, which had forced him to go back on his word to a dangerous gangster, thus jeopardizing his own life. "Franklin," he had said, "the only reason I let you in was so I could tell you no myself, in person. No."

Fogbound felt that Smith never should have given his word to a gangster in the first place. He considered that by virtue of his lack of human qualities, Smith was unfit to be a promoter, in which position he had so much influence over the lives and fortunes of others. "To my estimation," Fogbound said, "that Smith is completely nothing."

These academic points — and the headache he announced he contracted thinking about them — aside, Fogbound was resigned to failure with Smith and was thinking gloomily about offers of fights in Indianapolis and Des Moines. Aubrey took the prospect with equanimity. For one thing, he wanted to examine market possibilities for British products in parts of the country other than New York. For another, he wanted to test for himself the theory he had often heard about the natural democracy of the Middle West, and its more genuine Americanness. Did it, for example, make for any difference in tipping?"

I leaped in. "Juan Peron," I said, "in his first presidential administration in Argentina, from 1946 to 1955, declared tipping humiliating to workers and replaced it with a service charge. However, the service charge soon was augmented by a small voluntary payment, generally known as a tip."

Aubrey ignored my learned contribution. "Tipping practices tell a great deal about a people," he said. "Ours is an increasingly service-oriented society. Basic industrial and agricultural production require a smaller and smaller proportion of the work force. We must define our attitude to the service trades. We must decide whether tipping is consonant with dignity in the workplace. My own view is that it probably is not."

Fogbound listened with the mixture of awe, incomprehension, and mild annoyance with which he had come to greet Aubrey's disquisitions. To him, the future of tipping was without interest. So, in all their aspects, were Indianapolis and Des Moines.

"Des Moines," I said, "was founded as Fort Des Moines in 1843, and Indianapolis —"

Fogbound held up a hand. He wished the two cities well. To him, they were simply places where a fighter of Aubrey's standing should not be performing. To go there would be to admit that any hope of the championship was finished.

He brightened when Fredda came to his office to announce that she believed she had a solution. She prepared the ground by making certain that Fogbound had abandoned hope of melting Smith's heart and that no one else was pulling strings for him. This established, she said that she was applying herself to the problem.

"You?" Fogbound asked.

"Me. Pardon me. I."

"You know somebody?"

"I know somebody."

"Who?"

"Spare me," Fredda said. "This is a time for action. I go. You will not see me again until I conquer."

"So go."

"What will you do?" asked Aubrey.

Fredda raised an eyebrow. "I will get you the fight you need."

Late the next day, Fredda summoned us to her apartment. We had not heard from her in the interim, although Aubrey felt that she should have checked in periodically, much as a pilot keeps airport control advised of his whereabouts.

"Good evening, gentlemen," she said, as we came through the door. "I shall not visit you at the training camp this time. It might bring you bad luck."

Fogbound looked at her imploringly. "What happened?"

"Aubrey fights Proletariano at the Sportitorium six weeks from Friday. And for God's sake, have him in shape. I'd like him to win."

Aubrey and Fogbound spoke together: "What happened?"

Fredda scowled. "What happened? Nothing happened."

"But we have the fight?" Fogbound asked.

Fredda scowled again. "You have the fight. I've already told you that."

"You don't seem pleased," Aubrey said.

"I'm not pleased," Fredda declared. She had spoken to Smith on the telephone, making an appointment and explaining that she wanted to help Aubrey, but that Smith's attitude was perfectly understandable. Couldn't they talk? She had arrived at Smith's office charming, reasonable, and playful, intending to lead Smith to believe that she was ready to give her all, or at any rate to make it available for a while.

"My idea," Fredda explained, "was to offer the villain the fruits of his villainy. But he sees the vulnerability beneath the carefree laughter. There is a slight edge of hysteria. And his better self asserts itself. He rises above temptation and shows his innate decency by giving Aubrey the fight. It worked."

Aubrey threw his arms around her. "You're super."

Fredda submitted patiently, then pushed him off. It had all been too easy, she complained. She had not expected Smith to foam at the mouth or paw the ground, but there should have been some signs of inner anguish. Smith's better self asserted itself almost without a struggle.

"It didn't do much for my confidence," she said, "though at one point, his nostrils did dilate in the approved manner and he excused himself and left the room. I thought he was going to leave orders that we were not to be disturbed. But when he came back —"

"Nostrils back to normal?" I asked.

Fredda turned her tawny eyes on me in what a critic once called her basilisk stare. "Back to normal. All he said was that he had been expecting Sam for days and the papers were ready to be signed."

"You saw the papers?" Fogbound asked.

"I did. You're getting the very short end of the purse."

"That was dodgy," Aubrey said. "Suppose that Smith's better nature had not prevailed. What would you have done?"

"I would have got you the fight."

Aubrey took her hand. "How?"

"What kind of question is that? How many ways are there?"

"After Aubrey beats Proletariano, what about a title fight?" It was Fogbound. "You talked about that?"

"I did not. I thought I did very well to get what I did. I yielded no territory in return."

"How short is our end of the purse?"

"I told you. Very. You'll see for yourself."

For the first time in days, Fogbound smiled. "You're right. Sign first and ask questions afterward." He turned playfully to Aubrey. "It's an old Greek saying, like yours."

"I have some contemporary American sayings, Sam," Fredda said. "I.e., go. Take wing. Sign the contract."

"May I add an English one?" Aubrey was smiling. "Beetle off."

"I can take a hint," said Fogbound. And he was through the door.

24

DURING THE SIX WEEKS before the return match, both Aubrey and Proletariano searched unremittingly for that intangible asset, the will to win. Aubrey thought of the friends who were standing by him — Fredda, Fogbound, me — and was moved. He was, after all, an alien, even if legally admitted, and we were helping him. The magnitude of the sacrifice Fredda had been willing to make left him determined that even though it had not been made, it should not not have been made in vain. She had deprecated it characteristically, of course, and camouflaged it with her toughness. But Aubrey was coming more and more to believe that that toughness was a sham. He knew what her decision to make the sacrifice must have cost her.

For six weeks, Aubrey's jaw remained grimly set. My opinion was that this was probably a record, but there was no way to be sure, because this is one of the few athletic activities on which no statistics are kept. Fredda, on the other hand, was cheerful. She had done her part and had the comfortable feeling that it was for others to try to measure up to it.

A new obsession gnawed at Fogbound: When Aubrey lost, had it been an off night or had Proletariano solved his style? Aubrey was ungnawed by the question; "It had nothing to do with his style or mine. It was my inner self that was playing me up."

"He means a little off," I told Fogbound.

"Nonetheless," said Aubrey, "I shall show him something new. He is the kind of fighter known among British amateurs as a crouching weaver. I shall straighten him up with a right uppercut delivered after a left jab and followed by a left hook. No airy-fairy theories. Basic boxing. The British heritage."

Almost as preoccupied as Fogbound with the fight's outcome were Simco Savory, Webster Bindle, and Sir Giles Threave. Savory knew that Aubrey was finished as a party attraction if he lost again; our Washington bureau described him as "anxious." At the British Economic Mission, which I telephoned, snapping off a businesslike "Mercer, *Star-Telegram*," in response to "Threave here" when I was put through, the subject, because of its economic consequences, was taboo. I asked Threave whether there was anything he wanted to say about the fight, and he replied, "Oh, goodness gracious, no."

As for Bindle, he had begun to see possibilities for himself as an international statesman. He reasoned that success for Aubrey would strengthen British pride and self-reliance and that this would spread to the Dutch and the Italians and the rest. "This may be a pivotal moment," he called a news conference to say. "I see a more viable alliance and perhaps a lightening of the burden carried by the United States."

On the other side, Barbetta, sensing that Proletariano might feel that another easy victory was in the offing, was again hard at work with an appeal to his man's pride and emotions. Not that I knew this at the time. It came to me ex post facto when I acquired a well-placed informant. Barbetta did nothing so blatant as pointing out that another victory would put Proletariano in the big money. He reasoned that Proletariano could work that out for himself. Instead, having heard from Doreen about Aubrey's former occupation, he tried to impress upon Proletariano that there were few things a man could do as shameful as losing a fight to a clerk. Proletariano's mother, Barbetta said, would be shunned by her friends, while his father would be held up to scorn by much of the working population of Wilmington, Delaware. If Proletariano had any young brothers or sisters, they would have to leave school, and probably would become juvenile delinquents and end up gangsters, like Barbetta. He enjoyed it himself, but it was a hard life and not to everyone's taste. Finally, word would get back to the old country and the name of Proletariano would be a *ludibrio*, or laughingstock, for years to come.

Proletariano pondered all of this for a moment. "My sister's a clerk," he said.

To Barbetta, this seemed to clinch the argument but Proletariano was not easily derailed. "Only if it's so bad to lose to clerks, clerks must not be very good fighters," he said. "And if they ain't good fighters, I got nothing to worry about."

Barbetta thought fast. "He's a fake clerk. Not many people know it but it looks the same on your record."

Proletariano nodded. "I see," he said.

There was one small crisis to be overcome before the fight could go on. Anti-tax groups around the country had sent

Proletariano telegrams of congratulation after the first fight and had passed resolutions censuring Aubrey for interfering in United States affairs. This Aubrey denied: "I would not dream of abusing the hospitality of this great and generous nation. Yet neither will I check my beliefs at the port of entry. Your Constitution guarantees freedom of speech to all within the confines of this land. I must say what I believe. To do otherwise would be to diminish the American people as well as myself."

Aubrey's explanation did not block more telegrams to Proletariano from the anti-taxers, and it did not prevent pickets carrying signs that said, "AUBREY, GO HOME," from marching outside the Sportitorium. When Aubrey arrived for the weigh-in, he stopped to explain his position on taxes to the pickets. "They seemed rational," he told me later, "especially the one with the handcuffs. Rather a motherly type." As he stood there, with Fogbound saying urgently, "After the fight, after the fight," there was a small stir in the cluster around him and Aubrey looked down to find himself manacled to one of the pickets.

"Now, young man," she said, smiling brightly under her gray hair, her pug nose wrinkled, "you will understand what has happened to private enterprise in this country because of your beloved taxes. It is handcuffed."

"I told you after the fight," Fogbound shouted. "Get the police."

"Madam, do you mind?" Aubrey said. "I do have a weigh-in to get to. You've made your point. I appreciate the symbolism. Would you mind very much unlocking these?"

"I can't unlock them," the picket said, looking up at him. "I don't have the key. And I don't have any incentive to unlock them. Incentive is being destroyed in this country. You and your kind should have thought of that."

"She threw away the key," Fogbound shouted. "Get the police."

The picket, her face pointed toward the sky so that she could look Aubrey in the eye, next explained that early suffragettes in his country had chained themselves to railings outside 10 Downing Street and that her protest was in that spirit. "The tax burden must be lifted," she said. "Industry is being crippled. Middle income people are being crushed. Equity —"

Aubrey, staring down as though looking for a coin that had fallen, was saying, "My dear woman, it is for the American people to decide these questions. Now please do let me go," when the police arrived. Sweeping us along with them, they moved in a phalanx into the Sportitorium, the picket, about a foot off the ground, shouting to the newspeople who pushed in, "My name is Mary Jane Reifsnyder. I am from Oconomowoc, Wisconsin. I am only four feet ten inches tall. By profession, I am a teacher's aide. I am married, with two children."

In the dressing room, Aubrey was told to strip down for the weigh-in. He pointed out that he could not remove his shirt, undershirt (he called it a "vest"), jacket, or waistcoat without removing Mary Jane first. "We'll make allowances for that," Jack Smith said. "Proletariano's manager has no objection and he has waived his right to be present."

Aubrey removed his shoes, socks, and trousers. "Avert your eyes, Madam," he said.

"I'm old enough to be your mother," said the redoubtable Mary Jane, "and I'd like to know how many hidden taxes there are on those shoes. Probably not even made here." She reached down, picked one up, examined it, and said, "I might have known. Holmes of Norwich. Imports."

So it came about that Aubrey was weighed while wearing

most of his clothes and handcuffed to Mary Jane, who stood to the side of the scale, pointing out that none of this would have happened if Aubrey had not forced his views on taxation on the American people. After he was weighed, Mary Jane was lifted onto the scale while he stood to the side. This resulted from a hypothesis that his weight could be more accurately arrived at if hers also was known, but the hypothesis was not thought through and nothing came of it except that Mary Jane appeared to weigh one hundred two pounds.

"The handcuffs make me heavier," she said.

"After the fight, I told him," Fogbound said. "After the fight."

Eventually a policeman found among his keys one that fitted the cuffs, and Aubrey was set free. Fogbound looked for signs of injury and found none, probably because Aubrey's wrist was so thin that the metal had barely touched it. He swung around, found Mary Jane, and shouted, "You should go to jail."

"I shall not prefer charges," Aubrey said. "I know that emotions run high on this subject, and I have not been damaged."

"Thank you, sir," said Mary Jane. "You are a prince. Would you ask the police to return my handcuffs? I paid for them."

"They should put them on you," Fogbound bellowed.

"I am sorry, Madam," Aubrey said. "That is for the police to decide."

"Aubrey," Fogbound said. "I think a postponement. You're maybe again wonky."

"Not in the least," Aubrey declared. "I'm perfectly all right and we don't want to give Smith a pretext for calling this off. Not after what Fredda has done."

"You're right," Fogbound said. "But didn't I tell you, after the fight?"

Aubrey spent the rest of the day in his apartment, where Fogbound and I stood guard. We went to the Sportitorium that evening in a limousine provided by Jack Smith and only slightly smaller than Barbetta's, and with a security man in the front seat. There were no incidents.

This was how the fight went, as reported by the sportswriter who had affiliated himself with the sardonic school while in Pittsburgh. He had in the meantime read something about rhythmic prose and periodicity and now abjured the journalistic cliché of the short sentence:

Aubrey Philpott-Grimes, the English middleweight whose skeletal appearance belies a stout heart and no mean boxing ability, last night put himself back in line for a shot at the title by outboxing, outthinking, and outfighting Rocky Proletariano, a hard-swinging youngster from New York's working-class lower East Side, thereby undoing the damage Proletariano had done the Briton's cause by outpointing him seven weeks ago in Pittsburgh against the expectations of boxing men everywhere.

Philpott-Grimes, sporting fancy footwork and a six-inch reach advantage, had no trouble in avoiding Proletariano's head-long rushes and in tying him up when the powerful youngster got inside, and he rained left jabs on Rocky's unprotected face, while unleashing an occasional right uppercut that lacked knockout steam but nonetheless often stopped the East Side boy in his tracks.

At his best from the opening bell, Philpott-Grimes employed every punch in his extensive armory, and grew in stature as the evening progressed, using the ring like a master, and even managing to end most rounds in his own corner, leaving his opponent to plod wearily across the ring, a trek made the more wearisome by Proletariano's ineffectual pursuit of the clever Englishman, who fought with immaculate artistry.

Middleweight champion Mike Turner, the lion-hearted Irish battler, was among the 15,000 who looked on at the Sportitorium as Philpott-Grimes gave everything he had to avoid the plunge into anguish and oblivion that another defeat by Proletariano would have meant, a loss that would have signified the end of the studious Philpott-Grimes as a drawing card and his probable return to his post in the London stock exchange, where he acquired the understanding of his country's financial problems that has made him fight.

After this, the sentences became somewhat shorter but the reporter, missing a spot of human interest, did not note the presence at ringside of a man who seemed to know Aubrey and who shouted over and over again, "He knock you out this time, Philpott-Grimes." The man, who kept up his shouting to the end, began to sound rather desperate from the fourth round on, and the girl seated next to him seemed at times not to know which contestant to cheer. I could have told him who they were, but it was only later that I learned what the man muttered when the fight ended and Aubrey was declared the winner. It was: "That Philpott-Grimes. I maybe rub him out."

25

IN THE WEEKS BEFORE the Turner fight, a number of people in a number of places were making their plans for Aubrey. Aubrey himself, and Fogbound, knew that it was not safe to count Barbetta out completely, and neither would have been surprised had he tried to intervene on behalf of the champion, as he had with Proletariano. I had a fantasy in which he told Turner that Aubrey's family had been vicious oppressors of the Irish patriots, their reign of terror having begun with the Battle of the Boyne in 1690. "I'm surprised you don't know that," Barbetta said in the fantasy. "Philpott-Grimes, if that's *my* name, I'm afraid to mention it in Ireland. Too many people there, they remember." Then, as Turner prepared to swear eternal vengeance on the graves of his ancestors, Barbetta said slyly that Aubrey was sorry about it, sorry that Ireland was free: "He has his way, the English are still there." And Turner's wrath was terrible to behold.

This kind of thing Fogbound and Aubrey were prepared to accept as a normal hazard in a world where Barbettas were permitted to roam freely, but they were not aware of his intention to commit homicide, so Fogbound was able to keep his self-laceration down to manageable proportions. Aubrey's spirits were so high that he sometimes felt sorry for Turner, for he knew that no champion found it pleasant to be dethroned. He had the same impregnable confidence as before the first Proletariano fight, but without the emotional tension.

Fogbound had forbidden any visitors in camp, and any kind of contact with Sir Giles Threave and his colleagues, and this ban was accepted without a murmur. Aubrey might have been less malleable had he known about one request, but Fogbound kept it from him. It came from an interdisciplinary group of professors who, as they wrote, conjectured that it was possible to foresee Aubrey's tactics in the ring by reading his scholarly views, and vice versa.

"In both cases, they were carefully thought out," the chairman of the group, L. Peavey Hazard of the Center for Study of Reproducible Phenomena, Stillwater, Oklahoma, wrote to Fogbound, "and depend on impeccable execution. There appears to be little room for improvisation. We would like to see whether this insight can be supported empirically and, to that end, we ask your permission to send a small deputation to watch Mr. Philpott-Grimes from ringside as he trains. So far as we are aware, this would be the first scientific observation of synchronicity in ratiocination and professional sport, of which we believe Mr. Philpott-Grimes offers a rare example. The deputation's findings would in the first instance be circulated only within the profession. If, on the basis of further investigation, the theory can be proved out, it might open the way to a new field of cross-disciplinary study."

Fogbound had a ready reply: "After the fight."

Although the British Economic Mission wanted Aubrey

to enjoy serenity of mind, it somehow leaked out that he was to be rewarded with an appointment to the Mission if he won. One of those to whom word came of the pending appointment was my paper's diplomatic correspondent, and through him it came to me. He intended to print it as a relief from the leaden material he normally worked with and thought that I might like to tell Aubrey first.

"Thank you, Dipcor," I said, speaking in the cablese with which I sometimes enlivened the day. I then called Aubrey and relayed the information that the idea had originated with Threave, who had said, "If Aubrey boxes strenuously enough, there is reason to hope that he will be champion." Some members of the Mission thought it unfair that the appointment should be contingent on victory, but it was explained to them that appointing Aubrey to the Mission after a losing fight would open the way to levity at Britain's expense. A world champion, on the other hand, would make tangible the strength and dauntlessness with which Britain forged ahead.

After I gave Aubrey this news, there was a long silence during which, had I known what was happening, I might have whistled "God Save the Queen." For Aubrey was possessed by patriotic sentiments and by the thought of moving in the rarefied atmosphere of the Mission. At last he gulped out that he was too moved to know what to say.

I then explained that the Mission members had tried to keep word of the appointment from him because they remembered what had followed Sir Giles Threave's visit before the first Proletariano fight.

"The Mission need have no fear," Aubrey said. "I know the perils of becoming too tense."

"The proposal to appoint you went by pouch to very high

levels in Whitehall," I said, "and I understand that it was approved with unusual speed. You will be expected to concentrate on youth."

"Jolly good idea."

"There is a condition attached — that you pay your own expenses."

"Naturally," Aubrey said reverently.

Fredda also had plans involving the fight. She began by bidding for the television rights so that she could carry it on her show in place of the usual drama. She had the idea of rewarding the winner with the Fredda Plantagenet belt and went so far as to plan to make it adjustable, since one that would fit Turner would hang limply around Aubrey's skimpy waist. This, however, was only for form, for Fredda did not think it possible that Turner could win. She recognized that his presence in the ring was necessary but only so that Aubrey could have somebody to win the title from. The reason Fredda believed this so strongly was simple: Aubrey was in love with her, and Turner, so far as she knew, never having met him, was not.

It was also Fredda's intention to comment from what she called the woman's point of view, an idea she defended on the ground that at least it was something new, and the broadcasting of fights obviously needed something new. So, she felt, did her sponsor, Licentia Cosmetics, which made the hand creams and lotions that said, "Let's do it!" and which was trying to repel a challenge from another company that showed a girl with a satisfied smile over the slogan, "She did it!"

Cosmic's sports department, however, felt that Licentia's advertising messages were likely to be lost on much of the audience, and Licentia's advertising manager agreed, especially because most of the money he had available was to be used to push a revolutionary new product, developed after much research and expenditure in Licentia's laboratories, wigs with hair curlers attached. The curlers were to serve three purposes — to show that the woman wearing the wig was a busy person, to show that she cared about the appearance of her hair, and to make it appear that the wig was not a wig at all.

There was also a feeling at Cosmic that the relationship between Fredda and Aubrey made an impartial commentary unlikely. "I do not offer you impartiality," Fredda said. "I offer you spectacle and suspense." Despite the cogency of this argument, Licentia was asked to hold off, pending a final decision. Meanwhile, some time was sold to Knight In Armor men's cosmetics, which was trying to contain the advance of electric shavers and keep men using the razors and blades that enabled its styptic pencil business to thrive. Its message went like this:

Men, cutting yourself is half the adventure in shaving. Now, we're not telling you to slice yourself up just for the fun of it. But a man's life ought to have some danger in it. The Knight In Armor never ran from a fight. He put himself on the line. He took a cut and a trickle of blood in stride. They were badges of honor, for they proclaimed the knight. You should take them in stride, too, men. It's part of the adventure of shaving. Knight In Armour.

This was accompanied by shots of a knight, in armor but with his vizor raised and his face exposed, shaving happily and saying, upon cutting his lip, "Good. She'll think I got it jousting."

One of Knight In Armor's advertising men, a visionary

who had once unsuccessfully proposed that the company broadcast the New York Knicks' basketball games, had an idea for a new message. This was to wait for one of the fighters to bleed a little and then come in between the rounds with a plug for the styptic pencil, along these lines:

> Yes, folks, Jones is bleeding from a cut above the right eye and his seconds are trying to stop the flow and close the cut. And, men, if you should happen to cut yourself while shaving — and even the steadiest hand sometimes slips, men — there's nothing that will make that blood stay where it belongs like Knight In Armor's styptic pencil. Good old Knight In Armor. Now back to Hal Kelligan.

The proposal was rejected on the ground that styptic pencils were not used in fighters' corners, and people might notice, with the result that Kelligan's integrity would come into question.

Aubrey knew of the negotiations surrounding the sponsorship of the telecast, but such was his stability of temperament and his glowing satisfaction over the esteem in which the British Economic Mission held him that he was undisturbed, almost indifferent. He did recognize that Fredda at ringside with a microphone would carry interesting possibilities for him, his opponent, and the television audience, and might be distracting. When Fredda dropped out of the picture and was banished to a ringside seat behind the working press, the concern, mild at best, went with her.

26

A WEEK BEFORE THE FIGHT, Jack Smith summoned Fredda to his office "to iron out a few details." Fredda telephoned Aubrey's camp to say that she would let them know as soon as she could what the details were. The following noon, she called to say that it had all been taken care of.

"What sort of details were they?"

"Nothing you need bother your head about. You just go on training and let other people take care of these things."

"Sam would like to know."

"Tell Sam that Smith gives me no trouble at all."

"Was he difficult?"

"Only at first."

"Fredda, did you — for me?"

"No, as a matter of fact, I didn't."

"But you were prepared to?"

"Oh, yes. We can't turn back now. And I think that Smith does want to be dastardly. I think that's why he called me in. But he loses his nerve once I'm there. Poor fellow."

"I think he's rather a rotter. I count myself enlightened,

but I wonder whether the short, sharp shock of six of the best at an early age might not have made Smith a better man."

Fogbound took the incident personally. "Details, he has. I'm the manager. He should call me, not Fredda."

"*Quod ali quis facit per aliquem, facit per se.* What one does through an agent, one does personally. It is simply that Smith is a cad."

Fogbound nodded. "You run into all kinds of mixed bags in this business," he said.

Because of the depth and generosity of Fredda's love, Aubrey was determined to give his best and, if humanly possible, reward that love with victory. Fredda, acting on her own, came up with an additional means by which he could show his gratitude. She would marry Aubrey after his fight with Turner, marry him in the ring before as many in the Sportitorium as wanted to stay, and before a nationwide television audience. As Aubrey placed the slender gold band on her finger, she would place the championship belt around his waist. It would be a kind of double ring ceremony. Aubrey would be in his robe with a towel draped over his head but, naturally, with his gloves off. If Fogbound declined the honor, I would be best man.

As standby best man, I thought I had the right to ask the groom whether he had not always refused to take part in television advertising.

"I am not endorsing a product," he said, "except in the sense that I am endorsing Fredda, as in the same sense she is endorsing me. But neither of us is for sale. And our wedding ceremony will not be part of an advert. One has to be fairly dim not to see that."

"You do not think this falls under the rubric of commercialism, category crass?"

"I should say it is rather a reflection of Fredda's élan. She is not sullied by her association with advertising. She overpowers it. And as an earnest of her good faith, we're going to have it done properly by the vicar when we're in Steeple Bumpstead, with my parents present and giving us their blessing."

"Your honeymoon hideout?"

"I have suggested it. The Women's Institute has invited me to speak in the new village hall, and I would like to accept. Perhaps Fredda will speak as well, about the theater. I intend to compare the British and American systems of taxation."

This time, both Licentia and Cosmic fell in line, but an advertising agency man thought of a snag: "What if Philpott-Grimes loses?"

"He will not lose," Fredda said. "But if he does, I will marry him anyway. We are in love."

"Maybe so," the executive replied. "But is that the kind of publicity the client wants? I'm sorry, Miss Plantagenet, but I'll have to take this up at a higher level."

"Some people put a price on everything," Fredda said.

Somewhere on the higher level dwelled a gambler. He agreed that if Aubrey lost, the wedding in the ring might be less appealing. But on the other hand, would there not be something thrilling about a woman standing by her fallen hero? And Fredda was determined to marry Philpott-Grimes whatever happened. Licentia might as well get what it could out of it.

Fogbound, primed as always to plunge into a state of misery, began actively to fear the worst. "I want Aubrey and Fredda to be happy," he said, "and I'll be best man. But this opens up a whole new ball of wax."

27

BARBETTA WENT THROUGH two phases while Aubrey prepared for Turner. In the first he was determined to rub Aubrey out. It was his intention to do this as close to the day of the fight as possible, for he felt that this would be a nice dramatic touch, as in some moving pictures he had seen. It also was calculated to give Aubrey and his backers a maximum of work and investment before it was all brought to naught.

Barbetta's program put Doreen in a difficult position. She did not want to sing to the fuzz for she was Frankie's moll. Moreover, the fuzz might look askance at her association with him. And even if she were willing to wait some years for Frankie to emerge from prison to marry her, would he take the long view and forgive her for putting him there?

At the same time, she did not want to see Aubrey murdered. It was true that Aubrey and that Mr. Fogbound Franklin could have let Frankie buy in, but one should have the right to decide who owned one. Then, too, she'd heard some ominous mentions of accessories before the fact. She was not quite sure what they were, but she had visions of a headline that read: MOBSTER TO FRY: ACCOMPLICE GETS LIFE.

The upshot of all this was that she called me one morning from a pay phone in Grand Central. After biting out "Mercer, *Star-Telegram*," and hearing her story, I promised that I would help however I could; and she agreed to become my informant, which pleased me, for it made me a more complete newsman. I convinced myself that Doreen was an anonymous source and prepared to face future groups of inquiring journalism students with more confidence. During the next couple of weeks, the phone rang at 0730 hours (I use the military twenty-four–hour clock; it makes me feel more virile) when I was in the shower; at 1630 hours, when I was in heavy thought over an editorial titled "Whither Are We Going?"; at 0230 hours, interrupting a dream sequence just as I was about to receive the annual Prestigious and Coveted Literary Award for a penetrating psychological study of an Oriental fighter named Kid Pro Kuo, who gave as good as he got; and at other times of day and night. From these clandestine calls, during which I would have liked my informant to whisper and generally sound more harried than she did, I was able to piece together certain scenes.

They had just come from a Broadway show, a one-woman reading from the works of pioneers in psychiatry. It was a sellout, and Frankie had drawn up a diagram showing where pressure could be applied and influence brought to bear before he got a pair of seats. During the performance, while the simultaneous translation from the German came to them through headphones, he said a couple of times, "Maybe I buy a piece this show." Otherwise, he had been thoughtful and silent.

Now they were sitting on a gold brocade sofa in Frankie's

apartment. His Florentine leather boots were parked on the travertine coffee table and he was sighting along his right forefinger at the naked gilded bambino that formed the base of a lamp on his credenza. When Frankie pretended to be shooting someone, he used a silencer, so that all came out as he let the bambino have it was, "Pah! Pah!"

Doreen waited until the bambino had been annihilated, then said, "It's really very clever of you to pretend that you're going to rub Aubrey out. I know you're putting me on."

Frankie now was firing at a boxlike lucite container in which a small amount of blue water rolled from side to side, simulating waves. He thought he was picking off surfboarders. "No putting on. And I don't pretend. I rub him out."

There was a silence, during which my informant thought again about the headline, and then Frankie said, "You still like that Aubrey?"

My informant tried desperately to keep calm. "That's a giggle. The way he treated me — and all those boring lectures on the Eurodollar. No, it's just that — just that we used to be chums. And he has the dearest mum. I'd be sad to have to tell his dear old mum that her darling Aubs had had it. She'd be frightfully cut-up."

"Lately I don't like your conversation so good." Frankie looked into the mirror, pointed his hand back over his shoulder, and fired his forefinger between the pieces of a cut-glass chandelier. "Never touched it. Which is soon more than I can say for your Aubrey."

My informant waited a few days to try a different line. It came after Frankie, in reminiscent mood, had enjoyed a quiet chuckle over a piece of paper on which he had diagrammed the plot that originally intimidated Smith. Stretched out on the striped red-and-black silk chaise longue, and tossing aside a weekly newspaper headlined, VICE DOLL KEPT LIST, she said, "Shall I tell you why I liked you from the word go? Your brains. Other gangsters go about bashing people. You use your brains."

"That's right," Frankie said. He returned to a magazine article and an earlier train of thought. "I thought so all along. I find some doctor and make sure."

My informant leaned over and noted the title of the article. It was "Ulcers? Then You're A Potential Leader."

"Why, of course you are, pet," she said. "Just look at that deep medical article you're reading. Other gangsters couldn't begin to understand it. That's why I'm surprised about something you're going to do."

"What's that?"

"Rub out Aubrey."

Frankie said, "Yeah."

"I wish you wouldn't."

Frankie's head jerked up and my informant said quickly, "Don't get me wrong. I'd never ask you to go straight or anything like that."

"You're my moll."

"I'm your moll. It's just that really great leaders, like the Queen, don't use brute force to have their way."

"What she use?"

"Subtlety, pet. She influences events. She doesn't shoot anybody." My informant pointed to the diagram of the Smith caper. "I've seen you influence events, Frankie. You have a subtle mind, too. Like the Queen's."

At this juncture, Frankie rose and went to the bar to fix himself a rye whiskey on the rocks. Doreen had once tried to interest him in Scotch but he had told her that genuine gangsters drank nothing but straight rye. Then he turned.

"All the time the mob asks me what I'm waiting for. Because, the mob wants to buy in, nobody don't say no. I tell them it ain't easy. He's on television telling the clunks they should pay their taxes. And he's got the mouthpiece in that Congress. But the mob don't care. The mob is very tired of that Aubrey. Maybe soon the mob is tired of me. How it looks if I say I wait this long because my moll asks me?"

Doreen suddenly had a mental picture of a different newspaper headline: BODIES OF HOOD AND COMPANION FOUND IN CAR TRUNK — UNDERWORLD REVENGE HINTED.

She considered sobbing out that Frankie no longer loved her, but decided to hold it back as a last resort. She was thinking valiantly when Frankie's eyes suddenly lit up.

"The Queen, she ever change her mind?"

"Oh, I'm sure."

"I change mine. For a good moll, I do something. Aubrey wins, I still rub him out. But he don't win. I see to that. So for you, nothing to worry about." He picked up the pad and began the familiar diagramming. After a while, he held it up for my informant to see.

"I know that, Frankie," she said. "You've shown it to me before."

"Not this one. Nobody seen this one."

My informant leaned over and saw that the line of the diagram went in a puzzling series of loops until it ended in an X mark in the middle of the paper.

"Aubrey loses. So I don't got to kill him," Barbetta explained. "What you say my mind was?"

"Subtle."

"How you spell that?"

"S–u–b–t–l–e."

"What's the *b* for?"

"I don't know, I'm afraid."

"That's good, subtle?"

"It means you're extraordinarily clever."

Barbetta smiled.

"How does your plan work, Frankie?"

"You see. Soon enough."

28

WITH THE FIGHT NEAR, Bindle announced that he would attend as a one-man House subcommittee. He had recently
posted a map of the world on his office wall to show others,
and to remind himself of, the breadth of his concerns. "Our
policy," he had said, "must be national, but it must also be
regional, hemispheric, and global." Now he issued another
statement: "Our allies, and especially our British allies, must
see that we guard their interests as we do our own. I go to
New York with the firm expectation that the rules of fair play
will be observed and that justice will be done."

In New York, Bindle was interviewed during the pre-fight
broadcast conducted by Hal Kelligan, the eminent color man
and, during his football days, the best holder for points after
touchdown in the game until he tired, which he usually did
in the third quarter. Kelligan asked Bindle whether he was a
fight fan.

"Well, Hal," Bindle replied, "I have always taken a close
interest in sports. There is nothing more characteristically

American than intense athletic competition, conducted according to rules by which both sides abide."

"Thank you, Congressman," Kelligan said. "Have you a favorite in this fight?"

"My favorite, Hal, is what it has always been — the well-being of this nation and its friends. As I said earlier today in Washington, our allies, and especially our British allies, must see that we guard their interests as we do our own. Then, whatever the outcome, the mutual trust on which our alliance rests will be strengthened. I have come to New York with the firm expectation that the rules of fair play will be observed and that justice will be done."

Bindle was followed by Simco Savory, who had organized a group to cheer Aubrey on. Its members piled into the studio to laugh and applaud as Simco told Kelligan: "I'm ever so entranced. I feel almost as though I were going into the ring with that Turner fellow myself. We are here to say 'Bonne Chance' to Aubrey. We hope that our cheers will help him to victory.

Kellingan's next guest, after a commercial break during which Savory and his party left the studio, was Walter Haddon, a character actor who never missed a big fight.

"Well," Kelligan began, "how does it look to you, Walt?"

Haddon said it should be a great fight.

"You better believe it, brother," Kelligan said. "There's a lot of tension building up around here, and the fury will start with the sound of the opening bell. Now tell me, how do you size it up?"

"Well," Haddon said, "the way I look at it, Turner is the harder hitter but Philpott-Grimes is the better boxer and he moves faster. That's how I see it, puncher against boxer."

"Okay. Here's the bottom line. Who do you pick to win?"

"That is the bottom line, Hal. Turner punches harder but Philpott-Grimes is awfully clever. I think it'll be mighty close."

"Well, thank you, Walt Haddon. Walt, the fans who are listening know that you're a great fan. You never miss a big fight. Is there anything else you'd like to tell the fans before you go?"

"Well, just this, Hal. Turner's a great fighter and he's been champ a long time, but remember, when they get inside that ring, they both only have two hands."

"Well, thank you, Walt Haddon, and good luck with your new series, 'A Mouse in My House,' about a divorced father and his shy daughter who, unbeknownst to him, is not the timid schoolteacher she seems to be but a plainclothes detective as tough and resourceful as any man on the force. And does she have a time keeping the truth from Dad! You better believe it, brother."

"Thank you, Hal."

This brief exchange made things difficult for those who followed Haddon and for Kelligan himself, for Haddon had brought up both the punch versus boxing angle and the fact that each man would have only two hands after entering the ring, and Kelligan, earlier than he had intended, had let slip bottom line, which was his best phrase, and was afraid that he might have to fall back on nitty-gritty and sixty-four-dollar question.

That left those remaining with little new to say except that both men were in superb condition and that because Turner had been champion for some time, he might now be a little jaded whereas Philpott-Grimes might still be considered a hungry fighter. "He certainly looks hungry," one said, raising quiet but appreciative laughter. Another of those interviewed spoke admiringly of Aubrey's pronouncements on a common

West European monetary unit. Kelligan agreed. "He's a great articulator," he said.

Dr. Conrad Falkenhayn, the television psychiatrist, was asked what effect the planned wedding in the ring after the fight might have on both men. "It will act as a, y'know, re-inforcer for Philpott-Grimes," he said. "It provides inspiration without imposing any additional, y'know, duties on him. Fredda Plantagenet is there waiting for him as a bonus. Y'know?"

"And Turner?"

"It depends. It could affect him in two ways. If he wins, he will be, in a sense, y'know, a spoilsport. If that is the kind of thing he, y'know, enjoys, the wedding may make him a better and more malicious fighter. But if he has a spark of kindness and romance in him, it could, y'now, make him hold back."

Kelligan's last interview was with one of a contingent of British fight fans who had come over by chartered aircraft, and in this interview the color man felt let down by his producers. He had asked for an Englishman who would shout, "'it 'im, Haubrey," and who would render this for the television audience. The producers had come up with a company director whose English was in all particulars superior to Kelligan's.

After learning that his guest did not intend to shout, "'it 'im, Haubrey," or anything like it, Kelligan asked what he would shout if he were a cockney.

"I'm not very good at accents."

"What will you shout, then?"

"We shall just have to wait to see, shan't we?"

"I'm afraid our time's up," Kelligan said, then remembered that he had not worked "razor sharp" into the conversation. "I know one thing," he told the Englishman. "Aubrey's in top shape. Both fighters are. They're razor sharp. And men, when you're using that razor of yours, remember there's no better shaving cream, with or without brush, than good old Knight In Armor. And when you're finished, slap on Knight In Armor After Shave. It leaves you fresh and ready to frolic. You better believe it, brother."

The commercial was followed by the announcement from the ring of the main and stellar event of the evening, for the middleweight championship of the world, bringing together Aubrey Philpott-Grimes, the popular and capable challenger, from Steeple Bumpstead, England, and the titleholder, Irish Mike Turner, middleweight champion of the world, from Boston. Their weights were announced and the referee called Turner and Aubrey to the middle of the ring, gave them their instructions and told them to come out fighting.

While the referee was speaking, Aubrey told me later, "Turner seemed to be reaching into his memory for something. He looked as I've seen Fredda look when she was memorizing a part." Aubrey said he wondered about it, but did not think about it again once the fight started.

Perhaps I should have noticed Turner's expression, but my mind was on something else. I was looking at Aubrey's robe, the back of which, as usual, bore no emblem. I had suggested sewing the sign for the pound sterling there, and Aubrey had replied, "Forgive my candor, but that would be a frightful gaffe. The pound has a long and proud history. My part in upholding it should not be exaggerated. The pound will stand without me."

I stared at the narrow space where the pound sign might have been displayed and told myself that if any man had earned the right to wear it, that man was Aubrey. More precisely, I said to myself, "History will say that man was Aubrey." I often spoke to myself in that way. It kept me in trim for my job.

Fredda felt no pain when Aubrey was struck, struck ordinary blows, at any rate. She had seen too many fights for that. But she was by far the most acutely interested spectator in the Sportitorium. She told me later, when all of this could be recollected in tranquility, that she realized early that if Aubrey could keep it up, there was no doubt that he would win the title. She had a few anxious moments when Turner landed solidly and had Aubrey on the verge of trouble, but Aubrey always managed to get away, and his left worked with the monotony of a machine.

As round after round went by, Fredda became more and more exuberant, and she felt herself standing shoulder to shoulder with Aubrey in the ring. Her left moved with his, and when Turner banged a right into Aubrey's stomach, she said, "Ooh." By the late rounds, she was saying, "He's got it, he's got it," and she knew that only a catastrophe, a desperate punch, could prevent her becoming the wife of the middleweight champion of the world. She longed for the sound of the final bell.

The boxing correspondent of *The Times* of London, sent to New York for the event, saw things much the same way. His report, as it later appeared, ran thus:

Philpott-Grimes had a convincing reply for every stratagem that Turner employed and while his were not the heavier, they were certainly the more numerous blows. Philpott-Grimes' classic style, with the *sine qua non* left jab, made him far the superior at long range, in variety of moves, and in speed of attack. At in-fighting, one concedes, Philpott-Grimes did little or no damage, but he managed to prevent Turner from scoring any significant blows. An uninstructed onlooker might have been pardoned, as Philpott-Grimes piled up point after point, for mistaking the challenger for the champion and the champion for an excessively ambitious challenger.

Most of these nuances escaped Savory's party. In the early rounds, they squealed with glee if they happened to be watching when Aubrey ducked out of range or moved aside as Turner's punches whizzed by. But as the fight wore on, some of them became confused about just why they were there and cheered the wrong man. Bobby Lou Bridewell liked it when Aubrey hit the other fellow (her enchantment with Aubrey having steeled her to watch) "but he never seems to hit him very hard," she said, "and I'm so sad when the other fellow hits Aubrey."

I had some sympathy with the confused Savoryites, of whom Savory himself remarked gently that they were dear people, and ever so *simpatico*, but where boxing was concerned, not *au courant*. Aubrey's fights were interesting principally to connoisseurs of boxing, who were able to see how his style fitted his physique, how he slipped blows, and countered, and used his left, and led his opponents into weariness and frustration.

But the Turner fight had an aspect that distinguished it from Aubrey's other bouts and possibly from any other bout ever fought. I began to be aware of this in the fourth round, and I was close enough to the corner to hear Fogbound ask Aubrey, "What's all the talking?" when the round was over.

"Nothing important," Aubrey said. "He asked me what my percentage was. I told him, though of course he knew, and then he said there wouldn't be much left after I paid my taxes."

"No more talking," Fogbound said. "They don't give points for speeches."

Turner said nothing in the fifth round, but in round six he opened up again.

"What was it this time?" Fogbound asked.

"He seems to have adopted a scoffing tone," Aubrey said. "He said, 'You think you know economics?' I said yes, and he laughed."

"He wants to talk, let him talk. Not you. He'll take your mind off the fight."

"I think not," Aubrey said. "He's trying to distract me. I won't let him."

There was another exchange of words in the seventh round. Aubrey explained in the corner that while they were at long range and he had blocked Turner's left lead, Turner had said, "We'll see what you know about economics. What is Gresham's Law?" Aubrey had replied, after throwing a short right to the body, "Oh, dear, you'll have to do better than that. Named for Sir Thomas Gresham, a sixteenth-century English financier."

"Yeah," said Turner in the next clinch. "But what is it?"

Aubrey's reply was of necessity rather long, and to make it coherent, rather than speaking in fits and starts, he danced about, in and out of range, while delivering it: "If two kinds of money in circulation have the same face value but different intrinsic values, the money with the higher value will be hoarded and will no longer circulate. In short, bad money drives out good."

Before Fogbound could implore him not to talk but to punch, the bell rang for round eight. In this round, as we shortly learned, Turner asked about a cost-benefit analysis. We could see Aubrey shake his head and smile indulgently before he replied. "It was such an elementary question," he told Fogbound. "In a cost-benefit analysis, one simply weighs what one spends or sacrifices against what one gets in exchange for the spending or sacrifice."

"Aubrey, please," Fogbound begged. "Leave out the economics. Turner can get the answer in books. You'll *lend* him the books."

In round nine, Turner asked for a definition of *oligopsony*, no small achievement with a gum shield in his mouth, and Aubrey replied that it was a market structure in which a small number of firms did most of the buying. "I told him he'd have to do better than that," Aubrey advised Fogbound in the corner. "I told him that he was clearly losing the fight and the economics quiz, as well."

Aubrey was right on both counts and Fogbound said no more during the interval. In the tenth round, Turner asked Aubrey to tell him what a full employment budget was, and Aubrey, after landing two smart jabs on Turner's nose, told him instead that such elementary questions were insulting and did not deserve an answer.

"I told him he was putting up a poor show, Sam," Aubrey said after reporting this. "He's not unsettling me. My replies are demoralizing him."

Turner tried again in the eleventh round. As we learned after the bell, he asked about economies of scale and Aubrey said, "Very well. If you insist. Economies of scale come about when unit costs of production drop as output expands." That was a sufficient answer, but Aubrey, now conducting psychological warfare, tied up Turner, pushed him off, moved to the side as Turner rushed in, and added that economies of scale did not invariably accompany expanded output, and that the optimum size was not always the largest.

"Child's play," he told Fogbound.

At one minute and forty seconds into the twelfth round, Turner asked Aubrey to identify the author of the quotation, "Of all debts, men are least willing to pay the taxes. What a satire is this on government! Everywhere they think they get their money's worth, except for these," and, as he finished, swung desperately at Aubrey's jaw. He missed, and for a moment his hands were down and his chin exposed.

It was also at one minute and forty seconds into the twelfth round that the strain became too much for Fredda. Aubrey still was piling up points, but it seemed to Fredda that his thin left arm could not possibly hold the champion off for three rounds more. She had been hoping that somehow the suspense could be ended earlier, and had indulged in the fantasy that Turner might stun himself when he came in low by jamming his head against one of Aubrey's protruding bones.

Then — all of this I learned at a more propitious time — Fredda had an inspiration. In her Hollywood ingenue days, she had played in moving pictures about boxing in which the clean-cut young hero, on the verge of being knocked out, was inspired to a last desperate winning flurry by the sight of her, on her feet in the crowd, wringing her hands and shouting girlish words of encouragement. Now she remembered the first time she had seen Aubrey, and how he had knocked out a block of granite named Jim McGrath because McGrath had called him a Limey.

Fredda half rose from her seat. For a moment she hesitated, torn between the pressing need to end her suffering and the conviction that these things were best left to Aubrey and Fogbound. She was yielding to that conviction — after all, Aubrey did not tell her how to act — but in that moment, with Turner's chin unprotected, Aubrey missed the chance.

He seemed to be thinking about something. He didn't even swing.

It was too much for Fredda. She was overcome by anger at Aubrey's failure to deliver her from the exhausting tension. Maybe he didn't tell her how to act, but somebody should definitely tell *him* how to fight. Fredda nominated herself. She hoisted herself from her seat and cupped her hands to her mouth. Her voice, trained in the theater to project itself over large spaces and competing sounds, cut through the ringside noise.

"You skinny Limey bum," she shouted. "He was wide open!"

Although his mind was elsewhere, trying to remember whether he had ever heard the quotation before, the cry reached Aubrey's ears, and beyond his ears to his heart. It seemed to him that this was monstrous, that if ever he did not deserve such an appellation — and particularly from the woman he loved — this was the time. For nobody was more aware than he of the consummate performance he was putting on that night. "I have been astonishingly effective," he said to himself. "Quite remarkable, really." As Aubrey considered these matters, Turner was moving back into position after his missed swing. The champion's right hand swished through the air and landed on Aubrey's chin, now as unprotected as Turner's had been seconds before. Aubrey stiffened, then slid easily, section by section, to the canvas. Resting on his side, his eyes closed, a look compounded of resentment and pleading still on his face, he was counted out.

As *The Times* of London man wrote:

It was an astonishing dénouement. For much of the fight, one had had a wild chauvinistic urge for Philpott-Grimes' left jab to carry the day, though one knew that the thought was unworthy, for both men seemed equally deserving. Then, suddenly, there on the canvas lay the man who had carried Britain's hopes so high, now the very embodiment of mute frustration and agony. With the championship in his grasp, he had faltered — as so many British athletes seem to do in sight of victory — and during this momentary aberration Turner had seized his chance as a champion should and had unleashed the authoritative blow that felled his sufficiently formidable opponent.

It was a clean knockout, and one can only admire the fortitude with which it was consummated. It did not afford Philpott-Grimes' manager an opportunity for the protest against the decision that one associates with American boxing.

Fredda's reaction was less thoughtful. Thanks to her extensive training and experience as an actress, she was able to do almost anything in public without qualms. Now, as thousands of eyes focused on her to watch her dash into the ring and throw her arms around her stricken fiancé, she gathered her coat over her arm and walked out of the arena, the belt she was to place around the victor's waist still in the large handbag that she jauntily carried. In the seat on her right she left Licentia's advertising director. In the seat on her left she left Municipal Judge Itzhak Malfitano O'Rourke, a man New York Democrats had long hoped to persuade to run for political office because of his pre-eminent ethnic qualifications. He was to have performed the wedding ceremony.

While this happened, color man Hal Kelligan was setting the stage for the ceremony, explaining to his audience the poignant situation that had been created and the strange and affecting spectacle they were about to witness. When Licentia's advertising director recovered from his shock, he said, "Sorry, Judge," to O'Rourke, scribbled a note, made his way to Kelligan, and handed it to him. Kelligan then said that circumstances beyond the network's control prevented a telecast of the Plantagenet–Philpott-Grimes wedding and returned the audience to the studio.

Waiting to go on the air was the eleven o'clock "X-raying The News," anchored by the fast-talking twins team of Judy (female) and Jody (male), who abjured last names because they didn't sound friendly, and who had won many hearts with their personal touch and expressions of compassion. They had provided a sample of this at the end of the opening story, which was about an uprising in Central America:

"Isn't it a shame, Jody, that people can't live together in brotherhood and peace?"

"It is, Judy. When will we learn to love one another?"

"I wonder."

On this night, after a commercial for gerbil food, they used the fight as a closing item:

JODY: Oh, blimey. It's hard lines for our British cousins tonight.

JUDY: That's right, Jody. I'm afraid it is. Aubrey Philpott-Grimes didn't make it.

JODY: That's right, Judy. The Englishman was in there at the Sportitorium with the middleweight champ, Mike Turner, and he was doing all right until . . .

JUDY: Oh, Jody, that word, until! Until the twelfth round, when he took one on the chin from the champ . . .

JODY: . . . and down he went! And he was ahead on points at that time, and he couldn't get up.

JUDY: Though he tried so hard! And he was counted out. And there was no wedding afterward. Fredda Plantagenet, who was to marry him in the ring, win or lose, just got up and left. Did she jilt him, Jody?

JODY: Well, Aubrey *was* knocked out! Maybe she felt like that he left her waiting at the church! That's the news, folks. I'm Jody.

JUDY: I'm Judy.

JODY: Good night, Judy.

JUDY: Good night, Jody.

JODY: And good night to you!

JUDY: We love you!

Back at the Sportitorium, after the knockout, Aubrey had to be dragged to his corner and revived. He was in no condition to understand when Turner came over to see how he was and to say, "Tell him it was Ralph Waldo Emerson," but he was not badly hurt. He could not remember the precise sequence of events that led to his being knocked out, but he did recall that something had distracted his attention, though just what it was slipped his mind. In his dressing room, he was able to appreciate that the wedding plans could hardly have gone ahead. For one thing, there had been too long a delay while he was being brought around. For another, it would have been an anticlimax.

For Fredda, whose absence he noted, Aubrey reserved a special feeling of gratitude. In canceling the plan for a wedding in the ring, she had unerringly made the right decision. In the circumstances, it could only have been embarrassing and humiliating to him.

"I have disappointed her hopes," he said, "and she knows that I would be uncomfortable in her presence. She saves me that. As always, she thinks of others. I shall not intrude on her disappointment, as she has refrained from intruding on my grief. I shall see her tomorrow."

Brave words spoken, valorous Aubrey sagged. Rely on Fredda though he might, feel certain that she had done only what she should have, it was still a moment in which he needed consolation. He had lost his appointment to the British Economic Mission, he had seriously impaired his usefulness to the British Treasury, and he had let Fogbound down. This had been his night. He was unlikely ever to box that well again.

Fogbound managed to keep the press out, except for me — I was there ex officio — and he was determined that his man would have to answer no questions that night. He himself said nothing to Aubrey about the incident that led to Turner's landing that long right. Aubrey obviously did not remember. Fogbound had seen fighters in that condition before. It passed quickly enough. There was no point in rushing it.

With me, while Aubrey was in the shower, he was less restrained. "I told him no talking. Does Turner need economics lessons?" He paused. "Economics. That's something to ruin a fighter? And Fredda. I can understand no wedding. But does she have to shout at him? He's already fighting and answering questions."

"What about you, Sam? You're the innocent bystander in this. It's your loss, too."

Fogbound made a deprecating gesture with his hands, palms up. "Who's this Emerson?"

I told him.

"What did he say that was so important?"

"I gather it was something about men not wanting to pay taxes."

"It takes a big writer to know that?"

We heard the water go off in the shower. "I'm sorry for Aubrey," he whispered. "He brought it on himself, but I'm sorry for him. He could have been in the jaws of victory. Instead, he's in the spoils of defeat." Fogbound put a finger to his lips. "No more. Aubrey might hear."

29

THE TOMORROW to which Aubrey looked with so much hope Fredda looked to with distaste and impatience. From the dramatic point of view, she felt that it would be more effective if their affair died not with a strained and tired breakup but with the graceful, silent recognition that it was over.

She was also not happy with the papers. The sports page headlines did not trouble her:

KO'D AUBREY WITH ECONOMICS, CHAMP SAYS: BEAT HIM
    AT OWN GAME.
RALPH WALDO EMERSON WINS FOR TURNER
PHILPOTT–GRIMES, PUZZLED BY QUERY, IS KNOCKED OUT
TURNER USES RESEARCH AND BIG RIGHT HAND TO WIN

She wished that they had been different, but they pointed no finger at her. It was what was printed just below the headlines, in what we newspeople call decks, that made her uncomfortable:

Aubrey Loses Fight and Girl
No Wedding in Ring
Fredda Plantagenet Walks Out

There was also one that Fredda ignored:

Champ Won't Divulge Source of Tactics

And a headline that she did not see because Bobby Lou Bridewell had no New York newspaper outlets:

I WEPT BUCKETS

In the stories, Fredda found more detailed accounts of her conduct. One of them said,

Just before the fateful blow, Miss Plantagenet rose from her seat and shouted at her fiancé. This reporter, on the other side of the ring, was not able to make out what she said, but some who were in earshot believe that she called Philpott-Grimes a "skinny Limey bum." Whether this had any effect on the outcome of the fight, it is impossible to say. The Englishman was already distracted by Turner's question, and he might not have snapped back in time to avoid Turner's finishing right. But Miss Plantagenet plainly did not help Philpott-Grimes. She may have helped Turner.

Nevertheless, Fredda resigned herself to a final interview. As she told me when asking my opinion on whether her story might be sold to a popular magazine if fitted out with more prurient interest, she knew that Aubrey always wanted logical, explicit explanations of cause and effect. When he came to her apartment, having posed for the cameramen and promised a statement to the reporters, he looked desolate and apologetic. Fredda kissed him dutifully, sat him down, said, "Hard luck, darling," looked with real concern at his facial bruises, then said, "Aubrey, it's over." This began a painful conversation, during the first part of which Aubrey believed Fredda to be referring to his boxing career. When he understood what she meant, he said, "But, Fredda, after what you were ready to do for me?"

"I know," Fredda said, "but you lost. Anyway, it wasn't so much."

This seemed inadequate to Aubrey after the magnitude of their affair. "Because I lost the fight? Surely you don't think that I would turn my back on you if you were in a Broadway show that failed, or if your television series were canceled. That would be quite shameful."

Fredda sighed. Aubrey had no instinct about these things. "It was during round twelve. I didn't think you could keep Turner off for three rounds more with that spindle you call your left arm. And even if you did, I didn't think I could live through it. Then I remembered how you knocked out McGrath that first night because he called you a Limey. So I got up to call you a Limey, but I couldn't quite make up my mind to say it. And then Turner was wide open and you were thinking about that Emerson quote, which I still don't believe — Is there anybody more passé than Emerson? — and you missed the chance and I got so angry it just slipped out.

"Believe me, Aubrey, I am sorry from the bottom of my heart that you are not middleweight champion today. But I knew then that it was over. The skinny part doesn't matter, but you cannot breathe life back into an affair after the woman has called the man a Limey bum. The human spirit is capable of much, but it is not capable of that."

Fredda's speech brought back to Aubrey that moment in the ring when the phrase came hurtling at him. "Of course. Now I remember. *You* called me a Limey bum." He made a wry face as he pronounced it. "It was *you* who said that."

"It was."

"This is serious."

Aubrey stopped to think and Fredda could almost hear the files being shuffled in his mind "You say it was Emerson?"

"Haven't you read the papers?"

"Ralph Waldo Emerson? What has he to do with taxation?"

"It was a general observation, Aubrey. Emerson was within his legal rights in making it. Anyway, the next time you're asked that during a fight, you'll know the answer."

Aubrey caught Fredda's tone and the last tinge of apology left his voice. He put forward his analysis. "I leave aside the fact that you may have contributed to my defeat. I am a professional fighter and I should have kept my mind on my work no matter what was shouted at me or what questions were put to me."

"That's true," Fredda said. "I usually refuse to take academic examinations when I'm on stage. If you had asked me about it, I could have told you before the fight."

"I can also see," Aubrey said, "that in the aftermath of the fight you are under strong emotional pressure. I know what it is like when fate dashes the cup from one's lips."

"Fate would be acceptable," Fredda said. "This was Ralph Waldo Emerson."

"But all of that apart," Aubrey went on, "the knowledge that when I was in the ring with the middleweight champion of the world, you could address me in so vulgar a fashion, and with an epithet based on nationality" — Aubrey shook his head as though Fredda were defending herself — "I don't see how I could ever forget it."

Fredda did not know whether a good playwright would make her penitent or matter-of-fact at this point. She achieved a blend of the two. "I agree," she said.

Aubrey rolled on as though delivering a lecture. "It is not a foundation on which a happy marriage can be built. There is more to life than swanning about. And we have learned that when you are in a tight corner, your courage fails you. You pack up."

"I categorically deny swanning," Fredda said. "And if I were you, I wouldn't talk about failure. I have heard of men unable to attend their weddings because they were dead drunk. I can understand that. But to be out cold — you certainly rose to the occasion. Maybe we should have had a prompter at ringside to remind you to go on fighting when Turner asked that question."

"I may not have won the fight," Aubrey said. "I cannot see that that is any reason for not marrying me. Nor can I see that you should have married me if I had won, if that were the only reason. Marriage requires mutual respect, not hero-worship. You were to be my wife, not the head of a fan club."

"My dear boy," Fredda said distantly, "I shall be neither."

"Jolly good," Aubrey said. "This has been a close-run thing."

"Listen, my stringy friend, I gave you the best months you ever had. In your position, I would be grateful."

"You have this strange notion," Aubrey said, "that it lies within your power to dispense something unique. That belief, which I have always taken *cum grano salis,* with a grain of salt, seems to me to rest on a misunderstanding of the essential physical sameness of women, and of the size and distribution of the female population."

"If I were you," Fredda said, "I would not advertise my inability to appreciate true quality."

"Empty boasting," Aubrey said, buttoning his jacket.

"My God." Fredda addressed the world at large in round, tragic tones. "To think that I even read Milton Friedman with him." She enunciated clearly as Aubrey opened the door. "You remember the belt? My brilliant investment? I've sent it to Turner. And you are a skinny Limey bum. You are also a nut. Your attitude to the income tax proves it."

"One other thing," Aubrey said. "I have counted eighty-four electrically powered appliances in this flat. I had hoped that my example might lead you into a more sensible way of life. Have you ever used your television program to inform the American people about the realities of the international supply position? Have you ever, in that program, so much as hinted at the need to conserve energy?"

"I could go on at the beginning of the program and suggest that they switch off," Fredda said. "Would that satisfy you?"

"A typical response." Aubrey moved toward the door. "Taking the most extreme example so as to make the argument absurd. It is not that you are evil, Fredda, but you are unthinking. If the American economy should ever be brought low, it will be from within, and thanks to its casual and gluttonous consumption of natural resources. That is a considered judgment."

"Your considered judgment," Fredda replied as the door closed, "must be one of the least sought after in the English-speaking world."

These unsentimental messages were the last words to pass between them. Fredda sat back in her chair and smiled. What had happened was, in a way, too bad, but nothing lasted forever. And Aubrey had held up his end in the final scene better than she ever dreamed he would. She thought it had been carried off rather well, considering what a cliché it usually was.

Aubrey went from Fredda's apartment to Fogbound's office, where Fogbound and I were leafing through telegrams and looking at a cabbage pie that a well-wisher had sent to cheer Aubrey up. I thought of the phrase often used when prominent people are caught in crimes and not sent to prison — "He has suffered enough" — and suggested that the existence of the pie be kept from him. Among the telegrams was one from Savory saying that the fight had left him sad beyond his ability to, and that Aubrey would always be welcome at his parties. There was one from Bindle in which he congratulated Aubrey on his sportsmanship in not complaining about Turner's unorthodox tactics and said that there was a lesson in the fight for the western nations, which was that we could not dictate the weapons or strategy our adversaries might use, and so it was necessary to be ready to meet all eventualities. And there was one from the British Economic Mission which said, "LIP. STIFF. THREAVE (ON SECONDMENT)."

Aubrey's first description of his conversation with Fredda was given in Fogbound's office and was delayed while I informed him that the cuckoo clock had been invented during the bitter winter of 1640 by a Bavarian farmer who had little else to do.

"Fredda and I are finished," he said.

Fogbound, hardly surprised but playing along, asked why.

"We are poles apart," Aubrey said. "Success obscured our differences. Adversity has revealed them."

"You don't seem cast down," I said.

"On the contrary. I count myself fortunate to have drawn back from the brink."

This was true. Aubrey told the story of his breakup with Fredda with indignation rather than self-pity. Unable to use my patient smile or hollow laugh, I nodded knowingly, another of my acting accomplishments. The knowing nod seemed justified because I had once said that they were disparate types, which was not only a fair characterization but enabled me to use a word I had shortly before worked into an editorial.

Fogbound, though he clucked sympathetically at Aubrey's story, felt that his fighter was not angry enough about Fredda's intervention during the twelfth round. Fogbound did not believe that she should be hanged, but that was because she was a woman and he was old-fashioned about such things. A firing squad at dawn — and no blindfold — seemed to him sufficient.

"On Devil's Island," I said, "the executioner's pay after operating the guillotine was a can of sardines."

"Always fish," Fogbound complained. "From the beginning with Aubrey, mackerel. Then kippers. Now sardines."

There remained Aubrey's statement to the press: "I shall always admire Miss Plantagenet. However, irreconcilable differences have arisen, and she and I have agreed to go our separate ways. Her conduct during the Turner fight was a factor. I am obliged to add that my conduct during that fight was a factor, as well."

Fredda also played the game: "I shall always admire Mr. Philpott-Grimes. I think that his statement covers the situation and I have nothing to add."

Fogbound had a final comment. "High class," he said. "I almost forgot we lost."

30

IN THE NEXT forty-eight hours, during which Fogbound continued thinking of condign (an editorial writer's word, meaning appropriate) punishments for Fredda, Aubrey ate and slept and read parts of several newspapers. He granted interviews to British and American sportswriters, in which he refused to assign any blame to Fredda. "Nothing to do with it," he said. "It was my job to go on fighting. That's what I was in there for."

He also spoke well of Turner. "Extremely clever. Took me quite by surprise. Emerson is a bit off the beaten track when one thinks of economics. But he is a great American writer. And I have been made welcome in this country. It would have been no more than courteous for me to know."

Where had Turner got the idea and the question that beat him? Aubrey was gracious. "There are many intelligent Americans," he said. "Any number of them might have made the suggestion."

He was interviewed also by H. Barrington Whiteside, who had broadcast the fight home to Britain and who had announced not long before the end, "Turner is living on borrowed time and he knows it. Turner is desperately tired — unless, of course, he is acting. Who can tell?" In a reference to Aubrey, Whiteside went on, "But the man they said had no stamina" — who "they" were, he did not specify — "is showing them."

Unlike Fredda and Turner, Whiteside could not be heard by Aubrey and his remarks had no effect on the fight's outcome. When he interviewed Aubrey, it was principally to assure him that, even with the sour taste of defeat still in his mouth, his place in the history of British boxing was secure. And what were his plans, now that he had been battered insensible in his vain but glorious pursuit of the middleweight crown and had had some time to think about it? Aubrey said that he did not know but hoped that his usefulness to his country's well-being was not at an end. He wished this the more strongly, Aubrey said, because so many of his countrymen had been up in the small hours of the morning, listening to the Turner fight on the wireless. Their heavy consumption of energy, with its concomitant cost to the nation, had gone for naught.

All of this Aubrey managed in forty-eight hours, and he did it without Fogbound. Fogbound had not deserted him, however. With nice judgment, he had seen that Aubrey did not want his company at this time, and he had accepted that without shame or hurt. At the end of the forty-eight hours, Aubrey returned to Fogbound's office. Not that it was any more attractive than it had been — if anything, the dust lay more heavily than ever and seemed to add to the melancholy — but Aubrey knew that he would find tactful friends there.

"Tell me," he said, "why are there so many abandoned

mattresses in the streets of this city? Is there some significance here that I fail to grasp?

I asked whether he had seen an unusual number.

"It's a rare day that I don't see at least one. Are they put out as a signal of some sort? A code? It *is* rather grotty."

I said I did not know but that I would ask our city desk about it.

"And why will New York landlords put up signs that say, WILL BUILD TO SUITE? Don't they know that's wrong?"

Fogbound, sensing that Aubrey was under strain, cut in gently. "Aubrey, I'm surprised you're not reading your books."

"I tried, Sam, but I couldn't. Books are all very well. There is no substitute for action. I might have raised the morale of British workers, and productivity with it, simply by beating Turner. I failed."

Fogbound had just put his arm around Aubrey's shoulders, and had just begun to say that his wife would like Aubrey to come to dinner, and that she would prepare jam roly poly with custard if he wanted it, and another of Aubrey's one-time favorites, baked beans on toast, when there was a knock on the door. I opened it, and there stood Doreen, with Barbetta. He was dressed as I had not seen him before, in a brown wool tweed suit, with silk knit tie and a sleeveless wool sweater, a cotton square in his breast pocket, and a button-down shirt. He was hatless and, so far as I could see, subdued and ashamed. About Doreen, there was an air of dedicated happiness, as with a nurse on a recruiting poster, which she managed in spite of the sprinkling of Disco Dust in her hair, and in spite of being dressed in the soccer look, which included shorts, a tight-fitting half-sleeved shirt, knee-length socks, and, reaching above her ankles, rubber-soled shoes with reinforced toes. It was one of the popular costumes of the day, expressing the unity of women's fashion with the world of action. She began speaking as soon as she was through the door, but Fogbound interrupted her.

"A stranger in our mist," he shouted. "Nobody invited you. In here, we're friends. Barbetta we don't need." He pointed to the door. "Out."

Doreen ignored him. "I've brought Frankie with me," she said, making what seemed an obvious point. "I want all of you to know the real Frankie."

"Thanks." Fogbound was still shouting. "I know him."

"No, you don't. Not the real Frankie."

"Hold on, Sam," Aubrey said. "Give her a chance."

Fogbound subsided. "It wasn't the real Frankie we knew before? It was somebody different?"

"Somebody very different," Doreen said. "It wasn't the real Frankie at all."

"I have a split personality," Frankie put in proudly.

"Exactly," said Doreen. "He's slightly schizoid."

"I'd hardly say that," Frankie objected. "I'd describe it as more of a dichotomy problem. Bifurcation, if you like."

"Let me get this straight," I said. "I know Frankie the Barb, who threatens people, packs a gun, turns off air conditioners, and likes molls with nice teeth. Who is the other Frankie?"

"This very kind gentleman here," Doreen said.

"The other side of the coin, so to speak," Barbetta explained.

"What sort of talk for a gangster is that?"

"That's just the point," Doreen said excitedly. "This is the real Frankie, not the gangster. He's good, really he is, so good."

"Prove it," Fogbound said. Aubrey nodded agreement.

Doreen gave a cue line. "We're sorry Aubrey lost the fight, aren't we, Frankie?"

Barbetta, eyes on the ceiling, nodded.

I suggested that it had probably gone better at the rehearsal, and Doreen looked as though she might cry. "He tries to be good. But there are times when the bad side takes over."

"That's what it means to be dichotomous," Barbetta said.

"Dichotomous, schmichotomous," Fogbound said, in a dazzling display of vocal control, "all I know is he put us through plenty with that Jack Smith. And he's all the time going around with a gun. It's here" — Fogbound slapped his pocket. "It's there" — he put a finger to his left armpit. "Suppose he shoots me when he's the gangster Frankie. Will I get better when he's not?"

"That isn't fair," Doreen said.

Barbetta spoke up. "I can explain the gun. I've looked into these things. Violence is a power resource. The gun is a function of the dynamics of violence."

Fogbound shook his head impatiently and went on the attack. "How's the moll business?"

"I am his fiancée, thank you." Doreen extended her left hand to show an engagement ring.

Aubrey spoke up. "Even when he's in the gangster phase?"

Doreen blushed. "Then I'm his moll."

"How'd he get into this condition?" I asked. "Does he know what set him off?"

"It was his father."

"That's elementary. But what happened? Was he a child of the streets, an urchin?"

"No." Barbetta seemed humiliated by this shortcoming.

I had come across a sound I liked. "You never urched at all?"

"Never," Barbetta said in a strangled voice.

"So what's the trouble?" It was Fogbound.

Barbetta was barely audible. "It was psychic deprivation."

Doreen came to the rescue. "His father was emotionally absent. That was the root of the problem."

Barbetta took heart. "I'm complex. It goes deep."

"So control yourself," Fogbound said.

Barbetta exploded. "Control yourself! Control yourself! Don't you understand the concept of latent hostility?" He began to sob. "My case crystallizes the neglect of society."

Doreen took his hand. "You!" She faced Fogbound, who was looking on, astonished at the effect of his words. "You won't give him a chance. I brought him here so that you could understand him. Now see what's happened. And you!" She addressed Aubrey. "Our Mr. Broad-minded himself. You've given him no help, no sympathy at all."

"I haven't said a word," Aubrey said.

"Precisely. You haven't said a word. You see what he's wearing. That might have told you something."

"What should it tell us?" Fogbound asked.

Barbetta spoke disjointedly, through the tears. "You have to know what image you want to project, then find the kind of suit that will help you to project it."

Not having been denounced by Doreen, who had apparently overlooked me, I tried again. "Your father didn't beat you. He didn't disown you. What was it?"

Barbetta was calm now. "My parents simply did not provide the parenting I needed. My siblings suffered less. They were made of stronger stuff, and were more goal-oriented. But I was searching for a different role model, as young people will. There is money in the family, and I asked my father

to endow a university chair in self-awareness and self-actual-
ization. He wouldn't do it. He put the money into trust
funds for us, instead. Probably without knowing it, he was
telling me to be selfish. It did something to me, made me
bitter."

"Maybe it wasn't your parents' fault," I said. "Maybe they
had inferior parenting. Have you thought of that?"

Barbetta was not listening. "I shouldn't blame my father,
really. He couldn't know how much I feared rejection, how
it would hurt and warp me." Barbetta had delivered most
of the recitation in an emotionless voice, but here a note of
satisfaction crept in. "Now the split is out of hand."

"His analyst says it's one of the most difficult cases he's
ever seen," Doreen said impressively. "But we are not to give
up hope. Frankie is still telling him things he hasn't heard
before and he doesn't know when something Frankie says
will give him the clue he needs."

Barbetta was not satisfied that Doreen had conveyed the
full measure of his affliction. "I'm in analysis but I'm severely
traumatized." He nodded, as though to convince us. "The
analyst is baffled. I may be beyond help."

I suppressed an urge to say that millions would envy him,
and he continued in a heavy voice. "It isn't fair. Doreen
deserves a house, children, security, With me, what is there?
A sordid existence. Uncertainty. Fear. She should leave me.
It is the only way."

"I will never leave you," Doreen said simply, as a monarch's
consort might in time of danger. "Come along, Frankie. We
must go." She looked around the room. "I am asking for
nothing more than a little Christian charity." She opened
the door, and with Frankie too embarrassed to look back,
they left.

"Jewish charities, yes," Fogbound said, "A Christian charity I can't help her with."

I let it pass, and so did Aubrey, and there was a long silence before Fogbound spoke again. "That Frankie. A regular Jackal and Hyde. And you heard how good he talks? Just like the rest of us."

31

THE KNOWLEDGE that Barbetta was not a gangster, which should have brought us contentment, instead made Fogbound feel worse. It did the same to me. It is one thing to have your life complicated by a Mafioso. To have it complicated by someone who only thinks he is a Mafioso, and that only when his psychological disturbance is out of control, is another. I had, after all, investigated Barbetta. If I had won an award for my implacable digging, I might have made journalistic history by being forced to give it back. Aubrey's immediate reaction was mixed. He was, on the whole, glad that Doreen was not involved with a gangster, but he thought that this diluted her New York experience and he felt, as we did, humiliated.

It was a few days after the Barbetta visit that Aubrey received a telegram from Doreen. It said, "SO SORRY." Two days after that, Aubrey's telephone rang. It was Doreen. In a small voice, she asked whether he could come to see her. He was not to come to the flat. She gave him another address, which proved to be that of the Futuramotel, which stands on the West Side in the Fifties and is made entirely of glass and plastic. Signs in the lobby advertise its Salle Chateau de Richelieu, which offers Haute Cuisine Pour Le Gourmet, and its Honcho Room, where sixteen-ounce steaks are the specialty and the waiters wear ponchos and on them buttons that say, I'M A PONCHO HONCHO. There is also a coffee shop called The Minaret.

Doreen was waiting for him in the doorway to her room, and Aubrey's first impulse was to ask how she had chosen the motel, and his second to ask how it came to be built at all. She looked meek and frightened, and was clutching a hot water bottle, so Aubrey realized at once that she needed protection and reassurance. The hot water bottle was as close as she could come to home. He took her hand and she smiled bravely as she motioned him in and to a chair. As he sat down, she looked at him for a moment, then dropped her head.

"It's nice to see you again, Aubrey," she said primly.

Aubrey said that it was nice to see her, too.

Then Doreen looked tragically at the ceiling, cried out. "He's left me," and burst into tears.

Aubrey allowed national characteristics to take command. "I'll make you a nice cup of tea," he said.

Doreen put her hands to her face before she shook her head. Aubrey interpreted the movements to mean that there were no facilities for brewing tea in her room, though this was hard for him to believe. He sat still, helpless.

The tears showed no sign of slackening and Aubrey put his arm around her waist to show her that she still had a friend. In a moment, her face was pressed against his narrow chest, moistening his shirt. For a while he shook in rhythm with her. Then, gradually, the sobs became less frequent and

Doreen said, "He loved me only when he was bonkers. And when I thought he was out with the Mafia, he wasn't. He was seeing his psychiatrist. It's a moldy swizz."

She looked up at him, pushed back the hair that had fallen over her face, and dried her cheeks and eyes with his handkerchief.

"*Primum*," Aubrey said, "why not tell me what happened?"

Doreen straightened up, sat back, took a deep breath, and began. They had been at her place, listening to the radio. Frankie liked rock; he liked to sing along with the performers, and the sentiments appealed to him. His eyes would light up on hearing, "Break it up and break it down, / Vandalism Rock just owns this town," and "Eye for eye and tooth for tooth, / I don't care, call me uncouth, / You cross me once, I'll cut you dead, / And sink your body in a coat of lead."

"That's what I like to hear," he would tell her. "These songs. They got something to say."

On the fateful night, rock had given way to a program of old popular songs. "Played for our senior citizens," the announcer said, "but everybody's welcome to listen. They're great old tunes." Remembering a number of difficult incidents, Doreen got up to change stations, but Frankie told her not to. "Good old songs. They got something to say, too."

It began harmlessly with one of the big bands of the Thirties, with a girl vocalist and the drummer, who also did comic turns, in a lively, fun-loving rendition of "It Takes Two to Make a Marriage, It Takes Two to Make a Fight." Then came a romantic song that reflected the anticommunist mood of the late 1940s and 1950s, "Are You Now or Have You Ever Been in Love with Me?"

The trouble set in when the male vocalist took the lead on the third song, "You Rekindled the Flame." I remembered its being played in the final medley at college dances, with other sentimental favorites like "Goodnight, Sweetheart," and "Easy to Love," though it implicitly acknowledged the high rate of divorce in American life:

You rekindled the flame, you rekindled the flame,
When you took my picture out of the frame,
You rekindled, you relit the flame.
You restarted the game, you restarted the game,
When you said you'd abandon my name,
You rekindled, you relit the flame.
We expected happy wedlock, we seemed to merge so well,
But our life was one long deadlock, and so our joint stock fell.
But you rekindled the flame, you rekindled the flame,
Oh! I'll take the blame, if you'll make things the same,
For, darling, you rekindled the flame.

Frankie, who had barely stirred while the song filled the room, was transported. "A golden oldie," he said. "The kind my folks used to dance to." He smiled, rose, and began gliding around the floor, humming the while. Doreen rose to dance with him, but he motioned her away and stood still. "Gee, I wish my old man and me was friends. I'm thinking. Something that wise guy mediaman said. Maybe the old man had problems. Maybe him and his old man didn't get along so good."

"I do remember Mr. Mercer suggesting that your parents' parenting may have been shy of the mark."

"The old lady was all right," Frankie said. "For her, okay parenting. But the old man, maybe not."

"Do you think you've been too hard on him?"

There was no reply. Frankie was humming and gliding and he was speaking, so far as Doreen could see, to the wall, with his voice coming from the middle of his mouth, rather than from the gangsterish side. He sounded like the Frankie we heard during his recent visit to Fogbound's office, but happier. "Dad, may I cut in, please? I'd like to dance with Mother." He smiled, stood back, bowed, then extended his arm as though to encircle a partner, and began gliding once more. "Mother," he said, "I do so enjoy it when we're all together."

Doreen approached him again. She had not seen him this way before. "Frankie. Frankie, you did have some happy times with your father. There were times when you did get along. You just wouldn't own up to it."

Tension had made Doreen's voice loud, and it penetrated Frankie's reverie, "I'm not afraid to admit it," he said.

"Admit it, then," Doreen said.

Frankie fell silent. His jaw muscles tightened, he clenched his teeth and his arms grew rigid, and he seemed to be under physical as well as mental strain. Suddenly, a great wheezing sound came from him, he shook his head a few times as though to clear it, ran his hands through his hair, now wet with perspiration, straightened his shoulders, and rose. His voice was high and shaky. "It's finished. I've beaten it. My personality has been reintegrated. I can go home." His eyes, on Doreen, looked beyond her. "Home," he said again, dreamily.

Doreen, wanting to share his hour of deliverance, hugged him. Frankie stepped away. "I'll have to check this with Dr. Kindler," he said, "but I'm sure my recovery will depend on a complete break with the old life. I'm sufficiently familiar with the nature of my malady to know that."

"But Frankie," Doreen said, "we've waited for this moment. We've been everything to each other."

Frankie raised his hand before his eyes, as though to shut out argument and the past. "Really, it's pointless to argue. We mustn't jeopardize the cure. But I'll always be grateful. You made the cure possible. You made me face the truth about my father and myself." He took her hand and kissed it. "Please don't misunderstand me. I know there is no Morden fortune. Let me help you."

Doreen refused proudly. She had clothes, including a wine leather waistcoat, matching trousers with cummerbund and spotted shirt, a coordinated check shirt and rounded-collar blouse, a merino cardigan overblouse, sashed with a corded belt, and complemented by a velvet jacket. She also had jewelry, including an array of fashion glasses, and a range of wigs ordered from England, made of three kinds of fiber, and named for birds. Doreen's favorites were the Dove, Lark, Osprey, and Curlew. All of this had been provided by Frankie. If she needed money, she would sell them. She raised her eyes to his, crying a little. "Now go," she said huskily. Frankie turned quickly and left.

In a moment, he was back. "One last point. I'm sorry I used the name Barbetta. Italian-Americans have suffered enough because of the Mafia. I should not have contributed to that."

"You mean Frankie Barbetta is not your real name?"

"That's right."

"What is?"

"François Boisvilliers. We're an old Huguenot family."

"Why are you telling me this?"

"I thought it would interest you."

"You are round the bend," Doreen said.

Frankie nodded and left.

There was little more to tell, except how Doreen had left her apartment, even though the rent was paid for weeks to come, had found the motel room, and had mustered the courage to call Aubrey. She would never have called him, she said, if he and Fredda had not parted. But Americans seemed to have no constancy. Fredda and Frankie were apropos.

"Those rapid changes of character," Aubrey said. "They must have been tricky for you."

"Oh, not too bad. Suppose I was dressed for Frankie's gangster side and he changed. I'd wipe off some of the lipstick and the rest of the makeup and pull my skirt down and sit up straight. If he went the other way, I'd push out my chest and cross my legs and hike my skirt up a bit. And add makeup. Especially mascara. I could tart myself up and almost believe I was a psychiatric social worker. Frankie's ideas about these things were rather limited."

"You're a brave girl."

"Aubrey, do you still care for me a little? After all I've done?"

Aubrey was relieved to get to the point. "I'll take you back. I want you back."

Doreen snuggled her head precariously on his shoulder and sighed with satisfaction. "I'm a fallen woman."

"That's all right. I'm a fallen man. Knocked over, actually."

"On that point, Aubrey," Doreen said, "there is something you should know. It was Frankie who gave Turner the idea of asking you those rotten questions."

"Oh, no," said Aubrey.

"And Frankie supplied the questions."

"But how? He struck me as an economic illiterate."

"Oh, come off it, Aubrey. Frankie mugged up a few old textbooks and a volume of quotations, and there you are."

"But how did he get to Turner?"

Doreen reached for her handbag and took out a piece of paper. It had a straight pencil line running across it, and at the top, "I show them Frankie's no dummy." The line showed Frankie's approach to Turner's manager, who was told how Frankie had masterminded Proletariano's victory and his scheme for victory now. He would give them the questions; they would see how the fight went; they could use them or not, as they chose.

"And that was it?"

"I'm afraid so."

"You were at the fight, I suppose?"

"Oh, yes. But in rather distant seats. Frankie didn't want us to be seen. He thought you or Mr. Franklin might get the wind up about the quiz."

Audrey nodded. "Tell me. The driver chap with the gun — an actor?"

"A chauffeur. He'd been with Frankie for a while. He knew his part. Parts, really."

"It's time to face up to it," Aubrey said. "I have not been a mind-boggling success here."

"Nor I. Taking up with someone stark, staring, frothing mad." Aubrey was about to say something charitable and consoling, but Doreen continued. "Not that you did any better. I thought it was the Americans who went to England to get antiques, not the other way round."

Aubrey took his customary balanced view. "You are not being generous. And youth isn't everything. Will it take you long to pack?"

"Peasy. I've scarcely unpacked."

"Good. I'll just pop off to the flat and make things ready, and then I'll be back to fetch you. Better wear your mac. There may be a spot or two of drizzle."

"Mind how you go," Doreen said.

32

WE WERE HOLDING A FINAL POST-MORTEM in Fogbound's office, Aubrey and Doreen sitting cosily together on the high-backed bench and holding hands, Fogbound tilted back with his feet on his desk, and I standing meditatively by the window trying to coax some philosophic fumes out of my pipe.

"So it was Barbetta who inoculated all those economics ideas in Turner's head?" Fogbound remarked. "From experience, I thought I knew all the ways to lose, but this is the first time we're kayoed by a reference book."

"My fault entirely," said Aubrey. "I should have paid no attention to him, as you recommended, or else have done rather more supplemental reading."

"Still, I'm surprised," Fogbound observed. "He knows Ralph Walter Emerson and you don't. It must be the English schools — not so good."

"We must face facts," I said. "We perceived Barbetta as a typical Mafia hood. We had no contingency plans when he used the tools of a liberal education against us. And we must admit that getting Mike Turner to remember all those questions was one of the major pedagogical feats of our time."

"Frankie told you he was smart, but you wouldn't listen," Doreen joined in.

"Smart," Fogbound snorted. "He hurts law-obliging people. That's smart? Where is he now?"

"With his parents, I believe."

"They took him back?"

"Maybe they frisked him first," I said.

"One meets all kinds," Aubrey said. "Remember John-John McKenzie? An admirable chap. I've just heard from him."

"He wants another fight?"

"Not with me. But he does suggest that we meet and fire a few at the next England–West Indies test at Lords." He glanced at Fogbound. "That's cricket. I have accepted, of course. And he sent me a calypso he commissioned." He handed a sheet of paper to Doreen. "It's overstated but charming. I couldn't possible read it to you myself."

Doreen held the paper as though it were a scroll and she was reading a proclamation. "Ode On A Gallant Briton," she began. "Or Aubrey The Martyr:

"If there were more Britons with Aubrey's skill,
The British Empire might be existing still.
If there were more Britons with Aubrey's skill,
The British Empire might be existing still.
Imagine six hundred million people under one king.
That's what it was, a glorious thing.
Six hundred million on whom the sun never set,
The eighth wonder of the world, the finest empire yet.
Aubrey bust his head and do his best,
But what can one alone do against all the rest?
What they got now is the Westminster spectacle,
For truly Britain has become ramshackle.

The whole world looks on in wonderment
To see if Britain can again be prominent.
Great Englishmen like Raleigh, Drake, and Clive,
Would catch a disgust if they were alive.
Britons today really should be shame,
Every time that they hear Aubrey's name.
Her Majesty the Queen should give him the Garter,
For love of country, he make himself martyr.
The only living Briton who truly got the will
To deserve the mantle of Sir Winston Churchill."

Aubrey smiled in embarrassment. "The excesses might be less noticeable if we could hear it with the music."

Fogbound, who had worn a serious expression while Doreen was reading, probably because of the historic names recited, and who had applauded when she finished, now benignly had a little joke. It was about a fight in Syracuse and the need to go into training. Aubrey said there would be no fight in Syracuse or anywhere else — "*Non sum qualis eram*," he said, "I am not what I used to be" — and Fogbound burst into laughter which fifteen minutes earlier he would not have believed lay within him.

"Fellow colleagues," he said, "I can't call off the fight in Syracuse." He held up his hand to cut off protests. "I never booked it. I could see that Aubrey's boxing future was over."

Further conversation revealed that Aubrey and Doreen intended to be married. They had not settled this explicitly before, but when Fogbound asked what he proposed to do now, Aubrey said, "I hadn't thought about it. Get married, I rather imagine." Doreen had tittered agreement. It was the first time I had seen anyone do this, and I noted it with satisfaction.

Fogbound offered Aubrey congratulations and shook Doreen's hand, and I did the same. "But after that?"

Doreen, a little breathlessly and without clearing it with Aubrey, replied, "We're going back to England."

I objected. "Not back to England. You're accustomed to New York now. You're accustomed to the excitement, the bright lights, the *petites fêtes.*"

"We've lost our reason for being here," Aubrey said, "and our status. Wherefore, *cras ingens iterabimus aequor.* Tomorrow we embark again on the mighty ocean."

I suggested that they ask for asylum on humanitarian grounds to get away from the taxes, and that Threave apply with them. Aubrey and Doreen did not think this funny, and Fogbound chimed in. "Go back to England. There I think you're more at home. Only come back and see us some time."

"A little gray home in the West End," I said. "Suppose you had some offers to stay. Would that make any difference?"

It turned out that offers had come in, one of them a position as boxing coach and adjunct professor of humane values at a state university campus in Missouri, where Aubrey would also be expected to fight exhibition bouts from time to time. He thought Bindle might be behind it. "Also, a university dean called to ask whether I would be interested if they could find the money for a chair of Anglo-American Cultural Patterns." He drew some notes from his pocket and glanced at them as he went on. "He said that I would be expected to visit Britain at least every other year to observe emergent paradigmatic acculturation. And I would be free to hypothesize in a supportive environment. And there was something about team teaching in a hermeneutics seminar."

"Herman Noodnick, the promoter at the old Saint Nicholas Arena? He's teaching school now?" Fogbound asked.

"Hermeneutics. Having to do with interpretation."

"I was thinking of somebody else."

"None of that tempts you?" I asked.

"Not really," Aubrey said.

"Nor me." Doreen sniffed. "Frankly, I could never be happy in a country where leaflets turn up in one's post offering breath protection. I'm becoming rather browned-off about it. We don't need breath protection. We don't have strong mouth odor, thank you very much."

On cue from me, my brow furrowed. "What will you do?"

"I'm thinking of trying newspaper work," Aubrey said. "I've had no training, but it doesn't seem difficult."

"Why," I inquired with what I hoped was a trace of asperity, "do you say that?"

"I've watched. A smattering of literacy. A certain inquisitiveness. They seem to be all that is required."

"It may look simple," I said. "It's deceptive. The entire human comedy is yours to deal with. There may be a studied casualness in our manner. That is because we have learned to carry our weighty responsibilities without complaining and even with a certain grace. Anyway, I would have expected the two of you to open a tobacconist's shop."

"A tobacconist's," Doreen exclaimed. "Why on earth?"

"Aubrey doesn't smoke," Fogbound said.

"Nor do I," Doreen added. "So why a tobacconist's?"

I defended my position. "No reason. It is simply one of the things English people do. Or so I have always understood."

"It is true," Aubrey acknowledged, "that tobacco brings the Exchequer a large revenue and that taxes on tobacco can be raised to almost any level without discouraging consumption. That provides a welcome element of flexibility for the Chancellor. But I hadn't thought of becoming a tobacconist."

"You will not become a tobacconist," Doreen declared,

"whatever our American friends may wish. Nor will I. I'm sure the advice is well meant, but we'll live our own lives, thank you very much."

Doreen was becoming snappish. That "Thank you very much" had a distant tone. Fogbound cut in to ask when they were leaving, and they looked at each other before Aubrey said that they wanted to be married as soon as possible and it ought to be in their own country.

Doreen backed him up. "One wants to be in familiar surroundings. And if it's to be a church wedding, we might find ourselves with one of your hearty American clergymen. The kind who's written a book or two. The self-help sort of thing. I shouldn't want that."

A few weeks later, I ran into Fogbound in Paddy Hanrahan's. He was at the bar, where we had met on the memorable occasion when all of this began, and he was staring through the familiar cigar smoke. I greeted him with news garnered from my vast sources. First, Representative Bindle (D.–Mo.) had launched an investigation into the influence of Washington party-giving on the formation of government policy. Bindle was quoted as saying that he was not investigating lobbying as such but rather the manipulation that might take place at social affairs. A clever hostess might affect the decision-making process by her selection of guests and the way she seated them at the dinner table. There were people in Washington who gave parties constantly. Why? Bindle was also quoted as saying that the investigation was not to be interpreted as directed at Simco Savory. He would have to submit to the inquiry with the rest, but Bindle was confident that he would emerge in a favorable light.

Fogbound then challenged me to guess who had telephoned him that morning, and when I surrendered without trying, gave the answer. It *was* Savory, much troubled because he had lost a great attraction in Aubrey, and because letters to Barbetta, with whom he hoped to recoup, were coming back undelivered. The news that Barbetta was not a gangster had left Savory relieved. "I feared that his silence meant that the underworld had dealt out rough justice to one of its own," he had said. He told Fogbound that if anyone came to his attention who might help the campaign for the equality of the male party-giver, he would be ever so obliged if Fogbound would let him know.

I moved to my second item — Fredda Plantagenet and Jack Smith were being seen together. I had counted on this to inflame Fogbound; instead, he merely grunted automatically at the sound of Smith's name and gave thanks that Aubrey was not around to witness this act of perfidy. This brought Aubrey back into the picture, and Fogbound recalled the touching scenes before they parted.

Aubrey, who had taken all the punishment and gone through all the rigorous training, was returning to England with little more money than he had when he came. Fogbound had offered to give him some, or at the very least to lend him enough to get his marriage and journalistic career started. "I don't like to see you go back to England without renumeration," Fogbound said. But Aubrey, though much affected, had replied firmly that his money had gone to the Exchequer as the result of a policy deliberately decided on and soundly based.

Besides, Aubrey had said, they would have no trouble supporting themselves. If he didn't make it in journalism, he could go back to being a jobbing clerk, and Doreen would surely be a frugal housewife. She understood Britain's predicament. In dire circumstances, she could go back to the bank teller's career she was pursuing when they met in her pre-moll days. More important, he and Doreen understood each other perfectly. Only the day before, they had agreed at once, without argument, to alternate getting out of bed first in the morning to switch on the electric fire and make tea.

I told Fogbound that it was as well that Doreen did not know that the average housewife covered four miles and put in twenty-five hours a year just making beds. Then I sucked at my pipe. I still got tobacco juice in my mouth while doing this, but that seemed to me part (and parcel; why not?) of the editorial writer's burden.

Fogbound now returned to Aubrey. There had been a poignant reminder, a letter from a London firm of "Gentlemen's Outfitters" on Jermyn Street, which felt that Aubrey, with his devotion to his City of London garb, was giving Americans an incomplete impression of the range of British men's wear and actually choking off the exports he so dearly loved. The firm was enterprisingly offering to provide Aubrey with a complete wardrobe, so that he could show America British men's clothes at their best. Somebody had neglected to put air-mail postage on the letter, and it arrived after Aubrey's departure. Fogbound did not pass it along. He knew that the offer no longer held, and that even if it did, Aubrey's rigid standards would lead him to turn it down.

"You think he would have done better if he never met Fredda?"

"Irrelevant," I said, unable to avoid the direct question. "Also incompetent and immaterial. He did not beat Turner. Turner knocked him out. That's all the record books will show."

"I wish him luck. About Doreen I'm not so sure."

"I thought she behaved well at that last dinner at your house. As English molls go, she isn't bad."

"Maybe, but did she have to lean over to Aubrey and whisper about a jolly good tuck-in of English roast beef with Yorkshire pudding and sprouts? At the dinner table? That's manners?"

"How are you feeling these days about Fredda?"

"A Limey bum Aubrey wasn't. But between her and that Jack Smith, I'm on her side. I only hope she treats him worse than Aubrey." He looked at his watch. "Hey, I better go home and clean up. Pauline wants me to look nice."

"What's up?"

"Our anniversary. We're going to a play."

I said that I had not realized that he was such a social being, and Fogbound looked at me sadly. The week before, he had walked into the dining room, there to be confronted by a large sign leaning against the wall that read, DANCE TO PANCHITO THE RUMBA KING. He had escaped Panchito's exotic rhythms only by promising Mrs. Franklin this night out.

"What are you going to see?"

"I can't remember the name, but it's English. For my education. And training for our trip."

"What trip?"

"To England. I almost forgot. You're invited, too. Aubrey's going to be a knight." Fogbound pulled out a letter. "They're giving him initials. K.C.V.O. The K.C. I suppose stands for Knights of Columbus, which doesn't sound so big to me. We have them here. The V.O. I don't know."

"Knight Commander of the Victorian Order," I said. "A high honor. Aubrey will kneel before the Queen and be tapped on the shoulder with a sword."

"I hope she doesn't miss."

"After that, if my knowledge of heraldry serves me aright, he will receive, in what the British are pleased to call due course, the star of the order, which is a silver-faceted Maltese Cross, and a frosted silver facsimile with a badge in the center, and on the badge, the cypher *VRI* in gold. And he'll be Sir Aubrey and Doreen will be Lady Philpott-Grimes."

"That's what we'll have to call her — Lady Philpott-Grimes, who was not so long ago a moll?"

"I think she'll make allowances for old friends."

"I get a headache thinking about it. If he beat Turner, he'd be even bigger. King maybe." He shook his head. "That Barbetta. A calamity."

"Aubrey could not have become King," I said. "For one thing, he's not in the line of succession."

"He'll get in line," said Fogbound. "There's time."

I could end the story there, but there is a little more to tell. The Franklins did go over for the investiture, and this time Fogbound did not go to the Albert Hall. "No more English tigers," he told me when he got back. "How could I find one like Aubrey? But maybe another boy. Pauline says being with Aubrey made us younger. Retirement can wait."

Simco Savory also made the trip, unable to resist the prospect of giving a *"petite fête champêtre"* in London. "Another world to conquer," he told a Washington reporter. "I have already entered into correspondence with the catering firm of Justin de Blank of Knightsbridge. I hope that we will be *al fresco*. At this time of year, that is all but *de rigueur*."

Fogbound, reading this in a newspaper, could have used a translation but managed a comment without one. "Why not?" he said.

Bobby Lou Bridewell went along, to reassure herself that

the English still loved her and to get the first exclusive interview with Lady Philpott-Grimes, who told her, and through
her the American people, that the United States would always
have a place in her heart. Webster Bindle went to London
as part of his official duties. He issued identical press releases
there and in Washington, and thoughtfully sent me one in
advance. This, however, did me little good, because the release was embargoed until the moment the sword touched
Aubrey's shoulder. In his statement, Bindle pronounced the
Anglo-American alliance "the bedrock of our security system."
He went on: "I affirm that, even as I congratulate Sir Aubrey
and share his well-deserved joy."

And I, Mercer, *Star-Telegram?* I did not go, and so I
missed not only Aubrey's entry into the knighthood but his
debut as a journalist. He had become a columnist on economic affairs, his views appearing under the heading: by Sir
Aubrey Philpott-Grimes, K.C.V.O.

I had wanted to go, if only to tell him that bylines aren't
everything. But the editor had not yielded to my argument
that an editorial writer is virtually illiterate if he has not
made himself familiar with the great world capitals. "I need,"
I had told him, "the feel of London."

"You can write editorials without that, Mercer," he had
replied. "I've seen you do it."

"My editorials would be better informed, chief. They
would have more *gravitas*," I said, sounding, to my surprise,
rather like Aubrey.

"Not possible."

"More resonance, then."

"Mercer," the editor said, "in all my years in the business,
I have never run into editorials more resonant than yours."

"You know best, chief," I said.